ICONS OF JUSTICE

ICONS OF JUSTICE

ICONOGRAPHY
& THEMATIC IMAGERY
IN BOOK V OF
The Faerie Queene

JANE APTEKAR

COLUMBIA UNIVERSITY PRESS

New York & London   *1969*

This study, prepared under the Graduate Faculties of
Columbia University, was selected by a committee of those
faculties to receive one of the Clarke F. Ansley awards
given annually by Columbia University Press.

Copyright © 1967, 1969 Columbia University Press
Library of Congress Catalog Card Number: 79-79189
Printed in the United States of America

FOR
Bernard
AND
Rachel Miranda

ACKNOWLEDGMENTS

IN expressing my thanks to those who, directly or indirectly, contributed to the writing of this study, I must first name William Nelson, whose book, lectures, and discussions on Spenser inspired me to reconsider the poet, and whose kind criticisms moved my reconsideration to take the form it has. To Marjorie Hope Nicolson and S. F. Johnson, mentors to so many, I am indebted for some of my mind's basic books and for the idea of research. To J. A. Mazzeo I am indebted for the illumination of Machiavelli in particular, and for much scholarly excitement. To Angus Fletcher I am indebted for stimulating discussions on Spenser and on allegory. I am especially grateful to him for letting me read his study of Book V of *The Faerie Queene* in manuscript; I have made use of several of his valuable findings. To John Nelson and Ann Harris I am indebted for helpful criticisms on my manuscript; to Elizabeth E. Roth of the Prints Division of the New York Public Library, for advice on iconographical problems. I am more indebted than I can acknowledge or know to the writings and teachings of many great scholars: but I should like especially to thank Helen Gardner for introducing me to the Renaissance, to paradox, to scholarship, and to the discipline of writing about literature. Without my husband, from whom I have learned to look at the visual arts, and who has given me, with much else, Time, this book could hardly have been written.

J. A.

CONTENTS

INTRODUCTION

It is now clear to students of Spenser that *The Faerie Queene* is not, as was for centuries supposed, a mechanical moral allegory, sensuously and irrelevantly decorated with pictorial beauties.[1] To be sure, the poem is certainly an allegory and it is indeed vividly pictorial. But the real nature of Spenser's poem is only beginning to be understood in this age which has assimilated Donne and Joyce and accepted the critical validity of William Empson's "hierarchies of level"[2] and Northrop Frye's "structures of imagery."[3]

The allegory of *The Faerie Queene* is not the fourfold theological system which it is just possible to read into Book I,[4] or the detailed rendering of sixteenth-century political and religious affairs, which a number of early twentieth-century scholars have sought to find in the poem.[5] Nor is the poem a romantic *bildungsroman*, a psychological narrative of the maturing of the heroes' characters, as late nineteenth century readers tended to interpret it and as the author of the first published study devoted solely to Book V still maintains.[6] Nor is *The Faerie Queene* an encyclopedic presentation, through a language of moral abstractions, of the ethical and theological backgrounds to the Elizabethan World Picture.[7] On the contrary, it has recently been shown that Spenser's moral positions are frequently ironic, paradoxical, and aware of contrarieties.[8] And it is now clear that the sixteenth-century poet's allegorical method is more like that of James Joyce than like that of Guillaume de Lorris or the author of *Everyman*. To be sure, Spenser does have, like his predecessors, didactic and explicatory intentions; *The Faerie Queene* is certainly, as C. S. Lewis has insisted, a pilgrims' progress, and a great battle between good and evil, darkness and light.[9] But it is also more than this.

Indeed, the poem is too complex and many-faceted to be bound within any critical concept as limited as the traditional one of allegory. Only if the definition of allegory is stretched—as some recent writers have stretched it—to appropriately include *Ulysses* and the work of contemporary Italian film makers, may it also be elastic enough to fit *The Faerie Queene*.[10] For *The Faerie Queene* is not a narrative moralized to convey a "real" significance, such as the soul's search for God, goodness, or a lover; or the inevitable moral predicaments of holiness, temperance, and the rest; or the history of England—though it suggests all these.[11] It is, rather, the sum of innumerable intermittent narratives, conceits, and allusions. Spenser's allegory, as well as being a system of correspondences between events and persons within his poem and events and persons without—in literature, myth, and the scriptures, in actual historical events, and in various realms of abstract, ethical thought—is also a system of correspondences and of ironical, explicatory, and structurally cross-binding references within the poem.

Spenser uses not only the conventional method of allegory, which makes point-by-point correspondences between the realms he seeks to relate, between fiction and fact, and between icon and its signification; but he also uses names and figures with many complex, often apparently contradictory associations; and he connects all these by his own remarkable system of internal parallelism. *The Faerie Queene* as a whole is less an epic or a romance than, to pervert chronology, a widely expanded metaphysical lyric. Far from being enclosed within its own convention and confined to telling a pretty moral tale, it is a complex of reverberating imagery, of paradox, of logically developed sublevels, of great and various learning subtly, and often explosively, used.

One way to approach Spenser's allegory is through a study of his icons. The use of the word "icon" in literary criticism has been chiefly influenced by W. K. Wimsatt's explanation of his use of it for a book title. He writes:

> The term *icon* is used today by semeiotic writers to refer to a verbal sign which *somehow* shares the properties of, or resembles, the objects which it denotes. The same term in its more usual meaning refers to a visual image and especially to one which is a religious symbol. The verbal image which most fully realizes its verbal capacities is that which is not merely a bright picture (in the usual modern meaning of the term *image*) but also an interpretation of reality in its metaphoric and symbolic dimensions.[12]

Spenser's allegory *is*, indeed, a series of images which are in this sense icons—intensely visual images which are interpretations "of reality in its metaphoric and symbolic dimensions." More specifically, most of what are called icons in this study are images whose visual properties recall those of well-known iconographical traditions, and whose metaphoric and symbolic dimensions are in large part governed by the interpretative conventions of Renaissance iconology. In effect, many of Spenser's verbal pictures are allegorical images, or emblems; they visually resemble allegorical illustrations and paintings, or emblems, and they bear a stated or, more often, an unstated conceptual "signification."[13]

The popularity and the widespread circulation of emblem literature in the sixteenth century is well known. So is the fact that the first publication with which Spenser is known to have been associated was in fact an emblem book: Van der Noodt's *A The-*

atre (*of*) . . . *Voluptuous Worldlings;* moreover, *The Shep-heardes Calender* itself is illustrated by twelve rather emblematical woodcuts. Indeed, it has long been understood that icons and emblems entered into the imaginative fabric of Spenser's poetry as a whole. Many of the figures in Spenser's poem which to us must seem quaint, inventive, and of doubtful relevance are tradi-tional representations with a traditional significance that Spenser's readers would immediately have recognized. Rosemary Freeman has demonstrated in some detail that in *The Faerie Queene* many of Spenser's allegorical figures closely resemble their counterparts in the English emblem books.[14] She has even suggested further that Spenser, with his strong visual imagination, himself influ-enced some of the emblem writers who succeeded him.[15] And several recent scholars have had recourse to iconography to help explain particular puzzling incidents and images in *The Faerie Queene.* Rosemond Tuve has suggested that much allegorical imagery can be best explicated by reference to iconographical conventions, and has described the way in which allegorical imag-ery works in literature—and especially in *The Faerie Queene*—after and in the light of her analysis of how it works in emblems and moralizing illustrations.[16]

Until very recently, Spenser's imagery has been dismissed as irrelevant decoration. According to Douglas Bush's celebrated indictment, Spenser's metaphors are "patches stuck on rather than a growth from within."[17] In fact, on the contrary, as is shown in studies by Northrop Frye and the scholars who have followed him in closely examining Spenser's imagery and phraseology,[18] most of Spenser's images are the natural outcroppings of rich substrata of meaning.[19]

Rosemond Tuve once remarked that "What Spenser's images furnish of pithiness and apt significancy has perhaps been most ne-glected."[20] But no one could now accuse Spenser scholars of neglect-ing his imagery. Indeed, it is sometimes argued that the opposite trend may have gone too far, and that in a poet as manifold as Spen-ser almost any structures of imagery and of allegory may be detected by the ingenious reader. Several of the recent books on Spenser have, quite understandably, been attacked for their excessive ingenuity, for their tendency to erect upon Spenser's poetry a dramatic or allegorical or metaphorical or even a numerological structure which the poet's words and facts will hardly sustain.[21] But, in truth, though several of the recent studies of Spenser should certainly not be accepted in their entirety, they do bring a new dynamism to the study of Spenser.

The present essay, which discovers or creates structures of imagery as diligently as did its predecessors, is at least based rather more soundly in iconographical tradition than others have been in their concern with numerological mysteries or allegories of Christian sacrament. It may suggest new attitudes, directions, and possibilities; and it will certainly help to explain a number of details in Spenser's text which have hitherto been under discussion, or obscure.

We do not know and probably cannot ever know just how Spenser and his contemporaries were accustomed to read. What we do have in the way of marginalia in surviving copies of The Faerie Queene suggests that Spenser's contemporaries read allegory with some care and with close attention to semantics, the origins and associations of words, and the significance of images. One sixteenth- or early-seventeenth-century reader of The Faerie Queene was so absorbed in studying the poem's moral and allegorical significance that he got the characters and story mixed up.[22] The Elizabethan reader was prepared, it would seem, for complexity; but we just do not know how many different ideas and possibilities he could be expected to hold in his mind at the same time. The case of the reader who mixed up the story suggests that, despite the ubiquitous theory of less perhaps fourfold than severalfold allegory, and a universal symbolizing habit of mind, an Elizabethan would find it as difficult (yet as interesting) as would any modern to hold a number of tracks of vehicles and their tenors concurrently in his head.

Spenser presumably expected his readers at any given moment

to apprehend a number of different, simultaneous metaphorical possibilities; he expected his Elizabethan readers to be at least to some extent acquainted with conventions with which we today are almost entirely unfamiliar; he knew and assumed that his readers would know—and would use their knowledge of—various mythological, iconographical, and symbolical traditions.

This view of the real nature of Spenser's allegory can be well supported from a reading of one particularly neglected and particularly striking book: "The Legend of Justice." In this book Spenser puts forward his (and in many respects also his age's) ideas about justice through a number of separate themes that variously embody the complex, sometimes conflicting aspects of the virtue. These themes are presented through narrative and characterization and through several systems of allusion. They are presented, too, through various logically carried through, consistent threads of thematic imagery. Thematic imagery is imagery that implies, through direct statement, or allusion, or association, or pictorial convention, a particular theme; a theme which is recurrently implied, throughout the book, in widely scattered but strikingly interconnected icons and images.

Spenser's icons, images, and allusions set up three main threads of thematic imagery. The first of these threads seems entirely orthodox; but both of the others carry dubious, ironic undertones. Spenser's Legend of Justice explores, naturally, the nature of justice. But this justice is seen to be a more complex and contradictory virtue than one might have assumed. Book V is concerned, in the first place, in orthodox fashion, with justice's relationship to God; it is also concerned, more ambiguously, with justice's place in the ambivalent traditions connected with force and fraud, and with Hercules.

That it is God and the monarch whose function it is to administer justice is a commonplace of Elizabethan thought; Spenser's poem and Artegall's career illustrate the matter. God-serving and King-serving though Artegall is, however, readers have very often found him an objectionable hero and man. The standard defense is that the rigorous justice he exemplifies was accepted as legitimate by Spenser's contemporaries. Iconographical evidence indicates that this is not the case and that if we find Artegall objectionable it is probably for good reason. But if justice is in the first place to Spenser as to his contemporaries the respect in which the monarch imitates and represents either a merciful or a wrathful God, it is in the second place the quality, perfectly operative in the golden age, which crusades against the twin evils of force and fraud. Yet Spenser recognized the ironical truth that in the actual world of practical men, force and fraud, though they are less than honorable, less than good, are the very means which the governor must use in order to maintain God's justice. In the third place, Spenser's representative heroes of justice imitate Hercules, the great traditional exemplar of the virtue. Yet there was some suggestion, in the Renaissance, that Hercules was excessively cruel and concupiscent. The character of Artegall, who is ostensibly the proper instrument of God, is thus yet further ironically undercut by his relationship to the furious Hercules of heroic legend.

Accordingly, this book is divided into two parts, which treat of justice's orthodoxy and justice's dubiety, and three main sections, which are devoted to the icons and themes of God's justice, of force and fraud, and of Hercules.

It will be observed that this study gives very little attention to the matter that has in the past chiefly interested students of the Legend of Justice: the question of the Legend's relationship to history. Referring to *The Faerie Queene* as a whole, Spenser wrote in his Letter to Raleigh that "the generall end therefore of all the booke is to fashion a gentleman or noble person in all vertuous and gentle discipline." Now one may interpret "to fashion a gentleman" simply as "to portray a gentleman," or one may assume that the phrase has reference outside the poem and that Spenser was writing a courtesy book aimed at educating (or fashioning) actual Elizabethan gentlemen. But from either point of view it is clear that in *The Faerie Queene* there is a relationship between the heroes of the legends and the gentlemen of Spenser's England. And this relationship is necessarily stronger in Book V, the book of justice, of, largely, right political action, than in any other book in the poem. For many years students of Spenser's Legend of Justice have chiefly devoted themselves to exploring the book's historical references, to explicating its political allegory. They have demonstrated that many of the characters and actions in Book V are related to historical personages and incidents. And they have even with justice argued that the book as a whole is related to Spenser's own specifically political prose treatise, *A View of the Present State of Ireland*. But in this book very little attention is paid to these matters which have until recently been regarded as central.

To be sure, in one way or another many of Spenser's references to contemporary men and affairs are alluded to; but they are not emphasized. For one thing, they have been overemphasized already. For another, Spenser was more interested in what (for him) *is* than in what men were doing or should do: he was writing a philosophical not a political poem. His historical references are but some among many instances to support his theses about justice; his political allegories are, largely, only by way of confirmation or exemplification of his philosophical themes.

It should be noted that I do not at any point in this book suggest that Spenser was indebted to a particular emblem or painting for his visual details; I claim merely that there seems to have been a tradition to this or that effect. Therefore, out of the wealth of iconographical material that tends in the same direction, I have often chosen illustrations that did not appear until after the publication of Book V of *The Faerie Queene* in 1596. Sometimes I have had access only to a seventeenth-century edition of a work that was published earlier. Sometimes I have chosen a later version of a figure or scene that frequently occurred earlier, if that later version exemplified more of my points more clearly. Occasionally, though, I have used iconographical material which first appeared in the early seventeenth century and to which I have seen no earlier analogues. In these cases there is good reason to think that the artist was drawing on traditional material: usually most of the emblem's features are familiar, or the artist is known to have customarily depended on his predecessors' themes and images. In a few cases the development of an iconographical tradition is so significant as to the implications of an earlier emblem or idea and is in itself of such interest that I have followed it long after Spenser's time.

PART I
ORTHODOXY

CHAPTER 1

JOVE'S JUDGMENT SEAT

ONE of the most elaborate and carefully orthodox of the many icons which Spenser describes is that of Mercilla, as she sits enthroned in the midst of her monarchial court conducting her court of justice. Her person, accoutrements, and attendants are all described in a clear, detailed way that is almost heraldic; as in heraldry, each of the subject's attributes has its special significance. It is a set scene, like something out of a pageant, as Mercilla sits motionless and (from a realistic point of view) absurd with jewels, scepter, sword, and panoply, and with angels fluttering about her head and a bad-tempered lion beneath her. But realism is of course irrelevant. The visual details mark spiritual not actual realities. This is the case with almost all Spenser's icons; but it is particularly easy to see the symbolic force of the iconographical details in the description of Mercilla: monarchy and justice have always had their emblems. Most of Mercilla's attributes are familiar. Twentieth-century monarchs in effect still exist only by virtue of being the occasional carriers of such royal paraphernalia as hers. As for Mercilla's little angels: they confirm the monarch's closeness to God, recalling by visual association the bands of children dressed as angels who often attended the monarch-figure in sixteenth-century pageants.[1] The lion beneath Mercilla's throne has many significances—most of them familiar today; it is, among other things, England, monarchy, magnanimity, and might. But this is matter for a later chapter.

The familiar iconographical details in Spenser's description of Mercilla plainly mark her as a great and entirely orthodox monarch. They mark her, too, inevitably, as a judge. Now the act which best exemplifies good monarchy is the act of rendering justice: the act, in most cases, of making judgment. There is a many-faceted tradition to this effect. Ernst Cassirer has shown how the idea that the maintenance of justice is the first and principal task of the state developed from Plato, through classical and medieval political theories, into the Renaissance.[2] In England, the prince's original constitutional function was to act as judge. The highest courts in the country derive from the monarch's exercise of this function: the Court of the King's (or Queen's) Bench descends from the governmental and judicial council at which the monarch used to preside—on his judgment bench.[3] And the Christian view of the king fell together with this tradition. Spenser puts the matter very clearly, right at the beginning of the Legend of Justice. In the Proem in which he compliments the right and godly monarchy and justice of his own queen, his "Dread Soverayne Goddesse," he thus defines justice:

> Most sacred vertue she of all the rest,
>> Resembling God in his imperiall might;
>> Whose soveraine powre is herein most exprest,
>> That both to good and bad he dealeth right,
>> And all his workes with Justice hath bedight.
>> That powre he also doth to Princes lend,
>> And makes them like himselfe in glorious sight,
>> To sit in his owne seate, his cause to end,
> And rule his people right, as he doth recommend.

Dread Soverayne Goddesse, that doest highest sit
  In seate of judgement, in th'Almighties stead,
  And with magnificke might and wondrous wit
  Doest to thy people righteous doome aread,
  That furthest Nations filles with awfull dread,
  Pardon the boldnesse of thy basest thrall,
  That dare discourse of so divine a read,
  As thy great justice praysed over all:
The instrument whereof loe here thy Artegall.   (Pr.10,11)

Similarly, Jean Bodin, revolutionary though he was in some of his views of law and the state, is perfectly representative of traditional opinion in declaring that "the true function of the prince is to judge his people. He must of course be armed against the enemy, but justice is his necessary attribute in all places, and at all times." [4] This is the reason that Spenser's central and most formally elaborate icon of monarchy is in Book V: it is his description of Mercilla performing the same act as his Dread Soverayne Goddesse, the act of executing justice. For it is in this central incident that Duessa—that chief embodiment of evil through so much of *The Faerie Queene*—is at last arraigned. Mercilla conducts the trial with all due and detailed ceremony of prosecution, defense, and (offstage) sentencing: her judgment reflects, as the good monarch's must, "high heavens grace" (ix.42).

It is because monarchy and justice were traditionally so firmly interlinked that Spenser could appropriately open his legend of Justice as he does with the figure of the Dread Soverayne Goddesse (Queen Elizabeth) sitting in judgment, and could introduce his own monarch, in the person of Mercilla, into *The Faerie Queene* more fully in the Legend of Justice than in any other book in the poem.

Mercilla's palace and her porter actually resemble Queen Elizabeth's real ones.[5] Duessa represents (at this moment, though by no means in all her appearances in *The Faerie Queene*) Mary, Queen of Scots, her trial, Mary's trial, and several of her accusers, Elizabeth's ministers. Most of Mercilla's attributes, being exactly those which traditional monarchy and justice held in common, are, too, naturally enough, those with which artists endowed Elizabeth in contemporary portraits. Mercilla is even equipped with exactly the rusty sword which—as appears from the evidence of one of Elizabeth's own poems—was the queen's personal emblem of her peaceful reign.[6]

Most of Mercilla's circumstances have general heraldic or particular allegorical point. But this figure for England's Christian Elizabeth does have one seemingly rather unusual attribute in her strange group of attendants: the daughters of pagan Jove.

> And round about, before her feet there sate
> A bevie of faire Virgins clad in white
> That goodly seem'd t'adorne her royall state,
> All lovely daughters of high Jove, that hight
> Litae, by him begot in loves delight,
> Upon the righteous Themis: those they say
> Upon Joves judgement seat wayt day and night,
> And when in wrath he threats the worlds decay,
> They doe his anger calme, and cruell vengeance stay.
>
> They also doe by his divine permission
> Upon the thrones of mortall Princes tend,
> And often treat for pardon and remission
> To suppliants, through frayltie which offend.
> Those did upon Mercillaes throne attend:
> Just Dice, wise Eunomie, myld Eirene,
> And them amongst, her glorie to commend,
> Sate goodly Temperance in garments clene,
> And sacred Reverence, yborne of heavenly strene.   (ix.31,32)

It seems remarkable that we are to imagine Spenser's queen as being attended by some obscure figures from pagan mythology. It is even more remarkable, and significant, that we are to see Mercilla as being related, through a process of reflection, to Jove: that is, the service which the Litae do for her reflects the service which they do for Jove. But indeed the presence in the Court of Mercilla of the daughters of high Jove and of the overshadowing sense of Jove himself, far from being a learned and irrelevant decoration, in fact brings together and epitomizes the several orthodox central themes of the Legend of Justice. Jove is to be regarded as analogous, or equivalent, to God (vii.1). (Jove was the king of the Pagan gods and the greatest of the gods who ruled men; inevitably, the correspondence-finding Elizabethans took him to represent or to provide an automatic metaphor or mere pseudonym for the Scriptural God and King.) The relationship between Jove and the earthly prince which is suggested at the center of Spenser's most orthodox icon of monarchy and justice actually runs as a thematic thread through much of Book V; it is in its light that we should interpret many of the book's images, allusions, and incidents. As we read, we should be aware of the judgment seat of Jove or God as hovering not only somewhere above Mercilla, but indeed over most of the book in which Mercilla is only one of the several manifestations of monarchy and justice.

Jove reveals the skill of justice to princes' hearts; and the justice of earthly monarchs imitates and executes the justice of Jove (vii.1). Mercilla is the embodiment of a particularly merciful kind of justice. And she is influenced to make merciful judgments by the same Litae who influence Jove toward mercy. The Litae restrain Jove when in his wrath he threatens cruel vengeance and the world's decay. Similarly, though Mercilla sentences her rival to death (x.4), the poet nevertheless declares that she "would not let just vengeance on her light" (ix.49); influenced by the Litae and her own essential mercifulness, Mercilla pities Duessa and lets fall "few perling drops" for her (ix.50). The poet comments:

> Some Clarkes doe doubt in their devicefull art,
>   Whether this heavenly thing, whereof I treat,
>   To weeten Mercie, be of Justice part,
>   Or drawne forth from her by divine extreate.

This well I wote, that sure she is as great,
And meriteth to have as high a place,
Sith in th'Almighties everlasting seat
She first was bred, and borne of heavenly race;
From thence pour'd down on men, by influence of grace.   (x.1)

In all this, Spenser lets his queen have it both ways: at the same time that her rival is safely dead, Jove-struck, as it were, she herself is a paragon of the mercy poured down from "th'Almighties" judgment seat. In Mercilla's judgment, in fact, justice and mercy are reconciled.

Samuel Chew has made a fascinating study of the way in which the motif of the virtues reconciled recurs in iconography. For, as he has observed, "The conflicting claims of Justice and Mercy are as old as the dawn of man's moral consciousness." [7] In *The Virtues Reconciled* he traces, in a number of iconographical and literary contexts, the conflict between, and ultimate reconciliation of, the four daughters of God (on the one hand, Justice, and Truth or Fortitude, and on the other Mercy, and Peace or Prudence). There is, in the same tradition, a woodcut of the enthroned Queen Elizabeth being crowned by Justice and Mercy, supported by Fortitude and Prudence (Figure 1). A knowledge of this tradition illuminates Spenser's picture of Mercilla as at the same time just and merciful; it throws light, too, on the Litae.

There is no known single clear source for Spenser's Litae. As commentators have observed, he has run together more than one set of ladies. In Homer, the Litae are, as their name suggests, personifications of prayers; they are said to be daughters of Zeus who bless those who approach them; but they are ugly and wrinkled and have no specific names or number. According to Hesiod, the three fair ladies Dice, Eunomie, and Eirene are the Horae, daughters of Jupiter and Themis.[8] In Spenser, Jove's conciliatory daughters are "Just Dice, wise Eunomie, myld Eirene." (Temperance and Reverence, who are "them amongst," are clearly justice-associated virtues; but, as Spenser phrases the stanza, they do not appear to be actual daughters of Jove.) Now

Spenser's three daughters of Jove, Justice, and ("wise") Good
Law or Order, and Peace, are very close to God's traditional
daughters, Justice, Truth or Righteousness or Fortitude, and
Peace. And Mercilla, of course, is Mercy. Surely in these stanzas
Spenser is combining with the merged Litae and Horae of clas-
sical myth the Christian tradition of the four daughters of God.

FIGURE 1. Queen Elizabeth attended by the Daughters of
God. *Bishop's Bible* (London, 1569).

The function of the Litae is to restrain the anger and the cruel
vengeance of Jove. The function of all four of the daughters of

God, as Spenser shifts the tradition to his purpose, seems to be to avert the wrath of angry Jehovah, of the terrible God of the Old Testament of whom it was written: "Vengeance is mine, saith the Lord." It seems clear indeed that, as previous readers have suggested, the intervention of the Litae is an image of the mitigating of God's vengeance by Christ's love, of the difference between the Old Law and the New.[9] In the Four Daughters of God tradition Justice and Truth are in effect the representatives of the Old Law, Mercy and Peace the representatives of the New. Spenser uses all four ladies as an embodiment of a reconciliation of the opposing virtues; but it is a reconciliation that is weighted on the side of mercy and peace. "Mercilla," after all, is the name Spenser gives his queen, and "Irena" is the major objective of his chief knight's guiding quest. This is, too, much how Sir John Davies saw Queen Elizabeth: in his poem of compliment to her, *Astraea* (1599), he wrote:

> By Love she rules more than by *Law*
> Even her great mercy breedeth awe;
> This is her sword and scepter.[10]

Mercilla and the Litae are women. Now, though Spenser was by no means alone in the sixteenth century in considering that women rulers are in some circumstances legitimate, the weight of learned opinion had always been to the contrary.[11] Naturally the monarch must be a man; he mirrors God, and is toward his people as a father is toward his children. Spenser is no doubt making his contribution to the defense of Elizabeth's female rights through the argument-by-symbolism in his account of Mercilla.

The more orthodoxly princely male representatives of justice are very different from the gracious queen Mercilla. Artegall, and to some extent Arthur, too, executes not the merciful justice of ladies, Litae, and Christ, but the rigorous, righteously wrathful justice which typically emanates from Jove's judgment seat.

Stephen Batman, in *The Golden Booke of the Leaden Goddes* (1577), describes the various Greek gods and heroes in little verbal emblems; an account of its "Signification" follows each. He writes that "Jupiter was figured sitting in throne of Estate, with three eyes, and no Eares. . . . In his right hand he held Lightening, and in the left, a Scepter. Standing or treading upon Gyauntes." The signification of Jupiter's throne and scepter is that he is the king of gods and men. He has three eyes and no ears because his justice sees all and is deaf to pleas and bribes. His lightning represents his power. "His treading upon Giauntes doth declare him to be a punisher of those which are at defiaunce with him." [12] And this figure of Jupiter, or, as was more often written, Jove, constantly recurs: he is king and judge, power and punisher. And God. It is he whose presence is felt somewhere above Mercilla's throne, on his judgment seat, threatening cruel vengeance with, no doubt, his thunderbolt.

In one of the most popular and widely distributed of emblem books, the *Emblemata Horatiana* (1607, attributed to Otto van Veen, or Vaenius), there is an illuminating representation of Jove's judgment seat, and of the nature of monarchy and justice (Figure 2).[13] It is a picture of a king who is sitting on a dais addressing himself to a mixed group of his people below him. On one side of him, holding a scroll, stands a robed figure who represents the law, and on the other side an armed knight who represents justice's essential concomitant: executive force. Above the king, complete with the requisite cloud, eagle, and thunderbolt, is Jove. Just as Jove rules the king, the king rules his subjects: the king's gesture toward his people exactly imitates Jove's gesture toward the king. The monarch both acts as the representative and instrument of Jove and serves as the image of Jove. The emblem is called *Potestas potestati subiecta*. It demonstrates that even a monarch is ruled by a power greater than himself, that is, by God's justice. The emblematist shows Jove seeing to it, with threatening thunderbolt ready, that the king wields his sword justly, in imitation of the deity and in furtherance of divine ends.[14]

This king, who is ruling his people as Jove or God instructs or admonishes him, is in effect an ideal prince. He is, after all, rep-

FIGURE 2. *Potestas potestati subiecta.* From Van Veen's *Emblemata Hora-tiana* (Antwerp, 1607), p. 79.

resented in the most definitively kingly of postures: he is engaged in the monarch's proper task of judging his people. The editor of a later French edition of the *Emblemata Horatiana* certainly exhorts his readers to look upon the emblem in this light. He writes: *Venez voir, & estudiez le bon Roy que cette Peinture vous donne pour exemple. Il est environné de ses peuples. Il rend jus-*

tice a la Veufve & a l'Orphelin.[15] What is remarkable is that this exemplary king executes his justice by the use of a power that is parallel to the power of Jove.

It is clear that in Spenser's Legend of Justice the virtue-heroes combine in themselves the qualities of monarch and judge; as an almost inevitable corollary, they enforce their princely justice with Godly and Jovial power. This is particularly true of the chief knight of justice, Artegall.

Most of the first third of the Legend of Justice shows Artegall in his function of judge: in the first few cantos, in orthodox Aristotelian fashion,[16] he chooses between rival claimants, decides guilt, apportions punishment, and divides property. Indeed, in his very first act of judgment he clearly imitates the most famous of the judgments of Solomon, the exemplary Scriptural king and judge. Confronted with two men who both claim to be the lover of the same lady, Artegall settles the matter through recourse to the device of Solomon: he proposes to cut the lady in half. The true lover naturally relinquishes claim to his portion; he is then adjudged rightful owner of the whole. Spenser does not mention Solomon's name, but the allusion is very clear. And Solomon was the well-known type of the just monarch, of the archetypal king and judge. As Sir Walter Raleigh recommended, "The Prince himself is to sit sometimes in a place of public Justice, and to give an Experiment of his Wisdom and Equity, whereby great Reverence and Estimation is gotten, as in the example of Solomon." [17] And though in the second third of the Legend of Justice Artegall is, for various reasons and in various ways which we will discuss later, very much a mere man, he still has kingly qualities. He is, after all, as Spenser's genealogy makes clear, the ancestor of the British royal line (III.iii.26–49; V.vii.23). And when Britomart puts an end to the monstrous regiment of a woman in Radigund's realm and restores the populace "to mens subjection," she acts as though her lover were a king; she makes the Amazons "sweare fealty to Artegall" (vii.42,43). This princely "instrument" of

Elizabeth and of justice not only performs in his own person the king's function of judging but also has at his command the monarch's two executive instruments of power and law.

According to Stephen Batman, the signification of Jove's lightning bolt is power. In the Van Veen emblem *Potestas potestati subiecta* it is the power of Jove—embodied, indeed, in that bolt of his—which subdues the power of monarchs. The king in the Van Veen emblem wields a sword in exact reflection of the manner in which Jove wields the thunderbolt; at his side, moreover, is an armed knight, the representative and embodiment, and also the "instrument," of the monarch's power. Spenser's male representatives of justice likewise have power plainly at their command; they have at their disposal the power of brute (or, one should rather say, in view of Talus's role, mechanical) force. Since they are, directly or indirectly, the instruments of God, they also have, as it were by proxy, the order-keeping power of Jove. Each of them makes striking metaphorical or literal use of Jove's terrible weapons.

There is one emblem in which a noble figure, member of a house that was long a powerful executor for the crown, is so honored as to be represented wielding a kingly and Jovial weapon. This is the emblem honoring the current Earl of Essex in an anonymous collection of compliments to notable men: *The Mirrour of Majestie: or, The Badges of Honour conceitedly emblazoned, with emblemes annexed, poetically unfolded* (Figure 3).[18] The picture consists of a mailed hand emerging from a cloud, holding a thunderbolt. The oddly ungrammatical and quite unpoetical unfolding avers that the figure does not portend civil war (thus delicately the author passes over Elizabeth's Essex), but

> your Auncestrie, whose fame
> Like forked thunder, threaten'd cowards shame;
> Who fearing, lest on their debosh'd base merit,
> Heav'n should drop Bolts, by a flame-winged spirit.

In Spenser's Book V the representatives of justice are something of flame-winged, bolt-dropping, Heaven-serving spirits. They resemble the Earl of Essex in being so noble as to be empowered, or credited with the power, to wield the punishing weaponry of heaven.

Jove's most famous and terrible instrument was his thunderbolt. Artegall makes use of it through the implications of some traditional imagery. On one occasion Britomart makes clear metaphorical use of it: "Wroth," she descends on the two losels on Pollente's bridge like "flashing Levin" (vi.38–40). Mercilla by implication abjures it. Arthur, though, makes magnificent use of it.

As an embodiment, throughout *The Faerie Queene*, of the glories of magnificence, or magnanimity, and of England—and thus a very proper representative of monarchy and justice— Arthur is equipped with the weapons of God with which to main-

FIGURE 3. *Quis contra nos.* From *The Mirrour of Majestie* (London, 1618), Embleme 16. Courtesy of the Columbia University Libraries.

tain God's order. At the end of his fight against the Souldan
Arthur unveils his shield in front of the pagan's chariot-horses, to
thunderbolting effect:

> Like lightening flash, that hath the gazer burned,
>> So did the sight thereof their sense dismay   (viii.38)

There can be little doubt that this lightning-like flash has, orthodoxly, a Christian as well as a Jovial force. The drift of the
historical allegory and an analogous passage in Book I both suggest it. (During Arthur's fight with the ungodly Orgoglio in
Book I the veil falls from his magic shield; its effect on this occasion too is to render the foe helpless:

> As where th'Almighties lightning brond does light,
>> It dimmes the dazed eyen, and daunts the senses quight
>>>>>>>> (I.viii.21.)

It has long been apparent to Spenser scholars—Upton first
remarked it [19]—that in the Souldan incident Arthur represents and
is the instrument of the grace of God. It is clear that this is not an
isolated case, that the representatives of justice very often wield
weapons that put into effect less, in Book V as a whole, the grace
than the righteous wrath and just vengeance of God.[20]

The next four chapters will expand and deal with some other
aspects of the themes touched on here. We shall see that the many
Jove-associated allusions and icons in Book V set up a mythically,
theologically, and iconographically orthodox basis for Spenser's
treatment of justice. And in this thematic base power is a dominant motif: God, Jove, monarch, and judge, and their executors
or "instruments," all, in the Legend of Justice, orthodoxly maintain order through power.

POWER

CHAPTER 2

THE GIANTS' REBELLION

SPENSER's moral, political, and religious allegory has been fairly well understood for many centuries, often to the detriment of a proper understanding of the poem itself. It is only recently, however, that the threads of consistent, systematic allusion to myths and literary and other analogues have been recognized for the additional levels of allegory that they in effect are. In the Legend of Justice the myth which provides the dominant field of allusion is that of Hercules.[1] More intermittent and more sketchy, but as effective and as firmly *there* is the myth of Jove's wars against the giants and Titans.[2] According to legend, Jove engaged in two such wars. He led the first, in his youth, against the Titans: he dethroned his own father, Saturn, and assumed his place in heaven. More memorable and useful in Christian times was that other story of his war against the rebellious giants, who attacked him as Satan and the fallen angels attacked God.[3] Spenser followed the Renaissance tendency to run Jove's two wars together into one rebellion, and to regard the Titans and the giants as synonymous.

In Spenser's Book V the theme of the rebellion of the giants is introduced in the course of the first few stanzas and occurs again, most clearly, at the highest point of definition of the nature of justice, in the temple of Isis. This is how Spenser explains the priests' abstinence:

> Therefore they mote not taste of fleshly food,
>   Ne feed on ought, the which doth bloud containe,
>   Ne drinke of wine, for wine they say is blood,
>   Even the bloud of Gyants, which were slaine,
>   By thundering Jove in the Phlegrean plaine.
>   For which the earth (as they the story tell)
>   Wroth with the Gods, which to perpetuall paine
>   Had damn'd her sonnes, which gainst them did rebell,
> With inward grief and malice did against them swell.
>
> And of their vitall bloud, the which was shed
>   Into her pregnant bosome, forth she brought
>   The fruitful vine, whose liquor blouddy red
>   Having the mindes of men with fury fraught,
>   Mote in them stirre up old rebellious thought,
>   To make new warre against the Gods againe:
>   Such is the powre of that same fruit, that nought
>   The fell contagion may thereof restraine,
> Ne within reasons rule, her madding mood containe.
>
>   (vii. 10, 11)

The giants rebelled against Jove as the angels rebelled against God and as mutinous subjects would like to rebel against their monarchs. Much recent scholarship has demonstrated the six-teenth century's reliance on doctrines of order, hierarchy, and the unquestionable sovereignty of the king. The maintenance of the status quo, and of the position of the monarch, was regarded as essential for the health of the nation. Attempted rebellion against the monarch and effected usurpation of the place and the preroga-tives of the monarch are the state's worst evils; they are, according to the orthodox hierarchical systems, the worst enemies of justice. An ideal image for the proper putting down of rebellion, usurpation, and the opposition to God is the story of the wars between Jove and the giants.

The emblem of justice called *Potestas potestati subiecta* (Figure 2) is of considerable interest in this connection. The emblematist accompanies his engraving of the king sitting, god-imitative, in his judgment seat, with this significant passage from Horace:

> *Regum timendorum in proprios greges,*
> *Reges in ipsos imperium est Iovis,*
> *Clari Giganteo triumpho,*
> *Cuncta supercilio moventis.* (Lib.3,Od.1)

This suggests that Spenser is following an honorable tradition in defining right, just, God-directed monarchy in the light of Jove's dominion over kings and his suppression of giants' rebellions. And, indeed, a consistently recurring motif in Spenser's Book V is the systematic destruction by the heroes of justice of a series of ungodly, gigantic rebels.

At the very outset of Artegall's career Astraea equips him with the sword with which, Spenser specifically explains, Jove put down the giants' rebellion. This is Spenser's account of the way in which Artegall executed justice and served as instrument of and imitated the righteous wrath of God:

> Ne any liv'd on ground, that durst withstand
> His dreadfull heast, much lesse him match in fight,
> Or bide the horror of his wreakfull hand,
> When so he list in wrath lift up his steely brand.
>
> Which steely brand, to make him dreaded more,
> She gave unto him, gotten by her slight
> And earnest search, where it was kept in store
> In Joves eternall house, unwist of wight,
> Since he himselfe it us'd in that great fight

> Against the Titans, that whylome rebelled
> Gainst highest heaven; Chrysaor it was hight;
> Chrysaor that all other swords excelled,
> Well prov'd in that same day, when Jove those Gyants quelled.
>
> (i.8,9)

Now there is no tradition of Jove's having a famous sword with which he defeated the giants. Jove's usual weapon was his thunderbolt. It is with his thunderbolt that Jove throws down his rebellious attackers in the *Emblemata Horatiana* engraving entitled *Nequid ultra vires coneris* (Figure 4). The emblem is accompanied by this passage from Horace:

> *Caelum ipsum petimus stultitia: neque*
> *Per nostrum patimur scelus,*
> *Iracunda Iovem ponere fulmina.*   (Lib.1,Od.3)

Artegall is not equipped with Jove's angry lightning, but he is equipped with Talus, who is as absolute as any thunderbolt, and with his sword.[4] And on at least one occasion Talus has the same effect as does Jove's weapon. The Gyant who in the normal course of things would be thunderbolted for his defiance is destroyed by Talus. And Talus has the effect on the Gyant's "rascall crew" which the thunderbolt usually has. The rabble could do nothing against Talus's onslaught,

> But when at them he with his flail gan lay,
> He like a swarme of flyes them overthrew;
> Ne any of them durst come in his way,
> But here and there before his presence flew,
> And hid themselves in holes and bushes from his view.   (ii.53)

Furthermore, like a flush of ducks that have sighted a falcon, they

> Doe hide themselves from her astonying looke,
> Amongst the flags and covert round about.   (ii.54)

In Francis Quarles's *Emblems Divine and Moral*, in which the thunderbolt constantly recurs as the symbol of Divine Wrath,

FIGURE 4. *Nequid ultra vires coneris.* From *Emblemata Horatiana*, p. 175.

there are several emblems of men trying to hide from God's punishing bolt. In one, a victim crouches in a corner, trying to hide from thunderbolt-wielding God; beneath the emblem the poet writes:

> O! that I could some secret place explore,
> To hide me till the Hour of Wrath be o'er.[5]

Another emblem shows a number of men running in different directions to hide from God's wrathful thunderbolt.[6] It is in much the same manner that the rabble hides from Talus and his flail, frightened for fear of God into hiding in holes and bushes from his wrath.

But Artegall has a sword, not a thunderbolt.[7] From the iconographical point of view it is essential that Spenser's chief representative of Justice should have a sword. Astraea, Justitia, or the good English lady whose statue stands outside court houses to this day, invariably carries a sword. She frequently also carries a pair of scales. (Spenser makes use of this iconographical detail, too: he recounts how Astraea taught Artegall "to weigh both right and wrong/In equall ballance" [i.7] and describes the Gyant's misuse of the "huge great paire of ballance in his hand" —ii.30.) But justice's most notable attribute is a sword—a sword which also represents the proper executive and punitive power of the king.

That in itself is a good enough reason for Artegall to carry a sword. Moreover, though a sword was only occasionally associated with Jove in iconography, Spenser is able to make Artegall's sword very clearly Jovial, and so appropriate for punishing miscreants. For it is not only Jove's in the sense that Jove was its owner and user until Astraea stole it from him. It is also Jove's through the implications of its name, Chrysaor. Heroes of story, from Beowulf and Arthur onward, tended to wield famous, named swords. But among all the heroes in *The Faerie Queene* only one, Artegall, the executor for Jove, has a sword with an individual name. "Chrysaor" means "sword of gold"—fitting enough for a monarch and judge. The name has, further, several mythological associations.[8] Most relevant of these is its association with Jove: the name Chrysaoreus was, according to Strabo, a surname for the Carian Zeus.[9] Artegall's sword is Jove's by name as well as by origin.

Artegall wields Jove's sword and, by proxy and metaphorically, his thunderbolt to the same purpose: both are emblems and in-

struments of the just monarch's legitimate power. This power is
chiefly directed against the great literal and figurative traditional
enemies of justice. Clearly set forth at the beginning and in the
center of the Legend of Justice, the theme of Jove's quelling of
the giants is in fact a pervasive image for Artegall's chief task of
putting down gigantic, presumptuous rebels, usurpers, and tyrants. Most of these are, as rebels against God's duly appointed
monarch, automatically also enemies of God. And Artegall has
the sword of Jove to do it with.

Artegall first uses his "bright Chrysaor" to cut off the head of
the mighty pagan, Pollente. This wicked man is, if not gigantic,
at least, as his very name insists, "so puissant and strong,/That
with his powre he all doth overgo" (ii.7). Perhaps he exemplifies
the problem of the "over-mighty subject" which, understandably,
much troubled the Tudor kings.[10] Pollente, like the great English noblemen who retained their own armies, has assumed for
himself rights and privileges which—to the Tudor monarch's
mind—only the king should have. In this respect Pollente is a
rebel against and a usurper of proper authority. He is a twofold
foe of God, for he is not only a pagan but also a disrupter of
God's order and right government. He proves a tough adversary
for the hero of justice:

> But *Artegall* pursewed him still so neare,
>> With bright Chrysaor in his cruell hand,
>> That as his head he gan a litle reare
>> Above the brincke, to tread upon the land,
>> He smote it off, that tumbling on the strand
>> It bit the earth for very fell despight,
>> And gnashed with his teeth, as if he band
>> High God, whose goodnesse he despaired quight,
> Or curst the hand, which did that vengeance on him dight.

(ii.18)

The reference of the last line is significantly ambiguous. In the
first place the hand "which did that vengeance on him dight" is
the cruel hand which has just wielded bright Chrysaor to such

good effect; it is the hand of Artegall. But Pollente not only "curst the hand," but also "band High God"—cursed God himself. Everyone knew that vengeance is mine, saith the Lord. God-defying Pollente is felled by "that vengeance"; that is, by the vengeance of God as well as of Artegall—the vengeance of God as administered by the hand of his instrument, Artegall.

Then, again, the two great adversaries whom Arthur and Artegall encounter at the end of the Legend of Justice are, like Pollente, rebels, giants, and foes of God. They are rebels in that, like many of the evil characters in the book, they have taken over or are trying to take over the position that rightfully belongs to another. They have overrun, respectively, the lands of Belge and Irena. In that Geryoneo clearly and Grantorto perhaps by implication are represented as servants of the Catholic antichrist, they are foes of God. Both are unmistakably gigantic creatures. Geryoneo unseats Prince Arthur, who has undertaken to put down the tyrant:

> Whereof when as the Gyant was aware,
> He wox right blyth, as he had got thereby,
> And laught so loud, that all his teeth wide bare
> One might have seene enraung'd disorderly,
> Like to a rancke of piles, that pitched are awry.　　　　(xi.9)

And Grantorto is thus described:

> Of stature huge and hideous he was,
> Like to a Giant for his monstrous hight,
> And did in strength most sorts of men surpas,
> Ne ever any found his match in might;
> Thereto he had great skill in single fight:
> His face was ugly, and his countenance sterne,
> That could have frayd one with the very sight,
> And gaped like a gulfe, when he did gerne,
> That whether man or monster one could scarse discerne.

(xii.15)

Artegall destroys this last of the tyrannous enemies of justice as he had the first: he cuts off Grantorto's head with Chrysaor, the anti-giant sword of Jove. ("He stroke him with Chrysaor on the hed"—xii.23.)

But Artegall's most notable experience with a giant is his encounter with that rebellious, usurping, God-defying Gyant of Canto ii. This is the very Gyant himself, representative of all those giants who attempted the throne of Jove; he is the central exemplification of this one of Spenser's many themes of justice. Spenser does not distinguish this character, as his critics do, by adding any further identification; he is not merely the communist giant, the egalitarian giant, the demagogic giant: [11] he is absolutely "a mighty Gyant" such as were those who sought to overthrow the throne and the system of Jove.

Artegall and Talus come upon the Gyant standing on a rock with a crowd of people gathered round him. He is advocating universal cosmic and social equalization, and the downing of tyrants. He is a wicked man; an Anabaptist perhaps; [12] a Communist, as we would name him now with all that Elizabethan fervor of distrust and distress. He is proposing to challenge the very foundations of hierarchy and of the system of the Christian state: he is attempting to assume not only the king's power of governing but also God's power of justly apportioning the goods of the earth.

Artegall deals with the situation in an interesting and traditional way. He uses eloquence, which was considered to be the proper initial tool for dealing with rebellion and revolution. Artegall enters into a notably long discussion with the Gyant who is stirring up the mob to rebellion:

> All which when Artegall did see, and heare,
> How he mis-led the simple peoples traine,
> In sdeignfull wize he drew unto him neare,
> And thus unto him spake, without regard or feare. (ii.33)

His expostulation and the Gyant's reply, and his demonstration of the falseness of the Gyant's position and the Gyant's refusal to accept that proof occupy sixteen stanzas. The passage is so striking that most of Spenser's critics have commented on it, admiring or ridiculing the poetry, sympathetically explicating or crossly rejecting the philosophy.[13]

The reason Artegall enters into such a discussion at this point is that rebels and rabble-rousers should, if at all possible, the poet's contemporaries thought, be talked rather than forced into submission. At the beginning of the century Sir Thomas More had provided an object lesson in this vein; he had, so the story went, actually addressed and reasoned with a rebellious mob, speaking to the rioters near St. Martin's Gate and entreating them to disperse. Sir Philip Sidney imagines a similar scene in the *Arcadia*: when a rebellion against Duke Basilius arises Pyrochles goes to the Duke's throne to address the threatening crowd; his eloquence subdues and reforms the rebels.[14] Similarly, Sir John Cheke, in mid-century, actually composed an address to those of his fellow-Englishmen who were restless and rebellious; it touched a tender chord and was reprinted several times in the next hundred years. In his pamphlet Cheke explained that reason and natural law and our knowledge of the will of God make it clear that all men must accept their lot in life; he deplored "the usurping of authoritie, & taking in hand of rule, which is the sitting in Gods seat of justice, and a proud clyming up into Gods high throne." [15] Cheke describes the evil that men bring upon themselves through rebellion and ends with this peroration:

Wherefore, for Gods sake, have pittie on your selves: consider how miserably yee have spoiled, destroyed, and wasted us all: and if for desperatenesse yee care not for your selves, yet remember your country, and forsake this rebellion, with humble submission acknowledge your faults, & tarry not the extremity of the Kings sword.[16]

It appears to have been the standard, indeed inevitable, view that if eloquence could not subdue a mob of rioters, the force of the sword must do it. As the author of *The Cabinet Council* declared: "The first way to suppress Sedition, is Eloquence and excellent Persuasion, which oftentimes worketh great Effects among

the Multitude. . . . If Persuasion cannot prevail, then Force
must compel." [17] Eloquence does indeed fail to persuade the
Gyant; so Talus destroys him:

> Whom when so lewdly minded Talus found,
>> Approching nigh unto him cheeke by cheeke,
>> He shouldered him from off the higher ground,
> And down the rock him throwing, in the sea him dround.

$$(ii.49)$$

According to classical legend, the giants had made their attack
on Jove from a mountain which they had piled up toward the
heavens, rock upon rock, and from which Jove, aided by the other
gods and by Hercules, cast them back down.[18] The legend was of
wide circulation.

The *Emblemata Horatiana* emblem *Nequid ultra vires coneris*
(Figure 4) depicts an assault on the heights of Jove. A number of
men or giants are carrying great boulders up a mountain. There is
a tower in the background: the presumptuous climbers are trying
to build another tower of Babel. Above, Jove wields his thunderbolt; and, where he has struck, the aspirers fall tumbling down a
precipice. The emblematist is warning his readers not to attempt
things that are beyond the province of men. He quotes from
Horace several passages from odes in which the giants' war
against Jove is a dominant theme (Lib. 3, Od. 4; Lib. 1, Od. 3).
He comments on his own account: *Temeritas impetus est sine
ratione. Hac duce Gigantes caelum petunt, multique suis confisi
viribus, praecipites ruunt.*

The iconographical tradition illuminates Spenser's description of
the Gyant. It is for good reason that the journeying Artegall and
Talus "beheld a mighty Gyant stand/Upon a rocke" (ii.30); we,
too, are to visualize a giant on his appropriate heights of defiance.
True princes sit on high (cf. Pr. 11); the Gyant, a usurper, has
set himself up on a rebellious peak from which Talus, on behalf
of Artegall and Jove, casts him precipitately down.

For good measure, though, as many-leveled as ever, Spenser

associates the Gyant's end with another traditional fall: that from the top to the bottom of the wheel of fortune. The suggestion is made as it were at two removes. According to the narrative, a giant is pushed over a cliff. According to the accompanying simile, his end is like a shipwreck:

> Like as a ship, whom cruell tempest drives
>   Upon a rocke with horrible dismay,
>   Her shattered ribs in thousand peeces rives,
>   And spoyling all her geares and goodly ray,
>   Does make her selfe misfortunes piteous pray.
>   So downe the cliffe the wretched Gyant tumbled;
>   His battred ballances in peeces lay,
>   His timbered bones all broken rudely rumbled,
> So was the high aspyring with huge ruine humbled.   (ii.50)

The symbol of a ship on the ocean, subject alike to fair winds and to tempests and rocks, was a common one for fortune; the ship which so magnificently images the Gyant's great body is, indeed, specifically said to be "misfortunes piteous pray." But fortune causes falls, too. The wheel of fortune is one of the commonest images in iconography. Princes aspire: they go up the wheel on one side; they fall, are humbled: they go down it on the other. So was it in the case of the Gyant: "So was the high aspiring with huge ruin humbled."

It is notable that the immediately following episode opens, only a few stanzas later, with a description of Florimell emerging from the "stormes and tempests" of adverse fortune (iii. 1). Her good fortune coincides with the false, usurping Florimell's bad fortune: the false Florimell is "uncas'd" during the course of the episode which is thus introduced. Thus the wheel of fortune constantly reverses the positions of those who ride on it; it casts down to the very bottom those who, like the Gyant, are apparently at the very top.

All these ideas, images, and allusions make the crash of the Gyant's timbered bones reverberate.

CHAPTER 3

POWER AND LAW

IN THE EMBLEM *Potestas potestati subiecta*—that in which the king is depicted ruling his people as Jove, in turn, rules him—the king is flanked by two significant figures (Figure 2). That on the right is a man wearing robes and carrying a scroll; he represents the law. That on the left, standing, however, a little removed, is a ready-armed knight. He represents the prince and judge's essential executive force. Each of the legitimate monarchs and monarch-substitutes in the Legend of Justice is served by at least one of these figures: power. Some of them are also served by law, but a law which is more a matter of the force and enforcement that derives from a monarch than such a wise, peaceable, monarch-counseling kind of law as that depicted in the emblem.

It will be the purpose of this chapter to demonstrate that Artegall commands the just monarch's two executive instruments, power and law, and that in corresponding manner he himself embodies the power and law of a higher authority.

In the Proem to Book V Spenser praises his Dread Soverayne Goddesse for her great justice—"The instrument whereof loe here thy Artegall" (Pr. 11). On the literal narrative level,

Artegall is one of Gloriana's attendant knights (i. 4). But then he is also specifically said to be an instrument of the Dread Soverayne Goddesse; in a leap from the fictional to the historical world which blurs the logical levels of allegory and conveys them all, vehicle and its tenors, into an all-embracing fiction, Artegall is the instrument of Queen Elizabeth herself. Most commentators have, reasonably enough, associated Artegall, the instrument of the queen whose quest is to liberate Irena, with Arthur Grey, Lord de Wilton, the Lord Deputy of Ireland, with whom Spenser for a time served. Grey was specifically Elizabeth's "deputy." A deputy is one who fills the place of his absent principal; he has his attributes and performs his functions. In the Legend of Justice Artegall both, in his role of instrument, represents power and, in his role of deputy, uses it.

It is at the beginning of the fourth canto that Spenser most clearly declares that justice is and must be served by power. He writes:

> Who so upon him selfe will take the skill
> > True Justice unto people to divide,
> > Had need have mightie hands, for to fulfill
> > That, which he doth with righteous doome decide,
> > And for to maister wrong and puissant pride.
> > For vaine it is to deeme of things aright,
> > And makes wrong doers justice to deride,
> > Unlesse it be perform'd with dreadlesse might.
> For powre is the right hand of Justice truely hight.
>
> Therefore whylome to knights of great emprise
> > The charge of Justice given was in trust,
> > That they might execute her judgements wise,
> > And with their might beat downe licentious lust,
> > Which proudly did impugne her sentence just.
> > Whereof no braver president this day
> > Remaines on earth, preserv'd from yron rust
> > Of rude oblivion, and long times decay,
> Then this of Artegall, which here we have to say.   (iv.1,2)

Artegall has, it is clear, the requisite "mightie hands." Spenser has already explained that Artegall is descended from those other "knights of great emprise," Bacchus/Osiris and Hercules, who were the original, widely renowned great maintainers of justice (i.1,2). The poet now accounts for this tradition. The maintenance of justice is entrusted to heroic knights because it is they who have the power to enforce it. Artegall clearly executes the judgments of Jove and God with the power of his knightly sword. It is notable, too, that the monarch Mercilla has at her disposal both a sword and a lion which represent her power (ix.30,33).

At the beginning of Artegall's career Astraea gave him, in addition to the sword Chrysaor, the terrible creature whom Astraea herself has used as her own executor: Talus.[1]

> But when she parted hence, she left her groome
>   An yron man, which did on her attend
>   Alwayes, to execute her stedfast doome,
>   And willed him with Artegall to wend,
>   And doe what ever thing he did intend.   (i.12)

It was C. S. Lewis who observed that what Artegall is to the whole virtue of justice, Talus in turn is to Artegall.[2] And this is indeed the case. Both Artegall and Talus embody the power that is the right hand of justice. The iron Talus is Artegall's executor; Artegall is God's, Justice's, and his queen's.

Readers of *The Faerie Queene* have for the most part been agreed that Talus represents, or is the embodiment of, power. They deduce it, for one thing, from Spenser's outright statement that "powre is the right hand of Justice truely hight." For Talus is clearly Artegall's right-hand man.

That Talus represents power was first observed by Upton;[3] it has most recently been reasserted by Northrop Frye, who comments on "Spenser's conception of justice as the harnessing of physical power to conquer physical nature. In its lower aspects this power is mechanical, symbolized by the 'yron man' Talus. . . ."[4] Talus functions as a bloodhound and a police helicopter, an executioner and an army. (See V.ii.25; i.20; ii.26–28, 49; vii.36; xi.47; xii.7; etc.) But in all this he fulfills Artegall's purpose and will. It is his business to do the work that Artegall is too noble to do himself—he deals with vulgar mobs and women, and the slaughtering of the enemy (V.ii.52; iv.24). His difference from Artegall is largely one of degree: each of them performs the forceful acts suitable to his station. When, for instance, Artegall and Talus help Burbon deal with his oppressors Spenser writes:

> Those knights began a fresh them to assayle,
> And all about the fields like Squirrels hunt;
> But chiefly Talus with his yron flayle,
> Gainst which no flight nor rescue mote avayle,
> Made cruell havocke of the baser crew,
> And chaced them both over hill and dale:
> The raskall manie soone they overthrew,
> But the two knights themselves their captains did subdew.
>
> (xi.59)

The division of labor is clear: Talus is most effective against the base and raskall manie,[5] the knights against their peers.

Talus exercises his absolute power through his absolute weapon, his iron flail. This weapon has long interested Spenser scholars, who have speculated much about the origins of Talus and the significance of his flail. In fact the various iconographical and mythological associations of Talus's flail are relevant to, and indeed explicatory of, the relationship between justice and power.

The iron man himself is clearly derived from the Greek Talos, the brazen man who, according to Plato and other authorities, guarded the shores and helped to maintain the laws of Crete. Spenser's Talus is as metallic, as terrible, as law-keeping, and as magically fast-running as his forebear.[6] He resembles, too—more even than does the specifically brazen Talos of Crete—his more distant ancestors, the brazen men themselves. For of the men of the bronze age Hesiod wrote:

Zeus the Father made a third generation of mortal men, a brazen race, sprung from ash-trees; and it was in no way equal to the silver age, but was terrible and strong. They loved the lamentable works of Ares and deeds of violence; they ate no bread, but were hard of heart like adamant, fearful [Graves renders: pitiless [7]] men. Great was their strength and unconquerable the arms which grew from their shoulders on their strong limbs. Their armour was of bronze, and their houses of bronze, and of bronze were their implements [εἰργάζοντο]: there was no black iron.[8]

It is fitting enough, these men being brazen in a brazen age, that Talus should be iron in an iron age. Like the brazen men, Talus loves, or at any rate performs the deeds of Ares, or Mars. Like the brazen men he is terrible, strong, hard of heart, pitiless.[9] But Talus's most remarkable and apparently unprecedented characteristic is the flail which he carries; for neither the brazen men nor Talos of Crete carried such a weapon.

To be sure, Hesiod's brazen men carried, not weapons, but εἰργάζοντο: agricultural implements. These men did not eat bread and so probably did not grow the wheat from which bread is made: their agricultural implements were, as likely as not, their weapons. This was, at any rate, the belief of one English translator. The standard, often-repeated Latin translation of Hesiod's lines was:

> *His erant aenea arma, aeneaeque domus:*
> *Aere vero operabantur.*[10]

In this view, the brazen men had bronze tools to toil with. George Chapman, likewise, in a translation of 1618, leaves the brazen men weaponless:

> Their houses all were brazen, all of brass
> Their working instruments.[11]

But Thomas Cooke, in 1728, yields to a rational urge to endow the brazen men with weapons:

> Their houses brass, of brass the warlike blade.[12]

I have no evidence that any earlier translators or commentators saw Hesiod's working implements in terms of warlike blades. But it seems a very probable interpretation, the more especially in view of the way in which some agricultural implements—scythes and indeed flails—commonly had most violent and death-dealing associations.

There is in iconography one figure who quite often appears brandishing a flail; that is Mars, the god whose lamentable works the brazen men were said to have loved. Mars is usually and most orthodoxly represented as a young man, dressed in armour, riding a war chariot drawn, often through the air, by fierce horses, and brandishing a whip; he is accompanied by a wolf. But although he usually carries a whip, for the dual purpose of urging on his horses and threatening his enemies, he is frequently pictured as sitting—sometimes in a vehicle more like a farm cart than a war-chariot—with a flail over his shoulder instead of a whip in his raised hand (Figure 5).[13]

Such an attribute of the god of war makes a splendidly fitting weapon for Talus, that mighty swift-flying ironclad man, who on occasion functions as the power of an entire army.[14] One critic has, indeed, allegorized Talus in terms of the English army and his flail in terms of its newly developed musketry.[15] This is, of course, too limited a view. Others, still drawn to associate Talus with war, have suggested that his flail was a common medieval weapon. It was not such a common one as all that.

At least five mighty figures in medieval romances were equipped with iron flails. In *Huon de Bordeaux* (1400–54), the tower of Dunother is guarded by two men of brass, each holding an iron flail.[16] In the romance of *Partenay* (1475), a giant prepares himself for an encounter with the hero by arming himself with his falchion, his "Flaelles thre of yr," and his three iron sledgehammers. Again, in the romance of *Melusine*, "The geaunt toke hys flayel of yron, & gaf geffray a grete buffet." [17] It is from these flails, together with that of Talus, that the Oxford English

Dictionary derives the impression that the flail was a common medieval weapon. But Spenser specifically writes that Talus's flail was a "strange weapon, never wont in war" (iv.44). It is a much more terrible weapon than any common device from the medieval armory could be; it is much more terrible than a mere allegorization of the new Renaissance musketry; it is the weapon of Mars; it is the weapon which only giants and iron and brazen men are terrible and martial enough to use.

Flail-bearing Mars was often accompanied by a wolf: his creature, and the traditional emblem of terrible force. (In Figure 5, the artist has emphasized the relationship between flail and wolf through the central line in the woodcut: it runs through the bent flail, the front of the chariot, and then from the wolf's nose to his tail.) It is, perhaps, significant that flail-bearing Talus, too, is quite often presented in terms of wolf-imagery.

FIGURE 5. Mars. From *Ovide moralisé* (Bruges, 1480).

On one occasion, Radigund's Amazons are unable to stand against Talus,

> But like a sort of sheepe dispersed farre
> For dread of their devouring enemie,
> Through all the fields and vallies did before him flie. (iv.44)

Again, Talus pursues Dolon and his men so hard

> That here and there like scattred sheepe they lay. (vi.30)

Finally, when Envie and Detraction meet Artegall with, presumably, his iron groom,

> They both arose, and at him loudly cryde,
> As it had bene two shepheards curres, had scryde
> A ravenous Wolfe amongst the scattered flockes. (xii.38)

It is extraordinary that the hero of justice should be associated, even if from the viewpoint of two malicious old hags, with a ravenous wolf among scattered sheep; and Talus cannot but come very ferociously out of comparisons with a devouring, sheep-dispersing wolf.[18] To be sure, Spenser does not make much use of traditional Christian sheep-mysticism—in *The Shepheardes Calender* many of the pastoral figures are goatherds rather than shepherds; yet his sheep are usually innocent even if silly, and his wolves are consistently wicked. Though told that perhaps he should not, the modern reader persists in disliking Artegall and Talus; images such as these suggest that he is not wrong.

These scattered references to wolves make up a slight chain of thematic imagery linking Talus appropriately with Mars; they also fittingly reinforce Talus' association with power, for wolves are emblems of power. Good power is traditionally represented by lions. Wolves as consistently represent power's other aspect: armed and terrible force. They are the creatures of Mars, the embodiments of rapine, injuriousness toward everything, and insatiable greediness (which is why Spenser's wolves are such ravening, devouring creatures).[19]

Talus's ferocity is both confirmed and to some extent explained through his association with Mars. His odd relationship with Artegall and with justice may be illuminated by other significances which his flail suggests. For Talus's weapon is manifoldly remarkable in its associations. It may recall not only the flail which is the emblem of Mars but also the club which Hercules carries and the scourge which is the terrible instrument of Jove and of God's vengeful law.

In a Gaelic life of Hercules, *Stair Ercueil Ocus a Bas,* Hercules carries a flail.[20] It is possible that Spenser may have heard of this when he was in Ireland. Certainly in the light of it the flail that Talus carries is delightfully appropriate: it is the weapon with which Artegall is equipped in imitation of his predecessor Hercules,

> Who all the West with equall conquest wonne,
> And monstrous tyrants with his club subdewed;
> The club of Justice dread, with kingly powre endewed.   (i.2)

Hercules's club is an instrument for preserving law and the right. For Hercules is unlike the flail carriers which we have hitherto noticed: they were simply fearful, indiscriminately destructive giants. Hercules, though, and some other moral flail bearers of tradition, emphasize another aspect of Talus's flail.

In the *Lyf of Virgilius,* of 1518, an iron flail is carried by a virtuously superhuman figure who closely resembles Talus. It is the weapon of a copper horseman who goes about the country punishing wrongdoers; he suppresses "nyght ronners and theves."[21] This copper horseman is clearly a direct descendant of the brazen runner and lawkeeper of Crete. His flail is not a mere weapon for war and destruction, but an instrument of justice.

I have said that in Renaissance iconography Mars is depicted sometimes with a whip and sometimes with a flail. It appears that whips and flails were widely regarded as related to one another; in common usage they appear to have been interchangeable. Jean

Seznec attributes the variation between whips and flails in the iconography of Mars to a mistranslation, in one case at least, of the Latin *flagellum* by French *flayeu* (*fléau*).[22] But flails are associated with whips through their appearance and function as well as through their etymological origin (in *flagellum*). The entries in the Oxford English Dictionary on flails and threshing (the usual verb for the act of using a flail; Spenser calls Talus's flail a "thresher") suggest that flails were frequently regarded as interchangeable with whips, threshing with thrashing. According to Dryden's neat line, MacFlecknoe is "A scourge of Wit, and flayle of Sense": [23] the terms were, toward the end of the seventeenth century, as in earlier times, in effect synonymous.

Now any flail derived from or associated with the whip of Mars can have no moral force. But there was another classical god who wielded his own righteously vengeful weapon in a manner parallel to Mars: that was Jove himself. Taddeo di Bartolo represents Jupiter wielding his flames and Mars his whip in very much the same way (Figure 6). Sometimes Jove is described or represented as carrying, as Mars usually does, an actual whip, a whip that is assuredly a scourge of wrongdoers.

According to Macrobius, Jove is to be properly represented as brandishing a whip in his right hand—much in the manner of chariot-driving Mars, as succeeding painters and sculptors seem to have supposed.[24] In Macrobius's description, Jove's usually terrible and dominant thunderbolt is relegated to his left hand, along with a sheaf of wheat. He stands *dextra elevata cum flagro, in aurigae modum; laeva tenet fulmen, et spicas.*[25] There are several Renaissance representations of Jove which follow Macrobius's description. Notable among them is Agostino di Duccio's bas-relief of him in the Tempio Malatestiana.[26]

Talus and his flail are, like Chrysaor, the executive instruments of Artegall and of Jove. Artegall, Jove's executive, has in turn his own corresponding executive—Talus; as Artegall wields Jove's sword Chrysaor, Talus, it may be, wields Jove's scourge.

FIGURE 6. Jupiter and Mars. Taddeo di Bartolo, Siena, Palazzo Pubblico (finished by 1414).

Talus's weapon is in fact, though, not a whip but a flail. As such it is, I believe, as appropriate to the terrible harvester-God of parts of the Christian story as are scourge and thunderbolt to Jove. God's deeds are, especially in the New Testament, constantly being described in terms of husbandry. God seeks to sow good seed on good, not stony, ground. Death takes men as the mower takes the grass. At the last judgment the grain will be separated from the chaff. Now it is remarkable that on many of the occasions on which Talus punishes, executes, scatters, and slaughters wrongdoers he acts quite in accordance with the nature of his weapon: he is like a husbandman. And the imagery particularly tends to associate him with the most terrible of the deeds of the Christian farmer-God. For one thing, with ironical perversion, Talus sows death instead of life, corpses instead of good seed. He slaughters Grantorto's followers so generously

> That they lay scattred over all the land,
> As thicke as doth the seede after the sowers hand.   (xii.7)

Talus often, indeed, goes about with his flail much like death with his scythe (Figure 7).[27] On one occasion his dreadful appearance is said to be, like a falcon's to ducks, as death itself:

> As when a Faulcon hath with nimble flight
> Flowne at a flush of Ducks, foreby the brooke,
> The trembling foule dismayd with dreadfull sight
> Of death, the which them almost overtooke,
> Doe hide themselves from her astonying looke,
> Amongst the flags and covert round about.   (ii.54)

A flail is the implement which is used to beat out grain from its husk. The useless powdered threshed husk is called chaff. The chaff is winnowed from the heavier grain by a bellows or fan which blows it off and scatters it. God promised that at the day of judgment he would separate the bad men from the good like chaff from the grain. It is a central, often repeated image.[28] By reference to it Spenser suggests the true nature of Talus's acts. When Burbon is assailed by his enemies he is driven back

> untill that yron man
> With his huge flaile began to lay about,
> From whose sterne presence they diffused ran,
> Like scattred chaffe, the which the wind away doth fan.

(xi.47)

FIGURE 7. *Cunctos mors una manet*. From *Emblemata Horatiana*, p. 205.

No one need doubt the origin of that wind or the destination of that worthless chaff, those wicked men.

Whether Talus's flail is, at any given moment, to be associated with the flail of Mars, the whip of Jove, or God's combine harvester, it is, at any rate, clearly the instrument of his terrible power. For Talus and his flail are plainly, on the one hand, the embodiments of force. Like Artegall, they serve monarchy and justice in that essential executive capacity.

On the other hand, it is clear that Artegall and Talus also both represent the law.

Artegall has always been understood to represent justice: Spenser plainly declares as much in calling his fifth book "The Legend of Artegall, or of Justice"; and indeed he presents Artegall largely in terms of the traditional views of the virtue. Yet there are some times when Artegall is clearly conceived more in terms of law, and of law's relationship to equity, than in terms of monarchial absolute justice. Talus, too, has more than one significance. Though most scholars have always, very properly, seen him as the embodiment of power, others quite understandably consider him to be the symbol of law. The point is, of course, that the concepts of justice and law have always been closely interlinked; and, in Jean Bodin's view at least, the concepts of power and law may be regarded as interdependent.

Frederick M. Padelford thought that Talus represents the law; he argued on the grounds that "that which executes the judgments of justice, threshes out falsehood and unfolds truth, is . . . the law and its ministers." [29] There are, indeed, good grounds for associating Talus with the law. For one thing, what Astraea was actually said to have left to men when she went from the earth at the beginning of the iron age was a "testamentum" of laws.[30] Spenser's Astraea leaves Talus. Again, Talus is very clearly derived from that law-keeping brazen man, Talos of Crete. In Plato's *Minos*, Talos is associated with Rhadamanthus in the rigorous execution of the laws of Crete; he is said to be brazen because he carries the tables of the law engraved on a brazen tablet.[31] Indeed, in both classical and Christian tradition the law was characterized as something engraved on a tablet. In Greek and Roman tradition, the tables of the law were usually brazen; the Mosaic law was carved on stone. The identity of the robed man in the emblem *Potestas potestati subiecta* (Figure 2) is known chiefly by the fact that he stands holding a long scroll: he is the law. Talus does not carry a tablet or scroll. Yet Spenser's description of him at the beginning of the Legend of Justice has a close verbal correspondence with his description, in *A View of the Present State of Ireland*, of the law. Talus is "Immoveable, resistlesse, without end." And "the lawes," Spenser declares in the *View*, "oughte to be like stonye tables playne stedfaste and unmoveable." [32]

In the Van Veen emblem of justice the monarch is flanked by two separate and contrasting figures representing law and executive force. It is my contention that Spenser analyzed the component parts of justice rather differently; for him, power and law are not a contrasting pair but a pair with a related, even perhaps an identical function. According to this view Talus represents both the rigorous law which the sovereign decrees and the sovereign's power to enforce and maintain that law.

This is how Jean Bodin explains the orthodox view of the relationship between law and the monarch:

If we insist however that absolute power means exemption from all law whatsoever, there is no prince in the world who can be regarded as sovereign, since all the princes of the earth are subject to the laws of God and of nature, and even to certain human laws common to all nations. [33]

The figure of law who stands at the king's right hand in the emblem is advising the monarch from the tables of such prince-governing laws as these.

Beyond this, though, Bodin had his own particular, rather less orthodox view of the monarch and law. Whereas tradition had it that the monarch's definitive function is to administer justice, Bodin declared that the ruler's definitive function is to create law—if possible in accordance with natural laws but in practice, of course, often enough not. The ruler, in this view, is essentially a lawmaker and the enforcer of the laws he makes. Bodin wrote: "It is clear that the principal mark of sovereign majesty and absolute power is the right to impose laws generally on all subjects regardless of their consent." [34] And he declared that "law is nothing else than the command of the sovereign in the exercise of his sovereign power." [35] Law is, to a great extent, power, and power, law. Spenser almost certainly knew the work of the French jurist; the possibility that he may be indebted to it for some of his ideas, especially for some of those in his *View*, has been suggested by several scholars.[36] It may be that Spenser, like Bodin, regarded law less as a code by which the monarch governs his conduct and decisions than as an expression of and a vehicle for the king's legitimate power.

In Talus at any rate power is surely united with law—and that a law of the harshest kind. In this connection an early seventeenth-century English emblem of "The Rigour of the Law" is of some interest. In it is depicted a man on horseback who carries an iron yoke and brandishes a whip: he represents "the Rigour of the Law." The verses that accompany the emblem explain that the citizen who does not know how to ride and who therefore beats and maltreats his horse will not get the results he seeks; the case is exactly the same with those who apply "the Rigour of the Law" instead of "the gospel of Christ, which makes glad." [37] It is clear that one of the themes which Spenser manipulates in Book V is that of the relationship between the Old Law and the New. Jove is associated with the Old Law, and Talus's flail recalls Jove's whip. Swift iron Talus with his punishing flail would seem to be as clearly representative of the rigor of both man's law and God's as is the whip- and yoke-carrying horseman of the emblem.

It is in Artegall, however, that rigorous law and rigorous justice are most clearly exemplified; and it is through his relationship to Britomart that they are most clearly shown to be oversevere. For Artegall and the kind of justice which he represents is complemented by Britomart, who is specifically equated with "that part of Justice, which is Equity" (vii.3). Now equity is a branch of the law, that according to which, in fact, the English system of common law or law by precedent was instituted, and by which it was justified. Theoretically, equity can only exist in terms of, and in relationship to, the absolute law which it is its function to modify.[38] Spenser in effect says as much when he writes that Astraea taught Artegall to weigh right and wrong,

> And equitie to measure out along,
> According to the line of conscience,
> When so it needs with rigour to dispence.   (vi.7)

Although theoretically it was as much the function of equity to make the law severer where it was inadequate as it was to make it more lenient where it was too strict, in general practice the law would inevitably be equated with rigor, as it is by Spenser, and equity with "clemence oft in things amis" (vii.22). It thus appears that Spenser not only distinguishes the rigorous, Old, Jovial justice of Artegall from the merciful, New, Christian justice of Mercilla, but that he also distinguishes, in terms of the standard difference between law and equity, the legal justice of Artegall from the equitable justice of Britomart (who stands in the book in several respects parallel to Mercilla).

This interpretation may perhaps be supported by evidence that at least one influential iconologist distinguished the same two kinds of benevolent and rigorous justice. To be sure, the terms the iconologist uses are not the terms of law, power, equity, and mercy—those in which we have couched our discussion of the subject. But the relationship between rigorous male and pliant female kinds of justice is the same in Ripa and Baudoin as it is in Spenser. That Artegall's kind of justice did indeed have its place in the sixteenth-century scheme of things, and that that place was a less than supreme one, is suggested by a series of emblems in Ripa's *Iconologia*. They are translated, illustrated, and strikingly juxtaposed in Baudoin's French edition of the book (Figure 8).[39]

Ripa gives an account of four different kinds of justice, of which three are represented by women much like Mercilla; only

IVSTICE.   IVSTICE·INVIOLABLE.

IVSTICE·RIGOVREVSE.   IVSTICE·DIVINE.

FIGURE 8. Four figures of Justice. From Baudoin's *Iconologie*, II, 56 (Paris, 1644). Courtesy of the Art and Architecture Division, The New York Public Library, Astor, Lenox and Tilden Foundations.

one is represented by a figure which is probably that of a man. The first of the group is Justice. She is a beautiful young woman who is said to be, like Astraea, Britomart, and Queen Elizabeth, a virgin. She wears a crown and regal robes of gold to establish her queenly quality and has a jewel around her neck to show that justice is the most precious thing on earth; the jewel is cut in the form of an eye to show that it is like the sun in seeing everything.

Then there is Divine Justice. She is a crowned woman in a robe of gold tissue. Above her head is a dove ringed with the sun's rays and in her hands are justice's inevitable sword and scales. (Wavy swords such as this lady carries were traditionally associated with Jove's thunderbolt.) And Inviolable Justice is represented by a crowned woman wearing regal robes and carrying a sword and scales. At her feet are a dog and a serpent. (These creatures signify, Ripa declares, that she is faithful to virtue and hates vice.)

But the fourth kind of justice is rather different. Rigorous Justice is represented as a skeleton wielding, as usual, a sword and a pair of scales. This is, to be sure, a legitimate kind of justice; but it is a terrible one. It is usually Death who is represented as a skeleton (see Figure 7). Ripa in fact explains that *Giustitia rigorosa* is like death. It is like death in that it is never swayed by excuses and has no regard for persons; moreover:

La vista spaventevole di questa figura mostra, che spaventevole e ancora a' popoli questa sorte di Giustitia, che non sa in qualche occasione interpretare leggiermente la legge.[40]

Ripa's rigorous justice does not on any occasion interpret the laws leniently. And that is, most strikingly, Artegall's position, too. It is precisely Britomart's function, as equity, to interpret the laws in accordance with individual circumstances. It is precisely for her to modify with clemency the cruel dooms of rigorous Artegall.

The monarch in the emblem *Potestas potestati subiecta* was accompanied by those two separate and contrasting figures representing on the one hand wise and peaceable law and on the other executive force. Spenser combines these two into one figure which he sets up in contrasting relationship against a different set of concepts. Throughout his Legend of Justice he contrasts, not power with law, but rather, and with more many-leveled subtlety, masculine hardness with feminine softness, rigor with mercy, law with equity, vengeance with pity, and force, as we shall discover, not only with its common complement, wisdom, but also, in a striking and paradoxical departure, with fraud.

CHAPTER 4

LION

It is a remarkable fact that the iconographical tradition was one, the contrary of almost all others, in which monarchy, and the various attributes of monarchy and virtues connected with monarchy, were consistently represented in the figures of women. In detail after detail, Spenser's description of Mercilla corresponds with the emblematists' queenly representations of the royal virtues of justice, equity, magnanimity, clemency, and so forth. In detail after detail, too, naturally, Spenser's Mercilla resembles the Queen Elizabeth whom Renaissance illustrators and portrait painters saw: a lady heavily laden with symbolical accoutrements.[1] Spenser and the portrait painters were drawing upon the same tradition.

The tradition of representing royal virtues in the figures of queenly ladies derives no doubt from the classical examples of Astraea and Justitia, and from the habit of personifying many abstract virtues and magnificences, as Latinity suggested, by female figures. Spenser, like the Elizabethan portrait painters who represented their monarch in such iconographically orthodox terms, must have been delighted to have at his disposal at least this one tradition which accepted and presented a just and royal *woman*. As we have suggested in indicating Artegall's princely qualities, from the logic of analogy (which declared that the king is as a father, as God), and for other reasons, convention preferred, if it did not insist, that the ruler be a man.

Monarchy and justice were almost always pictured, like Mercilla in Spenser's elaborate description (ix. 27–33), as a young and beautiful woman; crowned—sometimes with the sun itself; richly bejeweled, and wearing regal, golden robes. They often had a scepter and a sword (cf. ix.30); they sometimes had captives at their feet (cf. ix.29); and again and again they appear seated on, or, like Mercilla, over, lions (ix.33).

We have already glanced at the three blazing, bejeweled, sword-and-scales carrying ladies through whom Ripa and Baudoin present different aspects of justice (Figure 8); Mercilla is just such a figure as these. She, too, is surrounded with gems, gold, and sunlight. She holds, the supreme emblem of monarchy,

> a Scepter in her royall hand,
> The sacred pledge of peace and clemencie
> With which high God had blest her happie land. (ix.30)

This is the scepter of royal power such as that which is wielded by Ripa's Magnanimity and by his Monarchy, and of course by Queen Elizabeth herself (Figures 10, 12, 15).[2] In Spenser, indeed, the scepter seems to have borrowed some of its significance from the cornucopia of peace and prosperity which representatives of monarchy frequently also carried (Figures 9, 10). In one hand, then, Mercilla holds a scepter. But iconographical figures almost always hold something in each hand. Having described the scepter Spenser goes on to complete his stanza with a description of what Mercilla would, in other circumstances, be holding in her other hand:

> But at her feet her sword was likewise layde,
> Whose long rest rusted the bright steely brand;

Yet when as foes enforst, or friends sought ayde,
She could it sternely draw, that all the world dismayde.

(ix.30)

This is an emblem of her ready but not-now-needed power. This is that sword of justice which figures representing the monarch frequently carried and those representing justice almost always carried. Indeed, the monarch in the emblem book *A Mirrour of Majestie* manages to hold the monarch's cornucopia in one hand and both the sword and the scales of justice in the other: he declares that he is

Thus arm'd with Pow'r to punish or protect,
When I have weigh'd each scruple and defect.[3]

But though Mercilla has, as clearly as does this monarch, the resources of power available to her, she is merciful. It is Artegall who punishes. Artegall's sword is of particular significance as the embodiment of his executive power; and complementary to that

FIGURE 9. *Nullum bonum inremuneratum.* From *Mirrour of Majestie*, Embleme 2. Courtesy of the Columbia University Libraries.

"cruell sword" (ii.18) of Jovial justice is the rusty, laid-aside sword of Mercilla's peaceful and merciful rule. Now the sword which represents Power was so regularly the attribute of monarchy that a poet who desired to emphasize the monarch's Mercy might indeed find himself obliged to exclude it. Spenser was not the only poet to do so. Sir John Davies, too, in his Hymne to Astraea's justice, lays his monarch's sword aside:

> Exil'd *Astraea* is come againe,
> Lo here she doth all things maintaine
> In *number, weight,* and *measure.* . . .
> In her left hand (wherein should be
> Nought but the sword) sits Clemency
> And conquers Vice with pardon. (Hymne XXIII)

William Nelson has pointed out that Queen Elizabeth, as emblem-conscious as any good Elizabethan, deliberately used the monarch's proper sword—but a fittingly rusty, resting sword—as her own symbol of her peaceful reign.[4]

Beneath the enthroned Mercilla there is also a fierce chained lion:

> Whylest underneath her feete, there as she sate,
> An huge great Lyon lay, that mote appall
> An hardie courage, like captived thrall,
> With a strong yron chaine and coller bound,
> That once he could not move, nor quich at all;
> Yet did he murmure with rebellions sound,
> And softly royne, when salvage choler gan redound. (ix.33)

That lion, like Mercilla's sword, clearly represents the power which is the right hand of justice; the fact that the lion is chained suggests, as does the rust on the resting sword, that the queen does not now need or intend to use her power—that she has not, indeed, used it for some time. That the lion represents power of some sort or other is very plain. In iconography lions very often do symbolize power or force, or some quality clearly derived from it. Ripa's *Iconologia* is full of the lions of force. But lions continually recur in Renaissance literature and iconography, and they recur with a great variety of meanings. Even the lions that queens are so often seated on or over differ from one another in significance.[5]

It is quite clear, to begin with, that Mercilla's lion does represent her royal power. Lions usually do. Were it only for this reason alone, the lion would be appropriately associated with Mercilla. Further, though, the lion is ideally appropriate within the historical level of the allegory. It is in part a figure of Mercilla's own particular function as representative of Elizabeth, monarch of England; the lion is the traditional royal beast. It is a lion that is begotten by Artegall and Britomart in the vision in the Temple of Isis; the priest explains that they are to have a son "That Lion-like shall shew his *powre* extreame" (vii.23; my italic). This lion represents the prince of the blood royal: for Spenser has firmly established Britomart to be the royal British ancestress (see also III.iii.26–49). In the emblem of the sword-and-cornucopia-carrying British monarch in *The Mirrour of Majestie*, the king is, naturally enough, depicted in the figure of a crowned lion (Figure 9).

The lion is a fitting symbol for the English monarch because he is a fitting symbol for monarchy in general. For the lion has a royal place in the universal hierarchy: he is king of the beasts as the king is prince of men. One of the many royal ladies who are depicted seated on lions in the emblem books is Magnanimity (Figure 10). She holds a scepter in one hand and a cornucopia in the other: for magnanimity is the supremely princely virtue. As Ripa explains, the lion represents magnanimity because he is king of the beasts just as magnanimity is king of the virtues. The system of correspondences is working once again. But the lion also represents magnanimity in that he is merciful and does not cause harm to other animals except in case of necessity.

The monarch's proper virtue of magnanimity is characterized

by a generous clemency; and it is just so that Mercilla, that magnanimous monarch, definitively embodies mercy. And we duly find yet another queen on a lion's back who represents the virtue of clemency. In Ripa's *Iconologia* the emblem for Clemency is a woman seated on a lion with a spear in her left hand and *una saetta* in her right (Figure 13). Ripa explains that clemency is sitting on a lion because the lion is in fact a symbol of clemency. Though the lion can very easily overcome men by his great force, he does not harm them without good reason—*non con legerissima scossa*.[6] By the middle of the seventeenth century clemency could be represented, with greater pictorial literalness, as a lion with an unharmed small dog beneath one of its paws.[7] Even in the nineteenth century the legend still had currency: Delacroix made a lithograph of a mountain lion gently holding a rabbit.[8]

The tradition which so consistently expressed queens' royal virtues by seating them over lions adds to the forcefulness and significance of the icon of Mercilla. However, if the association between lions and, in particular, clemency, had been generally regarded as very strong, Spenser would not, perhaps, have put chains on Mercilla's beast. He might have represented her mercy through the simple presence beneath her throne of the lion of clemency—not through her right restraint of the lion of force.

Ripa has a striking emblem in which queen, sword, and lion are

FIGURE 10. Magnanimity. From Baudoin's *Iconologie*, II, 133. Courtesy of the Art and Architecture Division, The New York Public Library, Astor, Lenox and Tilden Foundations.

in much the same conjunction as they are in Spenser's picture of Mercilla. The emblem is of force subdued by justice (Figure 11). In it justice, represented by the usual crowned, regally robed young woman, has, like Mercilla, a ready but not-now-needed sword. Her hand is on the hilt of her half-drawn weapon. She is seated on a lion. The emblem is entitled *Forza alla giustitia sottoposta;* Ripa describes it as consisting of

> *una donna, vestita regalmente, con una corona in capo, a sedere sopra'l dorso d'un Leone, & che stava in atto di metter mano ad una spada.*[9]

Now this lion is ambiguous. It may represent either the good force which is the instrument of justice but which Justice holds,

FIGURE 11. *Forza alla giustitia sottoposta.* From Ripa's *Iconologia*, p. 207 (Padua, 1618; 1st publication 1593). Courtesy of the Prints Division, The New York Public Library, Astor, Lenox and Tilden Foundations.

like her half-drawn sword, in abeyance, or it may represent the evil force of domestic wrongdoers and foreign foes, which Justice holds, with sword ready against rebellion, tamed as her very throne—as, indeed, part and sign of her glory. And the same dubiety is in Mercilla's lion. In view of the significance of Mercilla's sword, the rationality of parallelism suggests that the lion is a symbol of the just monarch's proper executive force, which the merciful monarch restrains. Yet on the other hand it might seem that a lion so terrible that it has to be kept thrall, chained beneath a prince's throne, must be a very dangerous creature, a foe the domination over which is part of the victor's glory. In both Ripa and Spenser, justice seated upon a lion is a figure ambiguous in both the conventional and the Empsonian senses: its significance is unclear; it appears to signify two different things at once.

On the one hand, Mercilla is seated above a chained lion in order to indicate that the just queen controls and dominates hostile force. Similarly, the monarch in Ripa's emblem *Monarchia mondana* has beneath her feet a number of subdued creatures, thus representing *il dominio de tutto il Mondo* (Figure 12).[10] Chained beneath her feet on one side are several prostrated crowned prisoners (*alcuni prigioni con corona in capo, incatenati, e prostrati in terra*). Now Mercilla too has at her feet if not captive at least prostrated kings. She sits

FIGURE 12. Monarchy. From Baudoin's *Iconologie*, II, 92. Courtesy of the Art and Architecture Division, The New York Public Library, Astor, Lenox and Tilden Foundations.

in royall state
Whylest kings and kesars at her feet did them prostrate.   (ix.29)

(We might note that one artist depicted the enthroned Queen Elizabeth as trampling on the Pope.[11]) Beneath the feet of *Monarchia mondana* are, besides prisoners, *un ferocissimo Leone, e un Serpente di smisurata grandezza.* One of her feet rests dominatingly on the dragon's back.[12] Mercilla has beneath her throne "an huge great Lyon" which is chained "like captived thrall." But he still roynes,[13] and murmurs "with rebellions sound."

The 1596 reading, "rebellions," was changed, in later editions of *The Faerie Queene,* to the apparently more rational "rebellious." But the concrete "rebellions" does accord with the interpretation I am suggesting: from one point of view, at least, Mercilla's lion may be regarded as the embodiment of hostile force, of English mobs as well as of Spanish armies, of, by contemporary definition, the forces of injustice.

On the one hand, then, Mercilla, with the huge great and most ferocious lion which she has quelled like a thrall, and with kings and kesars at her feet, has (or the poet politely wishes she had), like *Monarchia mondana,* dominion over a large part of at any rate the most important quarter of the globe. From this point of view the lion suggests the force of the queen's foreign and domestic foes.

But on the other hand and from another point of view, the lion also represents on the simplest level Mercilla's power, and on a more complex level her passions. Particularly suggestive in this connection are the iconographical associations of chains. The only emblem I have seen in which a lion is actually represented as chained is an emblem called *Virtu oprimée* which occurs in a late seventeenth-century emblem dictionary. The emblematist, Daniel de la Feuille, explains:

La vertu oppresse nous est icy representé sous le symbole d'un Lion chainé pour nous montrer que la force & le courage ne sont pas exempt des coups de la Fortune.[14]

The truth that even power and nobility are subject to fortune does not at first much help us in our understanding of Mercilla's lion. Yet De la Feuille's fine lion does belong to a tradition which can in fact throw some light on our subject. One of the earliest emblematists, Alciati, illustrated a point similar to De la Feuille's by a picture of two lions who are not chained, but harnessed. The emblem *Etiam ferocissimos domari* shows an armed charioteer driving two lions who are harnessed to a light chariot. The lions represent the noble force which, splendid though it is, may yet be unworthily enslaved. Alciati associates the charioteer with the tyrant Anthony, the lions with the senators and heroes of Rome. The emblem seems to have been an appealing one; it reappears, with a long commentary, in Baudoin's emblem dictionary.[15]

Both these emblematists' chained and harnessed lions are noble creatures subdued by evil forces; as such they are only indirectly relevant to Mercilla's lion. But the development and later interpretation of Alciati's emblem is of some interest. For the emblem of the harnessed lion naturally fell together with the widely used emblem of the curbed horse. Now the ability to curb mettlesome horses is the mark of the temperate man who, in accordance with Plato's often-repeated analogy, is able to curb passion in his own soul. Valeriano's emblem of *Justitiae cultus*, with its commentary, perfectly illustrates the matter. The emblem, which is of a woman seated on a lion's back, shows, Valeriano explains, that justice tames the passions just as a woman might tame a ferocious animal.[16] (Of course, the analogy which the Renaissance derived from Plato was that justice controls injustice in the state as temperance controls the passions in an individual. Valeriano has jumped a step. It is not usually justice's part to pass from the public into the private sphere in the way Valeriano suggests; it is not for justice to control the passions.)

In Baudoin's *Iconologie* an emblem of *Clemence* is very suggestively juxtaposed to an emblem of *Commandement sur soy-mesme* (Figure 13).[17] In this emblem self-restraint is represented, in the usual way,[18] by *un Hercule* subduing a lion—putting, in fact, the bit of temperance between the lion's teeth.

FIGURE 13. Clemency and self-control. From Baudoin's *Iconologie*, II, 115. Courtesy of the Art and Architecture Division, The New York Public Library, Astor, Lenox and Tilden Foundations.

Baudoin consistently combines his emblems in significant groups. In pairing clemency with self-command he is making the same observation on the nature of clemency as Spenser is. Mercilla, who is mercy, has to curb her own passions as well as—indeed, before she can—mitigate her might.

Actually, the complex and, in some respects, contradictory quality which iconographical parallels help us to see in the single icon of Mercilla's lion is typical of Spenser. The poet calls upon every available tradition to deepen his effect. He does not, however, do this in a doctrinaire manner: he merely hints at images which the reader should then create, in full, for himself, and afterwards apply back to the poem as explicatory emblems. Because Mercilla's lion is chained, royning, and rebellious, it cannot be *only* the lion of England, or of magnanimity, or of clemency, or of force; it must suggest also various complex psychological and political truths.

CHAPTER 5

SUN

I HAVE SUGGESTED that all the monarch-figures in Book V reflect in some way or another the power of Jove; all of them are also marked by another most orthodox characteristic of monarchy and justice: they are said to resemble or be symbolized by the sun. The sun-like-ness of the true representatives of justice, and the Phaeton-character of the false aspirers, constitutes a thread of thematic imagery in Book V which is similar to that concerned with the king's relationship to Jove and his putting down of the giants. The sun-theme comes up in some more unexpected places than does the Jove-theme: this has the effect of helping to unify some of the very varied elements in the Legend of Justice.

The sun and Jove themes are related, though. There is an early seventeenth-century emblem which perfectly illustrates the generally accepted connection between monarchy and justice, the God which they serve and mirror, and the sun. The emblem is entitled *Heureux celui qui fait le devoir de sa charge* (Figure 14). It is an emblem of justice. Centrally, there is a sun. Four arms and hands come from it at right angles. One of the horizontal hands holds a

sword, and the other, a balance: the inevitable attributes of justice. One vertical hand points down to a globe beneath, the other
up to a brighter sun above: the monarch rules the earth, imitating
God. He fulfills his proper function, does his God-assigned
duty. In this emblem the whole sixteenth-century political doc-

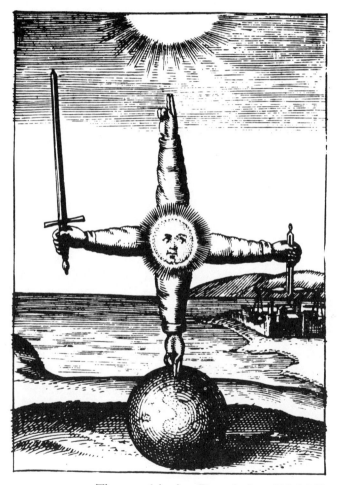

FIGURE 14. The sun of justice. From Andreas Friedrich's
Emblemes Nouveaux, p. 68 (Frankfurt, 1617). Courtesy of
the Columbia University Libraries.

trine which held that the monarch imitates and represents God, and that what God is to the monarch the monarch in turn is to the people, is epitomized in the single device of the sun. The monarch, who embodies earthly justice, can be perfectly represented in a sun, which mirrors the absolute sun: God.[1]

In emblems of monarchy and justice, the royal ladies who represent those virtues often have sun-crowned heads (Figures 8 and 12). And Mercilla is just such a sunny queen. This is how Spenser describes her as she sits enthroned in her Court:

> All over her a cloth of state was spred,
>> Not of rich tissew, nor of cloth of gold,
>> Nor of ought else, that may be richest red,
>> But like a cloud, as likest may be told,
>> That her brode spreading wings did wyde unfold:
>> Whose skirts were bordred with bright sunny beams,
>> Glistring like gold, amongst the plights enrold,
>> And here and there shooting forth silver streames,
> Mongst which crept little Angels through the glittering gleames.
>
> (ix.28)

There is a portrait of Queen Elizabeth, in an illuminated illustration, in which the queen is similarly represented as enthroned beneath a canopy; above the canopy the sun blazes (Figure 15).[2] It is of particular interest that Mercilla's canopy is like a sun-obscuring cloud. Bearing in mind all the strong traditional associations between monarch, Jove, and God, I would tend to view Mercilla's cloud-canopy in the light of Jove's cloud-throne. For, almost every time Jove makes a personal appearance in the emblem books, he is seated in a cloud behind which the sun is shining; the cloud is ringed with sun-rays (see Figures 2 and 4). In this Jove is, for practical reasons, veiling his blinding glory just as does Milton's God:

> thee Author of all being,
> Fountain of Light, thyself invisible
> Amidst the glorious brightness where thou sit'st

Thron'd inaccessible, but when thou shad'st
The full blaze of thy beams, and through a cloud
Drawn round about thee like a radiant Shrine,
Dark with excessive bright thy skirts appear

*(P.L.,*III,374–80)

Like God himself, Mercilla veils all but the skirts of her excessive
brightness with a cloud-like canopy. Spenser's thought is similar
to that of Sir John Davies, who, in his Hymne "To the Sun" in
Astraea, celebrates Elizabeth in terms of her sun-like-ness. The
compliment was, of course, a commonplace of love poetry; yet it
does fit perfectly aptly with our, and Davies's, themes of justice
and monarchy. He wrote:

Sweet, dazle not my feeble sight
And strike me not with blindnesse.[3]

Spenser in effect draws just such a portrait of his queen sedu-
lously restraining herself from dazzling her subjects. Not only is

FIGURE 15. Queen Elizabeth enthroned. Illuminated frontispiece to a
treatise entitled "Regina Fortunata,"
by Henry Howard, Earl of Northum-
berland, B. M. Egerton MS 944, f.iv
(circa 1576).

the sun above Mercilla's head very properly beclouded. Her head is itself like the sun, and she stoops to dim its brightness. When Artegall and Arthur were brought up to her and "Did to her myld obeysance, as they ought," she returned the salute; she inclined her head to them in "a faire stoupe":

> As the bright sunne, what time his fierie teme
> Towards the westerne brim begins to draw,
> Gins to abate the brightnesse of his beme,
> And fervour of his flames somewhat adaw:
> So did this mightie Ladie   (ix.35)

In fact the queen's bending head and the setting sun decline with the same motion. The conceit is as logical and audacious as one of Donne's. Yet since its terms are so firmly based in traditional imagery the reader can pass over it almost without noticing its implications.

It was in much the same way, very often, that Shakespeare used sun-imagery in connection with his monarchs. On one occasion a king rises as the sun does. In *Richard II* Bolingbroke thus describes the coming on to the walls of the king he has come to displace:

> See, see, King Richard doth himself appear,
> As doth the blushing discontented sun
> From out the fiery portal of the east,
> When he perceives the envious clouds are bent
> To dim his glory and to stain the track
> Of his bright passage to the occident.   (III.iii.62–67)

And then, descending toward his deposition, he with wry irony speaks of himself as Phaeton:

> Down, down I come: like glist'ring Phaeton
> Wanting the manage of unruly jades.   (III.iii.178–79)

Again, in *Henry IV*, Part 1, Prince Harry thus excuses his turpitude and promises reformation:

I know you all, and will a while uphold
The unyok'd humor of your idleness.
Yet herein will I imitate the sun,
Who doth permit the base contagious clouds
To smother up his beauty from the world,
That when he please again to be himself
Being wanted, he may be more wond'red at
By breaking through the foul and ugly mists
Of vapours that did seem to strangle him. (I.ii.218–26)

Mercilla, more noble than these and more assured on her seat, graciously dims for her guests the brightness that might be too much for them. In every other respect Mercilla holds her power and glory in check: successive stanzas describe how her sword rusts, how the Litae mitigate her wrath, and how her lion is chained (ix.30–33). It seems fitting that two stanzas before this sequence begins she should be seen clouding her sunlike glory (28), and two stanzas after it ends she should be described as bating, like the sun, her majesty and awe. Five successive images show how Mercilla moderates her monarchy.[4]

However, though Mercilla represents one legitimate kind of justice—that which is, in the long view, the best kind—there is in Book V another kind of justice which never dims its brilliance. The sun is as powerful an order-keeper as is the thunderbolt of Jove: the knights of rigorous justice make as relentless a use of it.

We have only to open Quarles's famous book of *Emblems Divine and Moral* to see that the sun is as much the standard emblem of God and the heavens as Jove's thunderbolt is the emblem of God's wrath.[5] Indeed, in popular mythology and iconography the sun was often associated, if not identified, with Jove. The sun was a standard symbol for God; the intermeshing of Christian and classical analogies inevitably resulted in Jove being associated with the sun. In the writings of Renaissance mythologists not only are Jove and the sun identified with one another, but detailed, esoteric grounds for the identification are given.[6] Jove even appears in Renaissance iconography with a sun-like head, such as that with which Apollo was usually endowed; he holds in his hand his usual thunderbolt (Figure 6).

Artegall is a hero who is endowed, through the implications of the imagery, with just such a head and just such a weapon. For he combines in himself both Jovial and Apollonian features. Spenser makes it explicitly clear that Artegall wields Jove's sword; and he is strongly associated with Jove in a number of other ways. He is also, through a dynamic, developing, many-layered thread of allusion, associated—even metaphorically iden-tified—with the sun.

It has been pointed out that from his first appearance in *The Faerie Queene*, long before the beginning of Book V, Artegall was associated with the sun. Britomart's first vision of him was of a comely knight whose appearance, when he looked forth from the magic mirror, was "as Phoebus face out of the east" (III, ii.24).[7] In Book V the sun imagery comes to its climax in Arte-gall's identification with Osiris (vii.2,22). Spenser makes the matter quite explicit: he describes the priests of Isis as wearing moon-shaped mitres

> To show that Isis doth the Moone portend;
> Like as Osyris signifies the Sunne. (vii.4)

Osiris was considered by many to be the Egyptian sun-god; sun-like-ness was, naturally enough, his usual attribute.[8] At least one influential Renaissance author automatically equated Osiris with the sun. This was Valeriano Bolzani in his *Hieroglyphica* (1556). Following the standard Renaissance doctrine as to the origins of devices, emblems, and the symbolical method generally,[9] Valeri-ano Bolzani purports to base his dictionary of myths and emblems on the Egyptian system of magical hieroglyphics. In practice all that is Egyptian about Valeriano Bolzani's work is his inclusion of a few Egyptian deities. Osiris twice occurs, and is each time primarily identified with the sun.[10] Spenser equates Artegall with Osiris because Osiris was, in the first place, the Egyptian god of justice.[11] The Renaissance associations between, on the one hand, justice, monarchy, and sun, and, on the other, justice, Osiris, and sun, provide a rationale for the way in which Artegall, too, at some points, is identified with the sun.

We have seen that one of Artegall's chief functions is to put down tyrants and rebels, and that he has Jovial weapons to help him in this task. More than once in Book V the same theme is expressed in another way: Artegall, and on one occasion Arthur, like true suns of monarchy and justice, oust Phaeton-like usurping suns from their bad eminence.

One of Artegall's earliest adventures is to take part, in disguise, in the tournament held by Marinell in honor of his marriage to Florimell. Artegall shows great prowess in the tournament and is judged the best knight. However, since he has borrowed Braggadocchio's shield for the occasion, and returned it to him afterwards, he does not claim his guerdon; he

> came not forth: but for Sir Artegall
> Came Braggadochio, and did show his shield,
> Which bore the Sunne brode blazed in a golden field.

> (iii.14)

The "his" is neatly ambiguous in its reference. In fact the shield is Braggadocchio's property. But it more properly belongs to Artegall—and the syntax permits such a reading. Braggadocchio, who pretends to an honor and a courage he does not possess, is equally presumptuous in bearing a shield emblazoned with the sun—a device which only Artegall, the true representative of justice, and the instrument, deputy, and image of the monarch, is entitled to use.[12] In that he usurps the sun—for however short a time—Braggadocchio is Phaeton-like. But Braggadocchio's outrageous assumption of a role too great for him gives Artegall an opportunity to reveal him for what he is, and for Talus to punish him home in the very respect in which he has offended: Talus

> Then from him reft his shield and it renverst,
> And blotted out his armes with falshood blent.   (iii.37)

Julius Zincgreff has an emblem of the sun representing the monarch: it is entitled *Unicus*. The monarch is always single, the emblematist explains; in this respect he is like the sun, for, as ancient authors say, two suns cannot be tolerated together in the sky.[13] The true sun, Artegall, cannot coexist with a second sun, an impostor. Braggadocchio, who represents a false honor and a false sun, is uncased by the true. Even more strikingly, in parallel wise in the same incident, the false Florimell melts and disappears when she is confronted by the true beauty and sun-like-ness of Florimell herself.

The false Florimell is, like Braggadocchio, a usurper. She pretends to the position and prerogatives of the true Florimell: she claims to be true beauty. When Braggadocchio is awarded the prize for his supposed prowess at the tournament he rudely tells the prize giver, Florimell, that his own lady excels her. He shows the false Florimell to the assembled knights and ladies, who are astonished:

> As when two sunnes appeare in the azure skye,
>> Mounted in Phoebus charet fierie bright,
>> Both darting forth faire beames to each mans eye
>> And both adorn'd with lampes of flaming light,
>> All that behold so strange prodigious sight,
>> Not knowing natures worke, nor what to weene,
>> Are rapt with wonder, and with rare affright.
>> So stood Sir Marinell, when he had seene
> The semblant of this false by his faire beauties Queene.   (iii.19)

Once again the truth is represented as one sun and falsehood as another. But the day of two suns is brief. On this occasion, just as on that on which Artegall confronted Braggadocchio, the false sun is undone by the true. As a matter of fact the false Florimell is so constructed that it is easy enough for the true sun to destroy her: she is a fake of the flimsiest kind: a snow-woman. On her first appearance she is described as snowy ("The Witch creates a snowy lady," III.viii. Arg.): she is thereafter repeatedly spoken of in the same terms—a constant reminder of her essential false-ness. At Florimell's end the habitual epithet rises into a fine thematically central image. Artegall settles the problem of the two apparent suns by bringing forward Florimell:

> Then did he set her by that snowy one
>> Like the true saint beside the image set,
>> Of both their beauties to make paragone,
>> And triall, whether should the honor get.
>> Streight way so soone as both together met,
>> Th' enchanted Damzell vanished into nought:
>> Her snowy substance melted as with heat,
>> Ne of that goodly hew remayned ought,
> But th' emptie girdle, which about her wast was wrought.

> As when the daughter of Thaumantes faire,
>> Hath in a watry cloud displayed wide
>> Her goodly bow, which paints the liquid ayre;
>> That all men wonder at her colours pride;
>> All suddenly, ere one can looke aside,
>> The glorious picture vanisheth away,
>> Ne any token doth thereof abide:
> So did this Ladies goodly forme decay,
> And into nothing goe, ere one could it bewray. (iii.24,25)

Both snow and rainbow melt at the appearance of the sun. The false Florimell had seemed to be a sun until the true sun came forth: then she is seen to be mere, insubstantial quickly melting snow and colored air.

In the Legend of Justice there is yet another occasion on which two suns appear in the sky. This time it is Arthur (who on so

many other occasions doubles for Artegall) who stands as the true
sun, who carries, as Artegall briefly, significantly did, a "sunlike
shield." The occasion is Arthur's defeat of the Souldan.

When Arthur unveils his shield in front of the Souldan's
chariot-horses they flee in terror

> As when the firie-mouthed steeds, which drew
>   The Sunnes bright wayne to Phaetons decay,
>   Soone as they did the monstrous Scorpion vew,
>   With ugly craples crawling in their way,
>   The dreadfull sight did them so sore affray,
>   That their well knowen courses they forwent,
>   And leading th'ever-burning lamp astray,
>   This lower world nigh all to ashes brent,
> And left their scorched path yet in the firmament.

> Such was the furie of these head-strong steeds,
>   Soone as the infants sunlike shield they saw   (viii.40,41)

In a moment of significant imagery a few stanzas earlier Arthur's
shield was "like lightning flash": it was the instrument of God's
wrath against wrongdoers. Now, in an equally significant moment, it is "sunlike." It represents, in the interests of a particular
image's consistency, the true sun, the bright height at which such
false would-be suns as the Souldan and Phaeton basely aim. (The
Souldan has, after all, been trying to destroy Mercilla, that true
and very sunny queen.) But two suns cannot be tolerated in the
sky together. The true sun uncases the false. Phaeton, who led
"th' ever-burning lampe astray," is put to flight by the appearance
of a second sun: "The infants sun-like shield."

Now the fall of Phaeton was sometimes attributed, as in Ovid's
account, to the terrifying appearance of Scorpio in the chariot-
horses' path.[14] This is the version of the story which Spenser
follows in stanza 40. But the most widespread version of the story
was that Jove felled Phaeton with his thunderbolt.[15] The reader
may, if he chooses, link the thunderbolt of that unspoken story

with that which he has momentarily glimpsed in Arthur's hand. I do not know of any suggestion in classical mythology that presumptuous Phaeton, the false sun, was destroyed by his father Helios, the true. But there is such a suggestion in an early and influential emblem book. In Alciati's *Emblemata* Phaeton is depicted at the moment of his fall from his sun-chariot; scattered horses rush from him in every direction. Above him is the sun; it is the sun's powerful rays which appear to have stricken the horses and caused the fall (Figure 16). Just so, in Spenser's account, does Arthur's sun-like shield "sore affray" and scatter the steeds of the Phaeton-imitating Souldan.

Actually Arthur not only has a sun-like shield, but he sets out on his Souldan adventure altogether in sunny brilliance:

> In glistering armes right goodly well beseene,
> That shone as bright, as doth the heaven sheene   (viii.29)

And the Souldan is Phaeton-like in more respects than one. It has been suggested that the Souldan's very name is meant to recall Sol: the sun.[16]

FIGURE 16. *In temerarios*. From Alciati's *Emblemata*, p. 209 (Paris, 1583). Courtesy of the Rare Book Division, The New York Public Library, Astor, Lenox and Tilden Foundations.

FIGURE 17. *Impresa* of Philip II. From Girolamo Ruscelli's *Imprese illustri*, p. 232 (1566).

Now, remarkably enough, there was one great sixteenth-century figure, a pagan, as most of his contemporary Englishmen would have in effect thought, whose *impresa* consisted of Apollo driving his sun-horses over oceans and cities; the motto was *Iam illus-*

trabit omnia (Figure 17). This person was Philip II of Spain. According to Girolamo Ruscelli's interpretation, the *impresa* is symbolic of Philip II's shedding glory and the true light of God over the nations.[17]

It has long been supposed that the Souldan, who supports Duessa's treasonous claims and who irreligiously opposes Mercilla, represents or alludes to Philip II.[18] And the battle between Arthur and the Souldan can very well be read as a little historical allegory of the scattering of Philip's Armada. Upton and others have pointed out that the Souldan's "charret hye/With yron wheeles and hookes arm'd dreadfully" is strongly reminiscent of the high ships of the Spanish fleet with their turrets,· hooks, and "piles." [19] It was, Protestant England thought, "by heavens high decree" (viii.40) that the Spanish navy was destroyed: Arthur's exploit against the Souldan represents England's defeating the superior forces of the Armada through the interference of divine providence—the unveiling of Arthur's lightning- and sun-like shield causes the routing of the Souldan just as the storm in the English channel scattered the Spanish ships.

The *impresa* of Philip II wonderfully illuminates Spenser's account of the Souldan. It enables us to see that through the Phaeton metaphor the poet is conjuring up Philip II's presumably well-known image of himself as the sun god in his chariot—but only to turn it wittily against him. For Philip's vision of himself as a godly illuminator, Spenser substitutes his own view of him as really an idol-worshiping pagan: a usurping Phaeton.

The whole passage is a marvel of many-layered metaphor; the images simultaneously support a vivid narrative, embody allegories, and work within the book's overall system of thematic imagery.

PART II
DUBIETY

CHAPTER 6

CROCODILE

It is inevitable that the hero-knights of justice should in some respects be associated with the sun; that is a traditional image. But Artegall is, rather more esoterically, also associated with Osiris, the Egyptian god of justice who "signifies the sunne" (vii.2,4), and, most mysteriously of all, with the crocodile.

In what is in effect Spenser's fullest definition of justice, his account of the Temple of Isis and of the vision which Britomart has there, Osiris is said to be embodied in the crocodile which the idol of the goddess Isis keeps subdued.

> For that same Crocodile Osyris is,
> That under Isis feete doth sleepe for ever   (vii.22)

As Osiris represents justice, Isis represents "that part of Justice, which is Equity" (vii.3). Though an icon which suggests that justice might lie beneath *anybody's* feet seems surprising, it is acceptable in terms of the relationship between justice and mercy, law and equity, that is established as a dominant theme and reiterated throughout the course of Book V; this maiden who subdues a crocodile stands in symmetrical, reciprocal balance against that other maiden who subdues a lion. Yet if Mercilla's lion has a number of possible significances, Isis's crocodile is dazzlingly complex.

Certainly, the crocodile quite orthodoxly represents Artegall, Osiris, sun, and justice; and certainly, again quite orthodoxly, Artegall's type of rigorous justice may very properly in certain circumstances be subdued. But the crocodile is also specifically said to embody "both forged guile,/And open force" (vii.7) and to tend to decree "cruell doomes" (22); it even attempts, as I interpret the matter, a sexual attack on Britomart (14–16). In fact, with all its strange aspects, the episode of the crocodile epitomizes Spenser's complex view of justice. In it are suggested both the orthodox kind of justice which was considered in the first section of this essay and the unorthodoxies which are the principal subjects of the two following sections. For the heroes of justice do tend to be over-forceful; they have just as much recourse to "forged guile" as does the crocodile which is a very symbol of fraud; and Artegall, in his role of Hercules-figure, seems to be as sexually reproachable as is the crocodile which is an outright emblem of lust.

The narrative brings Britomart to the Temple of Isis when she is on her way to rescue her lover Artegall from his shameful imprisonment by Radigund. She stays the night in the temple, falling asleep in front of the statue of the goddess Isis. This is Spenser's account of the priests' leading her to the idol:

> Thence forth unto the Idoll they her brought,
>   The which was framed all of silver fine,
>   So well as could with cunning hand be wrought,
>   And clothed all in garments made of line,
>   Hemd all about with fringe of silver twine.
>   Uppon her head she wore a Crowne of gold,
>   To shew that she had powre in things divine;
>   And at her feete a Crocodile was rold,
>   That with her wreathed taile her middle did enfold.

? his

(See p. 96)

One foot was set uppon the Crocodile,
    And on the ground the other fast did stand,
    So meaning to suppress both forged guile,
    And open force: and in her other hand
    She stretched forth a long white sclender wand.
    Such was the Goddesse; whom when Britomart
    Had long beheld, her selfe uppon the land
    She did prostrate, and with right humble hart,
Vnto her selfe her silent prayers did impart.   (vii.7,8)

As Britomart prays, she falls asleep, and as she sleeps she has "a wondrous vision." She dreams that she becomes, first, a priestess of Isis, then, a queen-like figure, crowned like Isis, but wearing a "robe of scarlet red" (the monarchial *purpurea?*) and not, like Isis, a silver-fringed linen stole. In her dream there arises "from below" "an hideous tempest," blowing the altar-embers "into outragious flames" which threaten to burn the whole temple. But the crocodile awakes,

    And gaping greedy wide, did streight devoure
    Both flames and tempest: with which growen great,
    And swolne with pride of his owne peerelesse powre,
    He gan to threaten her likewise to eat;
But that the Goddesse with her rod him backe did beat.

                    (vii.15)

There are, then, three distinct figures in Britomart's dream in the temple of Isis: the goddess, the lady, and the crocodile. But there is good reason for regarding Britomart, lover of Artegall, as, if not identical to, yet closely associated with Isis, wife of Osiris. The priest of Isis explains outright to Britomart that the crocodile "doth represent . . . thy faithfull lover," and that it is "like to Osyris" (vii.22). In that Osiris, embodied in the crocodile, lies beneath the feet of the goddess Isis, Artegall, by metaphorical extension, lies beneath the feet of Britomart. And this is another center of ambiguous, shifting values. For it is on the face of it strange that Artegall, Osiris, and Justice should be so debased as to be embodied in a crocodile—in, moreover, a crocodile that a mistress puts one victorious foot on.

The crocodile was regarded from two different points of view in the Renaissance. A few noble and godly crocodiles appear in the emblem books. These are the crocodiles traditionally associated with Osiris, and with the whole Egyptian tradition which was regarded as the very source of the art of hieroglyphics and emblems. For Osiris was seen as a hero, as the equivalent of Bacchus, as an archetypal maintainer of justice, as the sun, as a (perhaps *the*) god. His crocodile is a noble beast. But on the other hand Osiris was a heathen god, and, worse, being Egyptian, was associated with the dark and dangerous tradition of Hermetic magic.[1] His crocodile must be a terrible beast.

That Spenser was not the only Renaissance writer to have held in mind the two traditions of Osiris simultaneously is indicated by Stephen Batman's verbal emblem of the god. For that writer endows Osiris with a snake monster whose attributes have significances similar to, but as contradictory as, those of Spenser's crocodile. Batman writes:

Osiris was figured with a basket upon his head, in the which was a Serpent with three heades, holding the Tayle in his mouth.

Signification. . . . By the Basket the bondage of service under the which, all are held: By the Serpent with three heades, the first of a Lion, the second of a Dogge, the third of a Wolfe, The Serpent signifieth the prudence of Lawes, well to governe common Wealthes: the head of the Dogge, the auctority of nobility, the watchful barkinge of spirituality, to defende the oppressed from enormities: the head of the Wolfe signifieth oppression which proceadeth from the Kinge, from nobility, from spirituality, from Officer [*sic*] in auctority: from the kinge when he graunteth over much liberty, from the Nobilitie, when they regarde not magnanimity: from spirituality, when they defend not fidelity: from Officer [*sic*] in auctority, when by careless oppression, they consume poverty. These heades joyned on to on [*sic*] body, signifieth, the mutuall accord or consanguinity in evills, which as the Serpent devouring herselfe, by beginninge with her tayle, so are divers

= one /

Kingdomes, by oppressinge common Wealthes, made weake, and brought to confusion.[2]

As the universal "bondage of service" of justice, signified by the basket, is of prime importance to Batman, so is it, too, to Spenser, whose central icons are of right authorities holding something or somebody in service, and whose most puzzling narrative passage is concerned with justice's temporary servitude.

Justice, in Batman's view, may in large part be figured by a serpent in its traditional signification of wisdom. In fact, "The serpent signifieth the prudence of Lawes, well to governe common Wealthes." And indeed, Batman presents in conjunction with the serpent a symbol of wisdom in its particular aspect of prudence: the figure which has three heads, one of a lion, one of a wolf, and one of a dog is the "triciput," traditional symbol of prudence.[3] But it is what Batman makes of these heads that is of remarkable interest. In fact the three-headed snake loses one of its heads in the course of the "Signification." The emblematist is interested in recording a neat dichotomy: justice is made up of two forces in "mutual accord or consanguinity in evills"—on the one hand the dog-like watchfulness and protectiveness of those in authority, and on the other the wolfish oppression that may proceed from the same authorities. Similarly, the serpent seemed, at the beginning of Batman's account, admirable, prudent, lawgiving justice; by the end it has become a self-devouring monster —laws and lands preying upon themselves. And much as Batman's concept of justice and his symbolic serpent are divided, so too are Spenser's justice and his crocodile.

It is actually perfectly appropriate that Artegall, in his role of knight of justice and representative of God, be embodied in a crocodile. The chief point is of course that Osiris is associated with crocodiles.[4] In Egyptian mythology it was Sebak, the official crocodile-god, who was naturally usually represented as a crocodile. But this god, or a simple crocodile, is often depicted, both in Egyptian art and in Renaissance emblems, with Osiris or an Osiris-connected figure on his back. In an Egyptian bas-relief at Philae, Sebak is represented as bearing a handsome young standing figure on his back: the mummy of Osiris.[5] Then there is a sixteenth-century emblem representing *Dii Egyptiorum* in which a human figure with a dog-like head stands with one foot on a crocodile (Figure 18). The emblematist has little or no explanation of his icon beyond remarking, with the usual scorn, that the Egyptians worshipped monsters such as monkeys, ibises, dogs, and crocodiles.[6] In fact the figure in the emblem is the jackal-headed god Anubis who was Osiris's son and the lord of the dead. (Osiris too was lord of the dead.) And then there is Valeriano's interesting emblem entitled *Solis Simulacrum*. I have already indicated that, for Valeriano as for Spenser, Osiris signified the sun. Valeriano's representation of "an image of the sun" consists of a young man standing in a boat which is carried on a crocodile's back. The iconologist has a very odd explanation of this. He says that the young man represents the sun because he floats, like the sun, above the ocean; the crocodile represents the ocean itself because his tears are so plentiful.[7] The striking point is that here we have, whatever the particular rationalization, another young Osiris-associated figure standing on a crocodile's back. In fact it would appear that the figure of a young hero or god standing on the back of a crocodile is almost as iconographically orthodox as the figure of a queen sitting above a lion.

But in Spenser it is Isis, not Osiris, who stands, with one foot at least, on the back of a crocodile. It is the crocodile itself which symbolizes or is Osiris. In fact the true Egyptian crocodile god was Sebak. But Plutarch suggested another line of thought. He identified the crocodile with God; and the chief god of Egyptian mythology was Osiris. The relationship is as quaint as usual. Plutarch explained that the crocodile is declared to be a living representative of God since he is the only creature without a tongue; for the Divine Word has no need of a voice.[8] Valeriano gives as the primary significance of the crocodile: *Deus*.[9] And

ROMÆ IN HORTIS IVLII III. P. M.

ΘΕΟΙ ΑΔΕΑΦΟΙ.

Templa Paretoniis onerasse altaria monstris
Quis negat? inter quæ Simia & Ibis erant.
Et Canis, & vasto frendens Crocodilus hiatu.
Herbæ etiam cultu non caruere suo.

FIGURE 18. *Dii Egyptiorum.* From I. I. Boissard's *Theatrum Vitae Humanae*, p. 71 (Metz, 1596). Courtesy of the Columbia University Libraries.

again, from whatever tradition he may have derived the idea, Giordano Bruno writes of "the gods and the divinity in crocodiles, cocks and other things." [10]

Spenser then had plenty of precedents for his icon of a standing god with a foot on a crocodile's back, for his representation of

Osiris as a crocodile, and for his suggestion that the crocodile is a god- and justice-associated figure. But none of these explains why the crocodile should be subjected to Isis. True, crocodiles, according to Plutarch, show either fear or reverence for the goddess, so might be expected to lie at her feet.[11] But it is still strange that this particular crocodile, who is Osiris, Isis's husband and the embodiment of justice, should be so submissive.

The answer lies in the nature of those other, more usual kinds of crocodile which were available to Renaissance artists and poets. After all, when Christian apologists made much of Osiris's relationship with the crocodile they were paying the heathen god no compliment, recognizing no divine facts; they were discrediting him in terms of his connection with so vile a beast.[12] For the crocodile was most often representative of voracity and power, of lust, and of guile. Now Spenser specifically explains the meaning of his emblem of the idol of Isis with one foot on a crocodile in these orthodox terms: it is

> So meaning to suppresse both forged guile,
> And open force.   (vii.7)

Isis, that is, like Mercilla, suppresses bestial force; she also (again, indeed, like Mercilla) suppresses fraud.

In our next chapter, "Force and Fraud," we shall examine the significance of the pair force and fraud in Spenser's Book V and in the Renaissance generally. It is a central concept. Here it will suffice to point out how the icon of the crocodile suppressed by the lady is perfectly consonant with all the interlaced themes which come into their most marvelous knot in the temple of Isis.

Traditionally, the crocodile has the basically evil qualities of the eternal serpent and dragon; John Maplet, in his compendium of natural (and unnatural) history, *A Greene Forest*, describes it in these terms: "The Crocodile is called yellow snake for that he is a colour most Saffron like," and "It is a most glotonous serpent, and a verie ravener."[13] In its ravening, the crocodile is horribly forceful. In this matter, Valeriano and Spenser concur with Maplet. According to Valeriano, a crocodile is a *helluo:* a glutton; crocodiles signify greed and voracity.[14] According to Spenser, Isis's crocodile, "gaping greedy wide, did straight devoure" the flames and tempest in the temple; then he threatened "to eat" Britomart. It is of interest that Spenser described another such voracious, ferocious crocodile in the third of the sonnets in the *Visions of the worlds vanitie.* This "mightie Crocodile" is

> cram'd with guiltles blood, and greedie pray
> Of wretched people travailing that way.

His mouth is a "devouring hell." In the sonnet Spenser retells the story of how "a little Bird, cal'd Tedula" enters the beast's mouth to feed, "as Nature doth provide," upon the venom in its jaws (in Maplet's account, the Trochylos or wren enters the crocodile's mouth when it is sleeping, penetrates it, and eats its heart). The moral of the fable is stated in Spenser's question:

> Why then should greatest things the least disdaine,
> Sith that so small so mightie can constraine?

It is in effect the same moral that he draws from the ladies' suppression of their wild beasts in the Legend of Justice.

So much for the matter of crocodiles and of the "open force" which ladies and wrens are nevertheless able to control. As for "forged guile": it is a quality central to emblematic crocodiles. The crocodile may, as Maplet indicated, be equated with a snake: the snake's first function was to deceive. For Ripa, the crocodile is specifically an emblem of *Strategemma,* for Valeriano, of *Hypocrita.*[15] The crocodile owes his reputation for guile both to his association with snakes, and to the legend about crocodiles to which Spenser alludes in Book I of *The Faerie Queene* as well as in the previously mentioned sonnet. In Book I, supremely guileful Duessa is compared with the "cruell craftie crocodile" which, in accordance with the story reiterated throughout the Renaissance, feigns grief in order to catch travelers unawares (I.v.18).

Isis's crocodile is bisexual. Though predominantly male, and associated with the god Osiris and the knight Artegall, it is first described as a creature "that with *her* wreathed tail *her* middle did enfold" [my italics]. In its female aspect, the crocodile is associated with Duessa's snaky-tailed ancestress and prototype, traditionally guileful Echidna.[16]

Rightly regarded, the icon of the goddess over the crocodile embodies the whole significance of the Legend of Justice.[17] On the primary plane, it is an emblem of the proper submitting, as Spenser clearly declares, of the god to the goddess, of one aspect of justice to another, of rigor to clemency, and of law to equity (cf. vii.3,23). On a secondary plane, though, as Spenser just as clearly states, it is an emblem which suggests the essentially evil character of the justice which the first portion of Book V presents as so nobly Jovial. Though the crocodile be one way a god, the other he's a serpent. In dominating him, the goddess suppresses "both forged guile, and open force," and also restrains his "cruell doomes" (vii.23). Artegall represents force; there are times when force is not appropriate. He represents, as we shall see in the next chapter, fraud; fraud is the devil's device. He represents a justice that is rigorous even to cruelty; the mercy of Christ and of good queens must counterbalance it. Much of the importance of Spenser's great central icon is that it puts Artegall's absolute force into its proper, less than supremely just, place.

Yet there remains still another aspect of Artegall and of crocodiles. Granted that it is appropriate to one of the themes of Book V that Artegall be identified with a noble crocodile, with Osiris, the crocodile-associated god of justice; and granted that it is appropriate to another of the book's themes that Artegall be identified with a base crocodile, with the violent and guileful forces which a noble woman suppresses; yet why should Britomart dream, adding complexity to layered complexity, that her lover is about to devour her?

We may recall that Britomart dreams she is transformed from

a priestess of Isis into a queen like Isis. Then a hideous tempest comes up and blows the holy temple fire into outrageous flames. When Britomart and the whole temple are threatened with destruction the crocodile wakes up to save the situation and devour the flames. Then, though, it becomes "swolne with pride of his own peerelesse powre" and threatens to eat its mistress; she "with her rod him back did beat." The crocodile is instantly subdued "to humblesse meeke" and prostrates itself at its mistress's feet.[18] The goddess uses the crocodile's power to quell the tempest, restrains it from going on to devour Britomart. The crocodile is Britomart's assailant and her savior; he becomes, it would seem, her slave.

One tradition in which a man could simultaneously be a soldier attacking the fortress of his lady's heart and a captive enchained by the same lady's golden tresses was of course that which gave rise to and was embodied in the Petrarchan love poetry of the sixteenth century. And Petrarchism is, after all, though a convention, the expression of a number of psychological realities. Artegall is no Petrarchan lover. But he is a lover, and shortly to become a husband. One way by which Britomart's vision may reasonably be elucidated is by examining its relationship to the traditional iconographical and psychological symbolism of love and marriage.[19]

It is apparent that Book V of *The Faerie Queene* is, in one of its aspects, about marriage and the whole question of the proper relationship between men and women. One of the early cantos describes the events at Florimell's marriage to Marinell. Then, later, the whole Radigund episode is illuminated by the fact that one of Radigund's namesakes, Saint Radegund, was remarkable for her insistence on remaining a virgin after her marriage: from an anti-Catholic viewpoint, a notable example of wifely disobedience. Radegund's chastity casts an ironic light on Radigund's unchastity; but the ladies are alike in that they both exercise wrong female dominion.[20] Now questions of marriage, of the distribution of power within marriage, and of adultery all come within Aristotle's concept of justice.[21]

But what most essentially establishes Book V as a book of marriage is that Britomart's central vision there prophesies and in effect enshrines the union of herself with Artegall. A. S. P. Woodhouse has suggestively called it "that wonderful piece of dream psychology and symbolic art."[22] And several recent critics have thought that the whole matter of Britomart, the flames, and the crocodile have sexual significance.[23]

It is Britomart's vision of the relationship between herself and her lover—a lover who is in so many ways ambivalent—that is set forth in this puzzling series of icons. But it is part of Spenser's most human and ironic art that Britomart's vision of love and marriage is by no means identical with what the reader of the book, with his knowledge of events and of Artegall's character, can accept as valid.

The Petrarchan and the cynically realistic approaches to love have long existed side by side. Milton ascribes Adam's fall (his consenting to share the apples and the guilt proffered by Eve) to his forgetfulness of the right hierarchical relationship between men and women; Eve inevitably and blasphemously commends his Petrarchan devotion:

> O glorious trial of exceeding Love,
> Illustrious evidence, example high!   (*P.L.*IX.961–62)

A lover who, in "humblesse meeke," improbably prostrates himself at his mistress's feet is surely, from Britomart's point of view and in her dream, her Petrarchan servant.

Edwin Greenlaw has remarked that

Spenser's representation of Isis with one foot on the crocodile is not a happy one if, as he says, the crocodile is her lover Osiris; that is, it is not a happy one for the lover, or for romantic views of the marital relation.[24]

Perhaps the position this puts Artegall in is not one which the nineteenth or twentieth centuries would think romantic. More to the point, it is a position which is in direct contradiction to Spenser's specific statement a few cantos before; as a whole, in the Legend of Justice, Spenser puts forward the theologically and legally orthodox view that women must be subservient to men. Radigund is an outrageous example of a violation of this rule. Spenser comments:

> Such is the crueltie of womenkynd,
>> When they have shaken off the shamefast band,
>> With which wise Nature did them strongly bynd,
>> T'obay the heasts of mans well ruling hand,
>> That then all rule and reason they withstand,
>> To purchase a licentious libertie.
>> But vertuous women wisely understand,
>> That they were borne to base humilitie,
> Unlesse the heavens them lift to lawful soveraintie.　　(v.25)

In this stanza he specifically excludes from his general condemnation such righteous queens as Elizabeth and Mercilla. But that cannot account for Britomart's anomalous position as she stands over her meekly humble husband-to-be.

One explanation of the matter may lie in Britomart's dream-assumption of a Renaissance philosophy of love. Another may lie in her prophetic and hopeful application to herself of certain ideas which are illustrated in the iconography of marriage.

Ripa represents *Matrimonio* as a young person who has a yoke on her shoulders, stocks round her legs, a quince in one hand, and a viper beneath her feet (Figure 19). Fertility in marriage is represented by the quince which she holds in one hand; and sexuality by the viper at her feet. As for the yoke and stocks: Ripa explains that they show that marriage subjects gallant and carefree youth to law and family responsibility and the caprices of women. Now, though in Ripa's woodcut (and, even more clearly, in the emblems of Ripa's imitators), Matrimony is a woman, in Ripa's text, and in accordance, indeed, with the fact that *Matrimonio* is a masculine noun, Matrimony is represented by a man.[25]

It is clear enough that in a man-dominated world system marriage does burden and hobble women much as the woman in the woodcut is burdened and hobbled. It is also clear that, as Ripa writes in his text, marriage subjects young men to the burdens and restraints of family responsibility. There is, in this vein, a charming late seventeenth-century French engraving of Manhood standing with a *Chaine du mariage* attached to one ankle and a *Fardeau de la maison* perched on his shoulder.[26] On one level, Britomart suppresses the crocodile—which is Artegall, her husband-to-be—much as in general the institution of marriage subjects a man to the caprices and also to the responsible lawfulness of a relationship with a single woman. It will be remembered

FIGURE 19. *Matrimonio*. From Ripa's *Iconologia*, p. 320. Courtesy of the Prints Division, The New York Public Library, Astor, Lenox and Tilden Foundations.

that Britomart has her vision of Artegall as being a humbled crocodile during the course of her journey to succour her avowed knight; he, less responsible than he might be, is at this very time subjected in a dishonorable way to Radigund, Britomart's tyrannous and lascivious rival. Before she can beget the royal English dynasty Britomart will indeed have to subject her wayward lover to the discipline of marriage.

Yet all this is no more than *Britomart's* vision (and probably only her momentary hope, besides). The time will soon come, in actuality, when, although

> Such wondrous powre hath wemens faire aspect,
> To captive men, and make them all the world reject

> Yet could it not sterne Artegall retaine
> Nor hold from suite of his avowed quest,
> Which he had undertane to Gloriane;
> But left his love, albe her strong request,
> Faire Britomart in languor and unrest.   (vii.2,3)

Britomart might wish that her lover remain her captive; but his manly duty must call him away. It is she in fact who, in bringing Artegall's captivity by Radigund to an end, reasserts right hierarchy and with it her own essential captivity. Artegall does not yearn for Britomart; but she, lady-knight of chastity though she is, is as troubled by languor and unrest as ever was Cupid-ridden woman. (See also the extended account of Britomart's weak and womanly conduct in Artegall's absence: vi.3–17.) Love makes captives. But there is some question in Spenser's mind as to who is, and who thinks he is, and who should be the captive of whom.

The other amorous and marital ambivalence in Britomart's dream is that involved in the crocodile's being simultaneously both destroyer and preserver.

In that Britomart dreams that the crocodile devours the flames that threaten the idol of the goddess, the whole temple of Isis, and herself, she is creating an icon which has very clear traditional significance. In Alciati's *Emblemata* and all its many successors there is an emblem, entitled *Custodiendas virgines*, in which a beast is shown protecting a chaste maiden from the onslaughts of lust (Figure 20). It consists of a maiden who wears a helmet and carries a lance; she is standing before a temple. At her side lies a dragon. The maiden is, as the emblem-writer says and as the experienced reader of emblem books could tell at a glance, Pallas— goddess of chastity and, like Isis, of wisdom. The emblematist explains that the dragon is guarding Pallas against the dangers of lust and of indiscretion.[27] Similar to Pallas's temple is the temple of Isis:

Vera hæc effigies innuptæ est Palladis.eius
 Hic Draco:qui dominæ constitit ante pedes.
Cur diuæ comes hoc animal?custodia rerum
 Huic data.sic lucos,sacraq; templa colit.
Innuptas opus est cura asseruare puellas
 Peruigili.laqueos undique tendit amor.

FIGURE 20. *Custodiendas virgines*. From Alciati's *Emblemata*, p. 44 (Lyons, 1548). Courtesy of the Rare Book Division, The New York Public Library, Astor, Lenox and Tilden Foundations.

Borne uppon stately pillours, all dispred
With shining gold, and arched overhed   (vii.5)

As the dragon protects Pallas, in similar fashion that other beast,
the crocodile, protects that other chaste and Pallas-like maiden,
Britomart, from the flames in the temple. (That the flames which
the crocodile devours are, as likely as not, the flames of lust is
suggested by the fact that Amoret, too, was once surrounded by a
wall of flame such that only Britomart, or Chastity herself, could
penetrate.)

The commentator to the 1583 edition related the figures in the
Custodiendas virgines emblem to the goddess Isis. On Alciati's
question, in his little emblem verse, *Cur Divae comes hoc animal?* the commentator remarks *Huius quidem rei meminet obiter
Plutarchus commentario De Iside & Osiride.* Actually Plutarch
does not say anything about dragons; dragons do not figure
largely in Egyptian mythology. Indeed, the differences in the
various editions of the *Emblemata* suggest that opinions differed
as to what *was* the exact nature of the beast that defends the virgin. In the 1548 edition the dragon has quite a modest, doglike
tail. In the 1583 edition the tail has grown very much longer and
curlier. In the 1621 edition the dragon has shrunk to a definite
serpent. The commentator to this edition remarks that some have
thought the beast who guards Pallas should be a quadruped; he
claims, though, that such an opinion is due to an etymological
mistake. The same commentator explains that the guardian snake-
beast represents sapience—as indeed snakes usually did, unless
they alternatively happened to represent sin, or guile, or sexuality, or eternity.

Now, the crocodile at Britomart-Isis's feet is a very snaky creature. Elizabethans must have had access to correct descriptions of
crocodiles; and in fact most of the emblem book crocodiles that I
have seen lie as short and straight as logs. But Maplet did define
the crocodile as "a yellow snake." And the crocodile at the foot of
Isis is more like a snake or dragon than a real crocodile; it

was rold,

That with her wreathed taile her middle did enfold.   (vii.6)

On the one hand, then, chaste Britomart dreams, as any romantic maiden might, that her lover will defend her against assault as effectually as the dragon of the emblem defends the goddess and the temple of chastity. In fact, ironically, Britomart is at this moment on her way to forcibly extricate her lover from a dubious sexual situation: it is she, not he, who is actually putting up a fight for chastity.

By "chastity" Spenser does not in general mean total sexual abstinence; he means creative faithful marriage. The priests of Isis are presumably chaste in the stricter sense,

> For by the vow of their religion
> They tied were to stedfast chastity
> And continence of life   (vii.9)

They live so austerely that they sleep "uppon the cold hard stone," and they abstain not only from wine but also from "fleshly food"; "wine they say is blood,/Even the bloud of Gyants." Spenser is doing something very strange here. To a Christian, "wine is blood" is a special statement, embracing the highest of positive values. Isis's temple is the more mysteriously pagan in that it reverses the Christian formula: "wine is blood" is, in the pagan temple, not spiritual communion but dionysian release:

> Such is the powre of that same fruit, that nought
> The fell contagion may thereof restraine,
> Ne within reasons rule, her madding mood containe.   (vii.11)

The temple of Isis is altogether more ambiguously dionysian than one would have expected. Britomart's dream of tempest, fire, and impregnation is its fitting manifestation. Britomart, like the priests, sleeps on the floor. But though the priests sleep on cold hard stone, they "on their mother Earths deare lap did lie"—a sensuous and procreative place. And though Britomart merely unlaced her helmet and lay down at the altar's side, "her earthly parts with soft delight/Of sencelesse sleepe did deeply drowned lie": she could not have luxuriated more in piles of silken pillows. Moreover, the whole long account of the origins of wine dwells on how the earth swelled, and how the blood of the rebellious giants "was shed/Into her pregnant bosome," and how she brought forth vines. The passions of the giants are reflected, in the dream, in the force of the tempest and the fire; the fertility of the earth is embodied again, in the dream, in the way in which "of his game she soon enwombed grew" (vii.16). The "he" of "his game" is the crocodile.

Thus the temple of Isis, though it is apparently a temple of chastity, is in fact a temple which houses a great deal of sensuality and procreative energy. And it is as paradoxical with the crocodile in the dream: though in one respect, especially in that he devours the fire, he is the orthodox defender of chaste maidens, in another, he is the sexuality which is inevitably and necessarily directed *at* such maidens.

In iconography, crocodiles are often associated with lust. In Ripa's *Iconologia, Lussuria* is represented by a nude young woman whose hair is richly and artificially arranged. She is seated on a crocodile and is caressing a partridge (Figure 21). Both the crocodile and the partridge, the emblemist notes, are ancient symbols of concupiscence which occur in many writers.[28] Among the writers they occur in is Valeriano Bolzani, who declares that the crocodile represents *salacitas*. He explains that it represents lust because of its great fecundity and because it can convey lust by contagion to the victim of its bite.[29] With just such a fearsome, lust-moved and lust-moving mouth, perhaps, the crocodile turns to "eat" Britomart.

Possibly the vision of the crocodile's attack represents the sexual energy which must naturally seek its virgins; possibly it represents the psychic shock to the chaste maiden of the first experience (or, in this case, anticipation) of married sexuality. Possibly it hints at a topic that seems to have much interested Renaissance iconographers: the proper place of sexuality in marriage.

After his threatening attack has been subdued, the crocodile "Him selfe before her feete he lowly threw" (vii.16). In the emblem of *Matrimonio* (Figure 19) the lady is standing on a viper. This, Ripa explains, is a symbol of the suppression of sexuality. Ripa writes that the viper represents the lust which married people should trample on: they should avoid such practices as the viper's, which in its lust kills its husband. According to Valeriano Bolzani, a viper is the appropriate emblem of *Uxor inimica marito* because the viper, like the bad spouse, destroys its mate in

FIGURE 21. *Lussuria*. From Ripa's *Iconologia*, p. 315. Courtesy of the Prints Division, The New York Public Library, Astor, Lenox and Tilden Foundations.

coition. (The tale would have pleased Freud: she bites her husband's head off.) [30] Alciati uses the story to illustrate the truth that *Reverentiam in matrimonio requiri*. According to his version, snakes, both male and female, spit out their venom before coition so that they do not kill their mates.[31]

Spenser's paradoxes are consistent. Isis's crocodile simultaneously manifests the energy that is creative concupiscence and the energy that is destructive lust; in synthesis, it manifests, too, the sexuality and uxoriousness which must be rationally restrained in right marriage. Yet though there is reason enough to see such motifs of love and marriage expressed in the icon of Isis and the crocodile, these sexual motifs may simply be regarded as metaphorical parallels rather than as narrative or thematic statements. The temple of Isis is the temple of justice. And justice is as ambivalent as is sexual energy. The crocodile is simultaneously Osiris, god of justice, and the epitome of cruelty and guile. These excesses of guile and cruelty, though, are and should be harnessed beneath Isis's feet just as natural concupiscence is controlled in marriage. The crocodile represents the energy (which resembles, and derives from, and in part *is* sexuality) which justice uses and abuses; without this Dionysian (according to Spenser, this Bacchic—i.2) energy, there would *be* no justice.[32]

GUILE

CHAPTER 7

FORCE AND FRAUD

SPENSER significantly explains his icon of the statue of Isis standing with one foot upon a crocodile in terms of equity's suppression of "both forged guile, and open force." The relationship between Isis and the crocodile is parallel to the relationship between Mercilla and the lion.

For Mercilla's lion represents both the monarch's own mercifully restrained executive power and the conquered enemy power of rebels and foreign foes. And in much the same way, Britomart-Isis suppresses in the crocodile the worst aspects of the very justice of which she is the overall representative; and she also suppresses that ubiquitous Renaissance pair who are the principal enemies of justice: she subjugates both force and fraud. The complex relationship between justice and the pair of force and fraud is one of the themes round which the whole of the Legend of Justice is organized.

Classical and Christian tradition concurred in the matter of the relationship between force and fraud. From earliest times, the pair were mentioned together as brother evils—but fraud was generally regarded as the elder and worser. Actually, throughout *The Faerie Queene*, with the regularity of a time-honored cliché, force and fraud—or guile, or sleight—are mentioned in conjunction as twin attributes of the foes of goodness. But since the evils of force and fraud generally come within the field of justice they are, naturally enough, most deeply considered during the course of Book V.

The idea that force and fraud are among the chief threats to orderly government and the dynamics of human society can be traced back to Aristotle.[1] Significantly, he particularly mentions force and fraud in his *Politics*—a book largely concerned with matters which the Elizabethans would have regarded as belonging to the general sphere of justice. He discusses force and fraud at the beginning of his analysis of how revolutions are initiated and maintained, and how they may be prevented, writing that "the means used to cause revolutions of constitutions are sometimes force and sometimes fraud."[2] And Cicero saw evil in terms of the same categories. In a passage which found wide currency in the Renaissance and whose imagery was used again and again by other authors, Cicero wrote:

There are two ways or methods whereby one may injure or oppress another; the one is fraud and subtlety, the other open force and violence; the former of which is esteemed the part of a fox, and the latter of a lion; both of them certainly very unworthy of a reasonable creature, though fraud, I think, is the most odious of the two.[3]

It remained for Dante to make a central literary use of this pair of force and fraud, interpreting them in the light of the Church as well as of classical tradition. Of Dante's three great groups of sinners, the incontinent, the violent, and the fraudulent, the first comprises those whose sins of appetite do not endanger others, and the second the two great classes of men whose malice does injure others. Dante, following Aquinas, regards injurious *malitia* as the chief assailant of justice. But, like Cicero and like Aquinas,

Dante considers fraud more heinous than force because fraud depends on the misuse of man's higher intellectual faculty. In the *inferno*, fraudulent men are relegated to the deepest, most terrible circles of hell.

From all these points of view, then, force and fraud are the worst enemies of the stable state, of justice and peace, of good men, and of Christians. And Spenser's Legend of Justice is fully in accordance with this tradition: all the antagonists in the book are masters or embodiments of force or fraud or both.

Spenser's account of justice and of Artegall's education begins in the golden age. At that time, when perfect justice presided over the affairs of virtuous, happy men, the world was free from the twin evils of force and fraud. Spenser makes this clear in his definitive proem. He writes:

> For during Saturnes ancient raigne it's sayd,
> > That all the world with goodnesse did abound:
> > All loved vertue, no man was affrayd
> > Of force, ne fraud in wight was to be found:
> > No warre was knowne, no dreadfull trompets sound,
> > Peace universall rayn'd mongst men and beasts,
> > And all things freely grew out of the ground:
> > Justice sate high ador'd with solemne feasts,
> And to all people did divide her dred beheasts.   (Pr.9)

This ideal picture is in strong contrast to the poet's actual age. He opens the proem with a lament about present times, in which, he writes:

> > Me seemes the world is runne quite out of square,
> > From the first point of his appointed sourse,
> And being once amisse growes daily wourse and wourse.

> For from the golden age, that first was named,
> > It's now at earst become a stonie one;
> > And men themselves, the which at first were framed
> > Of earthly mould, and form'd of flesh and bone,

Are now transformed into hardest stone:
Such as behind their backs (so backward bred)
Were throwne by Pyrrha and Deucalione:
And if then those may any worse be red,
They into that ere long will be degendered.   (Pr. 1,2)

The golden age was frequently and inevitably associated with the
garden of Eden; the two provide parallel myths of man's decline
from a once-upon-a-time condition of goodness and happiness.
Classical and Christian story alike represented the first men as
happy and good, living at peace and in toil-free plenty. But the
fall, or the passing of the ages, brought iron, sin, and woe, and
force and fraud into the world. Once upon a time justice, order,
and God prevailed. Now the sun and the stars have gone out of
their appointed courses (Pr.4–8); Astraea has left the earth
(i.11); men have fallen into sin; tyranny, rebellion, and unjust
wars abound; and, as all the book's historical allusions are geared
to suggest, Antichrist, in the form of the Catholic Church, is
threatening the true faith on every front. Men are living in the
iron age, in the fallen world, in the city of man rather than in the
city of God.

Spenser first sets up the golden age from which his own age
falls so far short. He then appoints Artegall, Astraea's pupil and
representative, to administer justice in the imperfect actual world
of force and fraud. Even his assistant, Talus, is connected with
the myth of the five ages of man: he is, as we have seen, clearly a
man of the brazen race.

It has long been recognized that the Legend of Justice, in
which Queen Elizabeth is celebrated in terms of Astraea, makes
central use of the legend of the golden age: the age in which
Astraea lived and in which justice was as excellent as—the polite
Elizabethan might like to suggest—it was under Queen Elizabeth
herself.[4] Spenser, though, was not such a polite Elizabethan as all
that. He juxtaposes rather than equates the golden ideal, the
"image of the antique world," with the iron actual.[5] In fact the

characteristics of the world through which the knights of justice ride are very closely similar to those which were attributed to the iron age.

The authorities on the subject of the ages of man and of the world are Hesiod and Ovid. Both these authors write to the effect that the iron age was the age of war and the sacking of cities, when there was no respect for family ties or reverence for authority, and guest was not safe from host.[6] All these ills are characteristic, too, of the world in which Artegall has to wage justice. The last third of Book V is largely concerned with war and the sacking of cities; Pollente serves Munera as father never should serve daughter,[7] and the sons of Milesio dispute as brothers hardly should; Dolon's guests, moreover, are not safe from their host. And some further points of Hesiod's description of the iron age are of interest in relation to the Legend of Justice. Hesiod writes that:

There will be no favour for the man who keeps his oath or for the just or for the good; but rather men will praise the evil-doer and his violent dealing.[8] Strength will be right and reverence will cease to be; and the wicked will hurt the worthy man, speaking false words against him, and will swear an oath upon them. Envy, foul-mouthed, delighting in evil, with scowling face, will go along with wretched men and one and all.[9]

It is notable that the grim climax of Artegall's adventures is his confrontation with a similarly foul-mouthed Envy, and with representatives of the wicked who similarly hurt the worthy man by speaking false words against him.

However, it is in the matter of force and fraud that Spenser's iron age most nearly accords with that of classical tradition. Spenser maintains that during Saturn's ancient reign

> all the world with goodnesse did abound:
> All loved vertue, no man was affrayed
> Of force, ne fraud in wight was to be found.   (Pr.9)

As a matter of fact, it is not only in Book V that Spenser describes the golden age in these terms. In Book IV he declares that men of the golden age

> Ne then of guile had made experiment,
> But voide of vile and treacherous intent,
> Held vertue for it selfe in soveraine awe: . . .

> The Lyon then did with the Lambe consort,
> And eke the Dove sate by the Faulcons side,
> Ne each of other feared fraud or tort. (IV.viii.30,31)

The golden age was a time of perfect justice: there was then none of that force and, more especially, fraud, by which the iron age is characterized.

It was in much the same terms that Ovid had described the golden age. He wrote that at the beginning of the iron age

Modesty and truth and faith fled the earth, and in their place came tricks and plots and snares, violence and cursed love of gain (*fraudesque dolusque insidiaeque et vis et amor sceleratus habendi.*) [10]

Here in *fraudes et vis* are fraud and force themselves. *Dolus* appears directly in the poem in the character of Dolon; Malengin and the many other fraudulent characters have recourse to *insidiae*. It is not irrelevant, too, that Pollente and Munera, the sons of Milesio, the Souldan and his wife, and Duessa, all have what, in the case of Burbon, Geryoneo, and Grantorto, Spenser specifically calls "the love of Lordship and of lands" (xii.2)—in fact, *amor sceleratus habendi*.

Cesare Ripa has, by way of explication of his emblem for the iron age, a verse translation of the same passage from Ovid. For Ripa, too, the principal characteristics of the iron age are the pair of force and fraud. His emblem of *Età del Ferro* consists of an armed woman. She is, Ripa writes, of terrible appearance, and clad in garments made of iron. On her head she wears a helmet crested with the head of a wolf; in her right hand she bears a naked sword in fighting position, and in her left a shield. Depicted in the middle of the shield is fraud: that is, a figure with the face of a just man (*la faccia di uomo giusto*) and with the body of a serpent, stained and spotted with many colors.[11]

The woman is clearly an embodiment of force in that she is terrible, armed, iron-clad. At her feet are piled the instruments and accompaniments of war: *diverse armi, et insegne, tamburi, trombe, e simili*. Above all, the wolf on her helmet demonstrates her to be the mistress of war and terrible force. As for fraud: Ripa quite explicitly states that the symbols on the shield which the lady Iron Age bears signify this evil.

Most of the foes of justice that we have hitherto considered embody or make use of force. Indeed, the same set of wicked personages—Pollente, the Gyant, the Souldan, Geryoneo, and Grantorto—are appropriate simultaneously to the themes of Jove's quelling of giants, Hercules's destroying of tyrants, and justice's confronting of force. Pollente is, as the next chapter will show, not only the embodiment of power, as his name implies, but also specifically a user of "sleight." The two last great foes of Arthur and Artegall, Geryoneo and Grantorto, are "strong tyrants" (i.3; x.6), giant-like, powerful, mighty (x.8; xi.6; xii. 17–9, 24); but both of them have recourse to guile, too. Grantorto captures Irena "By guileful treason and by subtill slight" (xi.39) and entices Flourdelis away from Burbon by "many a guileful word" (xi.50). And Geryoneo is similarly guileful (x.12,13). It is, indeed, of the essence of Geryoneo and his monster that they equally and perfectly embody both force and fraud.

The common identification of the golden world with Eden no doubt made it inevitable that guile should be emphasized as the distinguishing characteristic of the fallen iron age: as the serpent destroyed Adam's paradise, fraud put an end to the age of Astraea. Rosemary Freeman describes an emblem in which the relationship between fraud, justice, and the golden age is particularly explicit; in it one of the several standard figures of fraud, two-headed "double fraud," is depicted in the very act of driving Justice from the earth.[12] From the Christian point of view, indeed, guile must always be the ancient opposer, the devil's instrument and the devil's self. Spenser's own version of the Arch-Enemy, Archimago, is a "guileful great Enchanter" (I.ii.Arg); and double Duessa constantly resorts to guile and to fraud. "Guile" and "guilefully" recur with very high frequency in the first book of *The Faerie Queene*, the book which describes all the inevitable encounters between Holiness and the powers of evil. In fact the only book in which these words occur more often is the Legend of Justice.[13]

It is in the nature of things that fraud and guile should be the basic foes of justice: the right execution of justice depends upon a knowledge of the truth. The chief issue in that central scene, the trial of Duessa, would seem to be the guilefulness, plots, and treachery of the accused queen. These were actually the central issues of the historical indictment of Mary, Queen of Scots, too.[14] Specifically excluded from Mercilla's court are "guyle, and malice, and despight,/That under shew oftimes of fayned semblance,/Are wont in Princes courts to worke great scath and hinderance" (V. ix.22). On the threshold is an exemplary spectacle of guile punished. Malfont, the wicked poet who "falsely did revyle,/And foule blaspheme that Queene for forged guyle" (ix.25) is nailed to a post by his tongue. All this makes it clear why it is Malengin, worst of guileful foes, whose name alliteratively matches and whose adventure shares a supreme canto with Mercilla's—best of mercifully just queens.

Malengin's name defines his nature. Upton etymologizes Malengin as "*Malum ingenium*"; and he quotes Le Duchet's definition: "*Malengin: dolus malus: c'est l'action d'une personne ingénieuse à mal faire.*" [15] Malengin is one of the central fraudulent characters in Book V. Dolon is the other. And Dolon, or *dolus malus* itself, is, as Angus Fletcher has shown, even more essentially the enemy of equitable justice than is Malengin. Dolon is the hypocritical host who just fails to entrap Britomart when she is on her way to rescue Artegall from *his* entrapment. Britomart represents equity. And *dolus malus* was traditionally, in Roman Law, the foe of equity:

Repeatedly the spirit of *aequitas* is opposed to *dolus malus,* and the form of *dolus malus* is *subtilitas,* or adherence to the strict letter of the law, in order to make it the means of an unscrupulous advantage. The essence of the wrong complained of is not that it is illegal, but that it is too legal.[16]

Rigorously lawful Artegall has fallen into the legal trap set by Radigund; he is as naturally disposed to legal as to various other kinds of excess. But though Dolon's guile has particular reference to the kind of fraud that can be perpetrated through legalistic ingenuity, it in general supports the theme that fraud and guile are among justice's chief enemies.

Thus it is that the iron-age world in which justice must try to keep order is populated by a number of violent and fraudulent characters. Indeed, Artegall is a true hero of justice *because* he destroys the traditional enemies of justice: oppressive and society-destroying force, and infernal fraud. Yet Spenser notes that to govern this world of fallen men and women, a less than perfect justice is called for: to control a world dominated by force and fraud, force and fraud are the indicated instruments. Throughout the Legend of Justice Artegall and his comrade, Arthur, repeatedly meet their twin foes, force and fraud, with the same twin means. Though force and, in particular, fraud are contrary to justice, though they are devilish instruments, again and again, in Book V, force is defeated by force, guile by guile. (Though noble force rightly used is the legitimate tool of true justice, it tends in all ages to be overused and abused, to become aggression and brutality. Similarly, justice's proper sagacity can drift soon enough to ingenuity, and thence to deceit.)

Generations of readers have disliked the Legend of Justice, principally because they have disliked Artegall.[17] C. S. Lewis's analysis, which is, surely, in effect that of most recent readers, is that, in Book V, Spenser "becomes a bad poet because he is, in certain respects, a bad man." [18]

This judgment from the guts is more to the point than those apologies contending that it is only realistic to recognize, as contemporaries did, that the Elizabethan world picture could only be rightly maintained through the exercise of a harsh justice, or explanations contending that the book must be as it is because Artegall and the whole of the end of the Legend of Justice is a particular impassioned defense of Arthur Grey, the Lord Deputy of Ireland. Indeed, Grey, whom Spenser knew and worked under, *was* very severe (guileful, too),[19] and Spenser, in his *View of the Present State of Ireland*, did praise and exonerate him. Accordingly, proponents of the sociological and biographical views of the Legend of Justice would maintain that it is unduly and unhistorically squeamish to regret the Irish massacres. Yet the great Burghley is supposed to have said "the Flemings had not such cause to rebel by the oppression of the Spaniards, as is reported the Irish people." [20] And Essex, whom Spenser may have had in mind as a suitable governor for Ireland, ordered the troops in his campaigns to offer no violence to man, woman, or child on pain of death.[21]

Spenser knew facts for facts as well as did these great men. Assuming this, some critics have tried to exonerate Artegall by dissociating him from the stern, harsh, and cruel acts by which the book's justice is so often executed. They do this by maintaining that Talus is a cruel executor but that the just Artegall restrains him, or by maintaining that Talus represents the harsh *method* of justice to which the man, Artegall, is necessarily, but not particularly willingly, committed.[22] To be sure, Artegall, like Britomart, does sometimes act to stop the slaughter that Talus is conducting.[23] But in spite of this, in the Legend of Justice slaughter is almost the condition of life. In fact, according to the Concordance, the word occurs eight times in this book—and only three other times in all the rest of *The Faerie Queene*. Talus is the executor for Artegall as Artegall himself is for Gloriana. The slaughter Artegall stops is the slaughter Artegall willed.

At the end of the Legend of Justice Artegall is directly accused of having resorted to guile and cruelty. Detraction makes the accusation,

> Saying, that he had with unmanly guile,
> And foule abusion both his honour blent,
> And that bright sword, the sword of Justice lent,
> Had stayned with reprochful crueltie   (xii.40)

Detraction is clearly not a reliable witness. On the first level her accusation may immediately be accepted as irony. The hero of justice cannot be tainted by any vice; it is Envy and Detraction who are the vicious ones. In fact, Detraction's charge has been connected with the widespread contemporary criticism of Lord Grey which led to his recall from Ireland. Artegall's recall probably reflects Grey's. The fact that the criticism is spoken by the foul hag slander has been thought to exonerate Grey: only slanderers could accuse him of baseness. But when it is recalled that both Artegall and Grey were in fact cruel and guileful we may conclude that in this case Detraction hits, in her evil way, on a vulnerable target.

The imagery confirms these ambivalent possibilities. When Envy and Detraction met Artegall on his way back to Faerie Court,

> They both arose, and at him loudly cryde,
> As it had bene two shepheards curres, had scryde
> A ravenous Wolfe amongst the scattered flockes   (xii.38)

The dogs which the two hags resemble may be currish, like that which traditionally accompanies Envy,[24] but they are at least guarding the sheep; the implication is that Artegall is like a wolf, the flock's fearful enemy. Again, on one level the hags are ren-

dered fouler and more ridiculous through their conducting themselves as though the hero of justice were a ravening wolf; on
another, though, there is the ironic suggestion that this is in fact
what he is. For it is not as though this were the first time Artegall
is associated with the ferocity of wolves; it is not as though it
were the first time he is called cruel and guileful. He has, after
all, been identified with that most violent and fraudulent of
beasts, the crocodile.

To be sure, in the Legend of Justice Spenser does orthodoxly
juxtapose the justice that is maintained by power with the principles of equity and mercy. But justice and mercy were regarded by
Elizabethans as both, equally, daughters of God. This is not
Spenser's view. For though some of Artegall's actions may be
regarded as rigorously just, and godly, others seem more ex-
tremely deceitful and cruel than is consonant with conventional
morality and religion.

In the first third of the Legend of Justice Artegall's orthodoxy
as noble prince, judge, and representative of God is clear. From
the point of his entrapment by Radigund, however, a number of
dubious shades appear in his character. He uses methods and
engages in activities which do not at all befit an ideal judge or
king. Artegall acts, in fact, less like a magic mirror of God than
like a man, and a Machiavellian man at that.

According to the classical-Christian tradition, perverted force
and fraud are inimical to justice and to God. Hence they must be
inimical, too, to the traditional prince or ruler—at least in so far
as he accords with the Christian, Platonic, and Aristotelian pre-
supposition that the monarch is the viceroy and mirror of God,
that the noblest faculties should rule both the individual and the
state, and that the best man will make the best governor.

Yet Renaissance theorists were practical enough to see that the
best man does not necessarily make the best ruler. Faith, charity,
and temperance will not suffice to keep order in a troubled state,
or to conduct foreign affairs with irreligious neighbors. Indeed,

practical observation must assure any realistic person that the state is not in fact governed according to the highest principles and that justice is not in fact maintained through Godliness alone. Statesmen had, in their daily political dealings, always used violence and policy—while paying lip service to higher principles.[25] Despite their professions to the contrary, princes had always known that the most effective methods of government were not the most high-minded ones. As Jean Bodin wrote:

> Those who go about uttering extravagant praises of princes who are mild, gracious, courteous, and simple, are greatly in error. Simplicity without prudence is dangerous and pernicious in a King, and much more to be dreaded than the cruelty of a severe, close-fisted, and inaccessible prince. Our forefathers did not without reason coin the phrase "a bad man makes a good king. . . ."[26]

Bodin was a practical man, and an analytical student of history; he was influenced by that supreme analytical pragmatist, Machiavelli. Machiavelli's prescription for the ruler was that he should both be the embodiment of justice, law, and reason in the traditionally orthodox way, and also maintain these goods by the only means practical: the prince, to be effective, must make use of exactly that long-reprehended pair of force and fraud.

In the first place, Machiavelli wrote:

> You must know, then, that there are two methods of fighting, the one by law, the other by force: the first method is that of men, the second of beasts; but as the first method is often insufficient, one must have recourse to the second. It is therefore necessary for a prince to know well how to use both the beast and the man. This was covertly taught to rulers by ancient writers, who relate how Achilles and many others of those ancient princes were given to Chiron the centaur to be brought up and educated under his discipline. The parable of this semi-animal, semi-human teacher is meant to indicate that a prince must know how to use both natures, and that the one without the other is not durable.[27]

Machiavelli saw his prince as half-man, with man's reason, law, and justice, and half-beast; Spenser's concept of Artegall as in one aspect the god-hero Osiris, and in the other, a crocodile, is analogous to Machiavelli's. Then Machiavelli went on to write:

A prince being thus obliged to know well how to act as a beast must imitate the fox and the lion, for the lion cannot protect himself from traps, and the fox cannot defend himself from wolves. One must therefore be a fox to recognize traps, and a lion to frighten wolves. Those that wish to be only lions do not understand this.

The analogy is from Cicero. Its terms are traditional and powerful: lions and wolves were the standard symbols of good and bad force; snares were the usual attributes and instruments of guileful persons; and foxes in fables and emblems were always associated with fraud.[28] Artegall, though he is never presented in so many words as half-fox, half-wolf, in fact has and uses these two beasts' qualities.

The whole matter, force and fraud, lions and foxes, and the relationship Machiavelli sketched between them, virtually entered into the Renaissance bloodstream. We find Bodin alluding to it in France and Raleigh, or who ever did write the *Cabinet Council*, using it in that most Machiavellian political treatise in England.[29] And inevitably, the image is in Ripa too. He describes the emblem for *Sforzo con inganno* as consisting of a robust young man with the pelt of a lion over one arm and the pelt of a fox over the other.[30] Again, Ripa's emblem of *Stratagemma Militare* is accompanied by an unusually long essay on the relationship between *dolo* and *vi, inganno* and *forza;* this culminates in the observation: *quando non bastava la pelle del Leone, faceva di mestiero cucirla con la pelle della volpe.* This is Machiavelli's advice.[31] The recurrence of these terms in iconography confirms their wide acceptance in the Renaissance; most men of the time knew at least this much of Machiavelli's political theory. And there is reason to believe that Spenser was quite a serious student of Machiavelli's writings.[32]

Certainly, Spenser's representative of justice is fully Machiavellian: Artegall is at the same time both God-like hero and beast; and in his beast-aspect he characteristically employs both force and fraud.[33]

It is scarcely necessary to point out again in this place that the representatives of justice use force. The theme is reiterated throughout Book V. Artegall and Arthur ride through the book wielding the sword and thunderbolt of justice; it is plainly stated that "powre is the right hand of Justice truely hight"; Talus is an embodiment of force; and the lion which lies beneath Mercilla and, in part at least, the crocodile which lies beneath Isis are traditional symbols of force. That Artegall's force is sometimes as ruthlessly absolute as that of the prince whose exploits Machiavelli celebrated is indicated by the number of massacres he instigates and by the fact that he, his sword, and his "dooms" are firmly called "cruell."

It remains to demonstrate that the representatives of justice also use fraud. Actually, at the very beginning of Artegall's adventures his use of guile is given more or less divine sanction. It is "by her slight" that Astraea has obtained for him the Titan-conquering sword of Jove:

> Which steely brand, to make him dreaded more,
>   She gave unto him, gotten by her slight
>   And earnest search, where it was kept in store
>   In Joves eternall house, unwist of wight.   (i.9)

Then Artegall's first act of justice is to imitate the most famous of the judgments of the wise—and crafty—Solomon. Having to decide between rival claimants to the same lady, he decides which man he thinks innocent, which guilty, and

> Did cast about by sleight the truth thereout to straine.   (i.24)

He proposes to divide the disputed property. The true lover objects. The three men have entered into a gentleman's agreement by which whoever dissents from Artegall's judgment shall have to carry a murdered lady's head for a year. According to Artegall's word the real lover, the dissenter, should get the head.

But the judge does not keep his word and it is the other man, the murderer and lady-stealer, who is justly punished. It would be hard to imagine a more guileful and dishonorable—and effective—process of law.

This is the book's first episode. The second episode, that in which Artegall encounters Pollente, is equally significant as an exemplification of the way in which justice deals with one of its chief enemies, power abetted by guile: Artegall destroys Pollente through force and fraud. He then goes on to beguile Radigund, to parry Clarinda's wile with equal wiliness, and to ensnarl the ensnaring Malengin.

And even the magnificent Arthur, though he is the epitome of all the Aristotelian virtues and instrument of the grace of God, is guileful in the Legend of Justice. After the two knights have come together in the act of rescuing a damsel in distress, they resolve to avenge the wrong done to this young lady, Samient, ambassadress of Queen Mercilla, by the wicked Souldan and his wife.

> But thinking best by counterfet disguise
> To their deseigne to make the easier way,
> They did this complot twixt them selves devise,
> First that sir Artegall should him array,
> Like one of those two Knights, which dead there lay.
> And then that Damzell, the sad Samient,
> Should as his purchast prize with him convey
> Unto the Souldans court, her to present
> Unto his scornefull Lady, that for her had sent. (viii.25)

In his adventures in the earlier books Arthur had not found it necessary to devise complots, or to lie and pretend to be what he was not.[34] His squire was equipped, in Book I, with a horn whose blast could make any door fly open (I.vii.3–5). He used this to get Orgoglio out of his castle. In Book V he still has that other important part of his equipment, the miraculous shield (I.viii. 19,20; V.viii.37,38), appropriate in both books in its allegorical

role of instrument of God's grace. Arthur would have used his
magic horn again, too, if there had not been good thematic reasons for him to use guile instead.

That guile is entirely too base a recourse for the standard
honorable knight is clearly demonstrated in Scudamour's plain
refusal to stoop to it in order to gain access to the Temple of
Venus in Book IV. His way is barred by Daunger, who, though
he is redoubtable in battle, is circumventable by guile. Some men
have

> Either through gifts, or guile, or such like waies,
> Crept in by stouping low, or stealing of the kaies.

> But I though meanest man of many moe,
>   Yet much disdaining unto him to lout,
>   Or creepe betweene his legs, so in to goe,
>   Resolv'd him to assault with manhood stout.   (IV.x.18,19)

Artegall and Arthur do not seem to be manly knights of this
kind. Yet they are involved in higher concerns than is Scudamour, bearer of the shield of love. They are, in many of their
actions, instruments of the monarch, Jove, and God.

Spenser has two universes simultaneously in view. In one,
God's representatives keep God's order through the use of God's
own weapons. The city of man strives to accord with the city of
God. In the other, men try to maintain daily political order by
such means as they can. (That these means are neither godly nor
good Spenser is as well aware as is the twentieth-century demo-
crat.) Men doomed to live in a fallen, iron world, a world of
force and fraud, a world from which justice has departed, must
execute such imperfect justice as under the circumstances they
can.

CHAPTER 8

SNAKES AND SNARES

THE traditional iconography of force is fully present in Book V, with its swords and thunderbolts, its lion and crocodile and wolves, its tyrants and giants, and its iron man. Fully present, too, is the traditional imagery of fraud and guile. This traditional imagery is centered, in Christian commentary, in classical rhetorical prescriptions, and in iconography, in themes connected with snakes and snares. The first snake in the garden of Eden was the father of all fraud; subsequent embodiments of deceit tended to be snaky. Ovid wrote of fraud's *insidiae*, and traps, snares, and nets recur as the inevitable instruments of guile. Indeed, it was precisely so that he should be able to guard against traps that Machiavelli had recommended that the prince should have the nature of a fox.

Pollente, whose name suggests his power, is the first embodiment of force whom Artegall meets. That this first giant-like tyrant is guileful as well as powerful is made plain by his dependence on the standard device of guile: a trap. The dwarf, meeting Artegall, explains that:

His name is hight Pollente, rightly so
    For that he is so puissant and strong,
    That with his powre he all doth overgo,
    And makes them subject to his mighty wrong;
    And some by sleight he eke doth underfong.
    For on a Bridge he custometh to fight,
    Which is but narrow, but exceeding long;
    And in the same are many trap fals pight,
Through which the rider downe doth fall through oversight.

                                                    (ii.7)

That particular spelling of "fals"—whether it is Spenser's or a
compositor's—underlines the way in which "false" and "falls"
run together. Falseness has from man's beginnings led to falls.
(Similarly, in a later canto, Britomart's bed in the house of her
treacherous host Dolon "by a false trap was let adowne to fall"
[vi.27]. Here the assonance confirms the pun.)

The powerful Pollente keeps control of his toll bridge through
guileful means: he has pitted it with traps. But Artegall out-traps
him. They encounter one another on the bridge:

                                        so both
    Together ran with ready speares in rest.
    Right in the midst, whereas they brest to brest
    Should meete, a trap was letten downe to fall
    Into the floud: streight leapt the Carle unblest,
    Well weening that his foe was falne withall:
But he was well aware, and leapt before his fall.   (ii.12)

When they are both in the river Pollente has "great advantage"
because he is accustomed to fighting in water and because his
horse "could swim like to a fish." But Artegall closes with him
and the battle between the two of them is

    As when a Dolphin and a Sele are met,
        In the wide champian of the Ocean plaine   (ii.15)

Pollente, the powerful man and skilled swimmer who rides a fish-
like horse, is suggested by the seal, and the nimble, crafty Arte-

gall, who uses guile against guile, is represented by the dolphin. For in Renaissance iconography the dolphin customarily represented guile. More particularly, it represented the guile which the good man employs in order to overcome an evilly guileful opponent. The dolphin figures largely in Ripa's discussion of *Stratagemma Militare*—a discussion that is most relevant to our present theme.

Stratagemma Militare is represented by the figure of an armed man whose helmet is crested with the head of a dolphin. He carries a shield on which are depicted a serpent, and a frog with a stick in its mouth. Ripa's explanation of his emblem indicates that he, like Machiavelli, was advocating the use of guile against the guileful, foxlikeness to avoid traps. The frog and serpent which Stratagem bears on his shield have this significance. The ever-guileful snake is foxed by the yet more wily frog, who carries a stick in his mouth so that he will be too big for the serpent to swallow. A story of the same sort is told about the dolphin. The dolphin is the emblem of that most crafty hero, Ulysses. This is why. The dolphin was able to defeat the crocodile, who has superior force (and is, of course, the embodiment of guile), by a stratagem: he attacked the crocodile's unprotected belly with the knife-like feathers on his back.[1] Artegall, dolphin-like, defeats, not, to be sure, a crocodile, but at any rate a seal.

On a later occasion "two losels," mistaking Britomart for Artegall, accuse her of killing their brother, Pollente's groom:

> But with thy bloud thou shalt appease the spright
> Of Guizor, by thee slaine, and murdred by thy slight.   (vi.37)

Artegall had in fact dispatched Pollente's groom quite straightforwardly before taking on his master.[2] But it is, perhaps, that anticipatory leap of Artegall's and his dolphin-like fighting techniques that they have in mind when they call him guileful.

Another notable trap in the Legend of Justice is that by which Britomart herself is threatened. This trap, too, is both a symbol

and a material manifestation of guile. As the Argument verse to
Canto vi puts it:

> Talus brings newes to Britomart,
> > of Artegals mishap,
> She goes to seeke him, Dolon meetes,
> > who seekes her to entrap.

But unlike the other knights of justice she meets this threat not
with reciprocal guile but with Christian watchfulness. She has to
deal with Dolon who is by name as surely identified with guile as
Pollente is with power. He too has a trap with which to get his
victims into his power. He has had a Poe-worthy bed built into
his guest room.[3] During the course of the night which Britomart
spent in this room

> She heard a wondrous noise below the hall.
> All sodainely the bed, where she should lie,
> By a false trap was let adowne to fall
> Into a lower room, and by and by
> The loft was raysd againe, that no man could it spie.   (vi.27)

Fortunately she was not in the bed. For one thing, she was too
painfully in love to sleep. For another, unlike the apostle Paul on
a central Christian occasion, and unlike, indeed, her own knight
Artegall, she was capable of keeping a faithful watch. The bed
was timed to fall at just the moment that a devout Christian
should have left it:

> What time the native Belman of the night,
> > The bird, that warned Peter of his fall,
> First rings his silver bell t'each sleepy wight,
> > That should their mindes up to devotion call.   (vi.27)

The passage both gives the grounds of Britomart's impregnability
—her true religion—and confirms the depths of Dolon's hypoc-
risy, his "double fraud." For Dolon at first appears to be an entirely good and, by implication at least, a religious man.

The most notable setter of snares in the Legend of Justice is

Malengin. He is the book's second great embodiment of guile; his name characterizes him as such as clearly as Dolon's did him. And his physical characteristics accord rather closely with the emblematists' representations of guile. In appearance Malengin is plain enough; unlike Dolon, he does not seem to be other than he is:

Full dreadfull wight he was, as ever went
Upon the earth, with hollow eyes deepe pent,
And long curld locks, that downe his shoulders shagged,
And on his backe an uncouth vestiment
Made of straunge stuffe, but all to worne and ragged,
And underneath his breech was all to torne and jagged.

(ix. 10)

Malengin both seems and is dreadful; he is dressed like the base person he is.[4] It has been suggested that his general shagginess, his long hair, and the strange ragged garment on his back are all drawn from Spenser's personal experience of the Irish mountain fighters.[5] It is possible, indeed, that Malengin's shagginess derives from Spenser's own observation of the Irish, who, he wrote, wore "mantells and long glibbes, which is a thick curled bush of heare, hanging downe over theyr eyes and monstrously disguising them."[6] It is equally possible that it derives from the traditional iconography of guile. One of Ripa's emblems of *Inganno* depicts a man with long shaggy hair and strange jagged garment (Figure 22); Ripa writes that he is covered by the skin of a goat in such a way that his face can hardly be seen.[7]

There is no doubt that Malengin carries in his hands precisely the ensnaring implements of iconographical guile. Many of Ripa's figures of guile carry, like Malengin, nets. But Ripa's chief emblem of *Inganno*, that for which he chooses to give a pictorial illustration (Figure 22), holds in his left hand a fishing net and in his right hand three fish hooks (but *molti hami*—many hooks— according to the accompanying description). It is closely in accordance with this tradition that Spenser describes Malengin:

And in his hand an huge long staffe he held,
   Whose top was arm'd with many an yron hooke,
   Fit to catch hold of all that he could weld,
   Or in the compasse of his clouches tooke;
   And ever round about he cast his looke.
   Als at his backe a great wyde net he bore,
   With which he seldome fished at the brooke,
   But usd to fish for fooles on the dry shore,
Of which he in faire weather wont to take great store.   (ix.11)

Nets are used for catching birds as well as fishes. Malengin's use of
a net to capture his victims and carry them away has been compared

FIGURE 22. *Inganno.* From Ripa's *Iconologia*, p. 257. Courtesy of the
Prints Division, The New York Public Library, Astor, Lenox and Tilden
Foundations.

with that of the giant Caligorante in the *Orlando Furioso* (xv.44,45); Caligorante used to spread his net in the sand and drive his intended victims into it.[8] But Malengin's net is really basically that of iconographical guile, and its use to capture fools and innocents and, within the narrative, Samient, is merely the logical application of an image.

Artegall and Arthur resolve to rid Mercilla's kingdom of the menace of Malengin. Having rescued Samient from some pursuing knights once, then used her in their "complot" to gain entrance to the Souldan's castle and rescued her all over again from that castle, they decide to make her their decoy to bring Malengin into the open. Artegall enters the Souldan's castle through a complot and destroys its inhabitants "with finall force" (viii.50); in the same way, the knights initiate their enterprise against Malengin guilefully, holding in readiness the final force of Talus. Talus will be the destroyer. Their part is to get hold of Malengin in the first place, to ensnare the snarer, to set a trap for the fowler and fisher of men. Once again the maiden Samient will have to serve as the guileful heroes' decoy and bait. She is to weep and wail, and when Malengin comes forth to seize her, as he surely will,

> They in awayt would closely him ensnarle (ix.9)

A snarle is a knotty, ropey matter, not unlike a net. The knights of justice justifiably use, once again, the weapon of guile against the guileful.

In Book V there is one other set of fisher-like ensnarers whom Artegall counters with right reciprocal guile. These are Radigund and her "trusty mayd," Clarinda.

In the first place, Radigund is guileful in that she practises *dolus malus*, setting legal traps for the unwary and honorable. She makes a bargain with Artegall: if he loses in single combat with her, he will become her slave. She vanquishes him through a woman's unfair ruse, disarming him with her beauty; he, how-

ever, honorably holds to his contract and keeps his word. Spenser
prefaces his account of the matter thus:

> Artegall fights with Radigund
>   and is subdewd by guile:
> He is by her emprisoned,
>   but wrought by Clarins wile.   (v.Arg.)

To be sure, there are general grounds for regarding Clarinda as
well as Radigund as necessarily guileful. They are women. It was
considered to be of the nature of all women to be guileful—and
to be largely the nature of love to depend on guile. This is as true
of innocent as of guilty love. So it is that lovelorn Britomart, as
she waits wakeful and watchful in the house of Dolon, apos-
trophizes her own eyes thus:

> Ye guilty eyes (sayd she) the which with guyle
>   My heart at first betrayd. . . .   (vi.25)

As Burbon understandably laments (his lady having been seduced
by Grantorto),

> Ay me, that ever guyle in wemen was invented.   (xi.50)

Eve, after all, was as deceitful as she was disobedient, inquisitive,
and greedy.

Radigund and Clarinda are women; Radigund and Clarinda
are, soon after meeting and capturing Artegall, in love. In fact,
Canto V of the Legend of Justice, which might seem largely a
romantic irrelevance, is central to one of the book's themes: it is
woven out of crisscrossed intrigues; it is entirely a tissue of guile.

When Radigund falls in love with her captive knight she sends
her maid, Clarinda, to woo him for her. Clarinda is to use
woman's usual guileful method of pleasing speech—the "art of
mightie words" (v.49). The wary Artegall strongly suspects that
Clarinda "some guilefull traine did weave" to impeach him for
treason or to destroy him in some other way; he receives her cau-
tiously but with interest (v.37–42):

She feeling him thus bite upon the bayt,
    Yet doubting least his hold was but unsound,
    And not well fastened, would not strike him strayt,
But drew him on with hope, fit leasure to awayt.

But foolish Mayd, whyles heedlesse of the hooke,
    She thus oft times was beating off and on,
    Through slipperie footing, fell into the brooke,
    And there was caught to her confusion.   (v.42–43)

Clarinda falls in love with Artegall. She now has a triple game to play: wooing Artegall for herself and offering him a freedom she has no intention of giving (v.56); pretending to Radigund that he rejects her overtures; and pretending to Artegall that Radigund is implacable:

    There all her subtill nets she did unfold,
    And all the engins of her wit display   (v.52)

Later, Radigund too is described in similar piscatorial terms. In justifying Artegall's fall to Radigund on the grounds that all men are subject to love, the poet writes:

    Nought under heaven so strongly doth allure
    The sence of man, and all his mind possesse,
    As beauties lovely baite. . . .   (viii.1)

It has been observed that "the Concordance shows that this figure of the bait is one of Spenser's most characteristic images. It occurs no less than 26 times. He was evidently a devoted angler."[9] An angler perhaps. A student of iconography and of the commonplaces of rhetoric certainly. Fishing hooks and nets have recurred from ancient even till contemporary times as metaphors for female attractiveness and the effects of love.[10]

One of Ripa's emblems of *Fraude* is a fishing maiden who has one victim caught on her line and others half-dead in her pail. For fraud resembles *il pescatore, che porgendo mangiare a'pesci, gli prende, & ammazza*.[11] Clarinda in like manner offers her fish something to eat—in order that she may capture it and, no doubt, destroy it. Such are apt to be the ways of love as well as of guile.[12]

In that Radigund and Clarinda capture and work upon Artegall like fishers they are indeed, as the Argument declares, guileful and wily. But it is just in this episode that Artegall himself is most notably guileful. Indeed, the guilefulness of his conduct in appearing to accept Clarinda's dishonorable proposals to free him from his servitude to Radigund has set afoot much questioning and answering among Spenser's readers.[13] Though previously Artegall could easily have ordered Talus, who always obeys him (v.19), to rescue him from Radigund, he stood to the "doome/ Of his owne mouth, that spake so wareless word" (v.17) as that which made him subject to the Amazon. Yet in conversation with Clarinda, though there has been nothing to release him from holding to his word, he declares that he would be delighted "if she would free him from that case" (v.40).

There are, to be sure, two traditions which justify Artegall's apparent willingness to break his word. According to Cicero, it is not necessary for a man to keep a promise that has been extorted by superior force or through deceit.[14] According to Bodin, it is against natural law to subjugate a man to a woman, and any contract to this effect must necessarily be invalid.[15] Yet the fact remains that Artegall originally planned to keep his word, and now considers breaking it. Moreover, though Spenser assures us to the contrary (v.56), his dallying with Clarinda does seem a trifle ungallant.

The best answer to such objections is that they are not, at this moment, the point. The climax to the exchange between Artegall and Clarinda is their interlocking in an intricate conflict of guile— of which Artegall is as much a master as are the ladies of Radigund's court. As on other occasions, Artegall simply meets guile with guile. He opposes Clarinda's machinations with a counter-ruse. There could scarcely be a more symmetrically satisfactory chain of deceit than this:

> So daily he faire semblant did her shew,
> Yet never meant he in his noble mind,
> To his owne absent love to be untrew:
> Ne ever did deceiptfull Clarin find
> In her false hart, his bondage to unbind;
> But rather how she mote him faster tye.
> Therefore unto her mistresse most unkind
> She daily told, her love he did defye,
> And him she told, her Dame his freedome did denye.   (v.56)

However, the whole affair of Artegall, Radigund, and Clarinda is merely matter for romance; the ladies' guileful snares are sentimentally interesting, not terrible. It is quite otherwise with the book's other embodiments of fraud, most of whom suggest the horrible man- or woman-monster which is fraud's most frequent emblem. Again and again, fraud is represented in iconography by the figure with the face of an upstanding man or a beautiful woman and the body of a dragon or snake. These figures—like that of the "double fraud" which has two heads, one of a young and beautiful maiden and the other of an old and ugly hag—indicate fraud's essential duality, the difference between appearance and reality, between what is professed or promised and what is.

The first of Ripa's many emblems of *Fraude* and *Inganno,* which the iconologist describes but does not illustrate, is

la fraude con la faccia di huomo giusto, & con tutto il resto del corpo di serpente, distinto con diverse macchie, e colori. . . .[16]

He goes on to explain why the figure of a man with a "just" face and a serpent's body should so perfectly represent fraud (compare, too, Figure 22). Ripa writes that it is fraud's intrinsic quality that he has the appearance of a just man. He has a benign face and speech, is modestly clad, walks with grave steps, and is pleasant in his manners and everything else. He seems to be a zealously religious and a charitable man. His appearance, Ripa repeats, is benign, and the words he speaks are caressing and intimate.

It is just in this guise of a venerable, benignant, sweet-spoken man that Dolon appears to his would-be victims. It is just so, too, that that epitome of guile, Archimago, who is in a manner the eternal serpent himself, appeared to his prey in Book I. Dolon, like Archimago and *Fraude*, is, to all appearances, an elderly man, decently dressed. (That the dress does or should reflect the nature and position of the wearer was a medieval and Renaissance commonplace.) As Britomart was riding in search of Artegall,

> She chaunst to meete toward th'even-tide
> A Knight, that softly paced on the plaine,
> As if himselfe to solace he were faine.
> Well shot in yeares he seem'd, and rather bent
> To peace, then needlesse trouble to constraine,
> As well by view of that his vestiment,
> As by his modest semblant, that no evill ment. (vi.19)

It had been in just the same way that Una and the Red Cross Knight had met Archimago:

> At length they chaunst to meet upon the way
> An aged Sire, in long black weedes yclad,
> His feete all bare, his beard all hoarie gray,
> And by his belt a booke he hanging had;
> Sober he seemde, and very sagely sad,
> And to the ground his eyes were lowly bent,
> Simple in shew, and voyde of malice bad,
> And all the way he prayed, as he went,
> And often knockt his breast, as one that did repent. (I.i.29)

He conducts her to his hermitage. Elderly knights were to be expected, like Malory's Sir Lancelot and the hermit of Spenser's Book VI, to retire from the world for the purpose of meditation; [17] Dolon is never actually said to be a knight of this kind, but that he well may be is suggested by the circumstances of his melancholy (he paced softly, "as if him selfe to solace he were faine—vi.19), his removed dwelling ("a little wide by West"—vi.22), and the imagery of Peter and prayer that is ironically associated with him (vi.27).

In the matter of his style of speech Dolon fully accords with the tradition of *Fraude*. As soon as he meets with Britomart he engages her in polite conversation. He speaks "curteous words, in the most comely wize" (vi.20). Now courtesy is a most dubious quantity, as Ripa's attribution of its various graces to his *Fraude* suggests—and as Spenser, too, well understands, for he explores the whole matter in detail in his Book VI. In the account of Britomart's quest in the Legend of Justice, Dolon prevailed upon the heroine to accept his hospitality since "shady dampe had dimd the heavens reach" (vi.21); at his home he "talk't of pleasant things, the night away to weare" (vi.22). Again, it is all just as it had been with Una, the Red Cross Knight, and Archimago. That incarnation of fraud first discussed the local news with the passers-by, then invited them, since the sun was low, to spend the night with him (I.i.30–34). On that occasion, too, host and guests spent the evening in conversation:

> With faire discourse the evening so they pas:
> For that old man of pleasing words had store,
> And well could file his tongue as smooth as glas.   (I.i.35)

It is, of course, precisely the *tongue* of the guileful poet Malfont that was nailed to a post at the entrance to the Court of Mercilla. Clarinda is to use woman's witty, man-charming trade, "the art of mightie words." And it is his smoothness of tongue that is one of the principal defining characteristics of Malengin. This embodiment of "Guyle" (ix.Arg.) is crafty and nimble and

> So smooth of tongue, and subtile in his tale,
> That could deceive one looking in his face;
> Therefore by name Malengin they him call   (ix.5)

Fair words are as likely to be deceptive as is a fair appearance; this is why iconographical guile is notably pleasant-spoken.

Ripa's *Fraude* and *Inganno* appear to be honest men but are in reality deceivers, serpent-tailed. Our first impression of Dolon and Archimago is of honest men; but they are both soon seeking to entrap their beguiled guests. In Archimago's case the imagery actually suggests that the hypocrite has, temporarily, metaphorically, a serpent's form. Spenser writes that Archimago has worked to separate Una from the Red Cross Knight in order to do her all the harm he can:

> For her he hated as the hissing snake   (I.ii.9)

We can read this ambiguous line in two ways. It either means that Archimago hated Una, as it were on principle, in the same way as the snake hates all good persons, or it means that Archimago hated Una as intensely as if *she* were a snake. The effect is by either reading the same. For if Archimago indeed regards Una as snake-like, the irony is so intense, the reversal of qualities so clear, that the reader must automatically make the appropriate rectification. It is Archimago who so well fits the devilish snaky body of fraud:

> He then devisde himselfe how to disguise;
>   For by his mightie science he could take
>   As many forms and shapes in seeming wise,
>   As ever Proteus to himselfe could make:
>   Sometime a fowle, sometime a fish in lake,
>   Now like a foxe, now like a dragon fell,
>   That of himselfe he oft for feare would quake,
>   And oft would flie away. O who can tell
> The hidden power of herbes, and might of Magicke spell?
>
>   (I.ii.10)

Archimago's turning himself into a self-terrified dragon is funny enough. The medieval playwrights knew, after all, that the devil is a comic, a fine butt for humor, one quite capable of scaring him-

self to death. But snake, dragon, devil: all are in effect synonymous; all are embodiments of essential fraud. And so, to Machiavelli, the iconographers, and the fabulists, was the fox. Archimago
is hardly disguising himself when he turns himself into a crafty
fox or a dragon: he is assuming his true nature.

Malengin, or "Guyle," is as significantly protean as is Archimago, or "Hypocrisie"; he turns himself into several of the same
forms. When Arthur and Artegall send Talus after the nimble
Malengin as he flees among the rocks, the guileful creature is
driven so hard that he is forced to the resort of Proteus and
Archimago: he proceeds

> To leave his proper forme, and other shape to take.

> Into a Foxe himselfe he first did tourne;
> But he him hunted like a Foxe full fast. (ix.16–17)

Thereafter he turns successively, and with delightful narrative
image-shifting logic, into the bush the fox hides in, the bird that
flies out of the bush, the stone that is thrown at the bird—and
falls, and the hedgehog that lies on the earth like a round, prickly
stone; finally "he would to a snake againe" (ix.19). Just as the
guileful Archimago was like a hissing snake, and was wont to turn
himself into a fox and a dragon, the guileful Malengin turns
himself into a fox and a snake. None of Spenser's sources for the
story of Proteus—or of Achelous, that more immediately relevant
shape-changer—mentions any change into a fox.[18] Here as elsewhere Spenser suits his images to his narrative and thematic purpose.

In the cases of Malengin and Archimago there is the barest
suggestion of a snaky reality beneath an apparently fair exterior.
And, though snakes are never mentioned in connection with him,
Dolon is a dual figure. But the figure in the Legend of Justice
which is most remarkably based on traditional snaky-tailed fraud is
Geryoneo's monster.

CHAPTER 9

GERYONEO

IN THE Legend of Justice Geryoneo is a terrible three-bodied tyrant who has seized the widow Belge's kingdom and is oppressing and destroying her people. He has set up an idol of his father Geryon, and beneath its altar he keeps a monster which lives on the carcasses of those sacrificed to the idol.

Geryoneo and his monster constitute a cluster of images and associations as complex as anything in *The Faerie Queene*. In fact they are perfectly exemplary of Spenser's allegorical method. Geryoneo is an important figure in the narrative; in fact it takes two cantos to describe Arthur's dealings with him. His function in the political allegory is transparent, largely because one set of references and associations connected with him fits so aptly with contemporary affairs. And he is a central figure in the myth which Spenser's heroes imitate—that of Hercules. The tyrant, usurper, giant, and Christian-destroying pagan accords with all Spenser's consistent, though indeed inevitable, orthodox themes of justice. And, finally, the imagery and associations connected with Geryoneo and his monster make the pair the perfect embodiment of the two central foes of justice at present under discussion: they epitomize force and fraud.

Spenser quite specifically, and twice over, states that Geryoneo's monster is guileful. He writes:

> An huge great Beast it was, when it in length
>> Was stretched forth, that nigh fild all the place,
>> And seem'd to be of infinite great strength;
>> Horrible, hideous, and of hellish race . . .
>> For of a Mayd she had the outward face,
>> To hide the horrour, which did lurke behinde,
> The better to beguile, whom she so fond did finde.   (xi.23)

The horror that lurks behind consists in her dog's body, lion's claws, eagle's wings, and

> A Dragons taile, whose sting without redresse
> Full deadly wounds, where so it is empight.   (xi.24)

Like the Sphinx, Spenser writes,

> So also did this Monster use like slight
> To many a one, which came unto her schoole,
> Whom she did put to death, deceived like a foole.   (xi.25)

This creature which seems fair of "outward face," but which is fair only so as to hide the hideous snaky reality of its body, clearly belongs to the iconography of guile.

Critics have pointed out that in his description of Geryoneo's terrible, specifically Sphinx-like monster Spenser is probably following Natale Conti's description of the Sphinx: *Caput et manus puellae, corpus canis, vocem hominis, caudam draconis, leonis ungues, alas avis. . . . cum alas haberet aquilae, citissimeque ad illos convolaret. . . .*[1] The physical details are indeed similar. But there is no basis in Conti's description for the extreme guilefulness of Spenser's monster.

In a recent study, Irwin Panofsky has discussed the iconographical tradition in which fraud is represented by a figure with a beautiful woman's face and the body of a dragon or serpent. He

discusses in the light of this tradition Bronzino's "Allegory" in
the London National Gallery; he explains that in this picture the
strange figure of an apparently beautiful young girl with a snaky
tail is a representation of fraud.[2] Several emblems in Ripa's book
confirm his thesis.[3] Geryoneo's guileful monster, with its maid's
face and dragon's tail, is indubitably of this tradition.

Ripa has this description of one type of *Fraude* (Figure 23):

*Donna con due faccie una di giovane bella l'altra di vecchia brutta,
sarà nuda fino alla mammelle, sarà vestita di giallolino fin'a meza gamba,
haverà i piedi simili all'aquila, e la coda di scorpione, vedendosi al par
delle gambe, nella destra mano terrà due cuori, & una maschera con la
sinistra.*[4]

FIGURE 23. *Fraude*. From Ripa's *Iconologia*, p. 209. Courtesy of the Prints
Division, The New York Public Library, Astor, Lenox, and Tilden Foundations.

Predictably, the iconologist explains that the two faces, the half-nakedness, the two hearts, and the mask demonstrate fraud's duplicity. The lady's scorpion's tail is a variation on guile's usual sting-pointed dragon's tail; Spenser's monster has such a tail. And her eagle's feet recall the lion's claws and eagle's wings of Spenser's monster.

As a matter of fact the type of Ripa's *Fraude* reappears most notably in the Duessa of Book I.[5] In the first place Duessa's name defines her duality—the essentially twofold nature of guile. She has, like Ripa's *Fraude,* in effect two heads and two aspects. Duessa is accustomed, too, to wearing, if not, like Ripa's *Fraude,* the mask, yet the appearance and clothing of a young and beautiful woman. But she is, in reality and underneath, a filthy, hideous old hag (I.ii.40,41; vii.46–49). Then again, beneath her gorgeous robes Duessa has a tail and "most monstrous," claw-like feet. One of her feet is, like the feet of Ripa's *Fraude,* "like an Eagles claw" (the other is "like a Beares uneven paw"—this being a symbol of asymmetry and irregularity). Spenser is relevantly original in the matter of Duessa's tail. He equips his guileful hag not with the customary (and impressive) serpent's, dragon's, or scorpion's tail, but with the supremely fittingly foul fraudulent tail of a fox:

> But at her rompe she growing had behind
> A foxes taile, with dong all fowly dight.   (I.viii.48)

And there is, in Book I, another creature which resembles the Legend of Justice's monster of guile: Errour. Errour is described as an "ugly monster"

> Halfe like a serpent horribly displaide,
> But th'other halfe did woman's shape retaine,
> Moste lothsom, filthie, foule, and full of vile disdaine.   (I.i.14)

Errour is, too, as hugely den-filling and as terribly armed as is Geryoneo's monster:

> Her huge long taile her den all overspred,
> Yet was in knots and many boughtes upwound,
> Pointed with mortall sting.   (I.i.14)

Error and guile are, after all, naturally associated; error is the aim and consequence of guile; Errour dwells within a beguiling maze, leads toward Archimago, and is a precursor of Duessa.

It is actually only too natural that Errour and Geryoneo's monster should resemble one another: both are closely related to Echidna.[6] The serpent-woman Echidna first appeared in Hesiod's *Theogony*. She quite often reappears in the Renaissance, usually as a symbol of a certain kind of guile—that involving specious argument, wrong learning, and hence, naturally, doctrinal error.[7] The Errour which spews out books and pamphlets of heresy and Catholic propaganda, and the monster beneath the idol of Geryon which reflects the Spanish Inquisition both accord admirably with the Echidna tradition.

It is of interest that another, very well-known monster belongs to the tradition we are discussing. This is Milton's Sin. It has been pointed out that Milton's Sin is indebted to Spenser's Errour;[8] and they are indeed similar even to their capacity for swallowing their own revolting young when danger threatens. In fact even the wording and cadence of Milton's description echoes Spenser's; for Sin

> seem'd Woman to the waist, and fair,
> But ended foul in many a scaly fold
> Voluminous and vast, a Serpent arm'd
> With mortal sting.   (*P.L.*II.650–53)

It is very clear that Geryoneo's monster, who has the outward face of a maid in order to hide the horror that lurks behind—a horror made up of a monster's body and a dragon's tail—belongs to a strongly established tradition. Her appearance proclaims her nature: she is an emblem of fraud.

However, this is not all. Not only do her appearance and the fact that Spenser specifically declares her to be guileful identify her; she is also characterized and identified through the names of her master and of the idol she serves: Geryoneo and Geryon.

In Dante's *Inferno* a monster named Geryon guards the eighth circle of hell—the circle in which the worst of sinners, fraudulent men, are punished. Except for the fact that it is male, this monster is just like all the serpent-people we have been examining. (As a matter of fact the sex of Geryoneo's monster is ambiguous: Belge describes it as a male—x.29.) That Dante's monster was well known is suggested by the way in which Ripa picks it up: he begins his description of the first of his emblems of *Fraude:*

Dante dipinge nel suo inferno la fraude con la faccia di huomo giusto, & con tutto il resto del corpo di serpente, distinto con diverse macchie, e colori, e la sua coda ritirata in punta di scorpione, ricoperta nell'onde di Cocito, overo in acqua torbida, e nera, così dipinta la dimanda Gerione. . . .[9]

But even better known and more frequently recurrent in books of mythology and in emblems is another, quite different creature named Geryon. For "Geryon" stands more often as a symbol of strength and unity than as a symbol of double guile; he perfectly embodies force as well as fraud.

Though its appearance shows it to be the epitome of guile, the monster does not actually *act* fraudulently. In fact, since it is confined beneath the altar and restricted to a diet of dead victims, it scarcely has an opportunity to do so. It is, indeed, called upon to exercise its force, its "infinite great strength," rather than its fraud. But Geryoneo does use both force and fraud; he is fraudulent particularly, as Machiavelli and common sense prescribed, in order to gain an initial advantage. It is through guile that he first obtained power in Belge's kingdom (x.12,13); it is with guile that he fights, using his natural physical advantages for a crafty piece of sleight-of-six-hands (xi.7). But Geryoneo, who combines the power of three in his triple-membered body, who is a "strong tyrant" (x.6), "one of matchless might" (x.8), and who has "double strength" in each of his six hands and arms (xi.6), is clearly an embodiment of force, too. Thus Geryoneo is, even more fully than Pollente, an exemplary embodiment of the two great forces which are the foes of justice: force and fraud.

Spenser's three-bodied Geryoneo resembles his father, Geryon, the powerful three-bodied tyrant whom Hercules slew. Spenser specifically says so (x.9–11). Moreover, he describes his Geryon-resembling figure in precisely the traditional way, so that he looks like yet another figure who has stepped from the pages of an emblem book. In particular, in his physical appearance and in the details of his parentage, Spenser's Geryoneo follows the Geryon of Natale Conti's account. The mythologist explains that Geryon is the greatly powerful creature whom Hercules slew; he writes that some believe him to have had three bodies because he ruled over three Spanish kingdoms; but that "others have believed that by the fable of Geryon, who had many legs, hands, and eyes, governed by one will, was symbolized concord among citizens, which makes them invincible when those who are just men act in concert, as Plutarch says in his Politics." [10] This account of Geryon occurs in the same chapter of Conti's work as does the account of the Sphinx upon which Spenser perhaps based his and Geryoneo's guile-monster.

The same Geryon regularly appears in the emblem books. He is a three-bodied crowned warrior who symbolizes concord and united force. Both Alciati and Ripa have this emblem. [11] According-ing to Alciati, Geryon represents *Concordia insuperabilis* (Figure 24). His figure of Geryon as a crowned warrior who has six arms and six legs is followed by these lines:

> *Tergeminos inter fuerat concordia fratres.*
> *Tanta simul pietas mutua, & unus amor:*
> *Invicti humanis ut viribus ampla tenerent*
> *Regna, uno dicti nomine Geryonis.*

Geryon, from this view, is a figure for the truth that strength united makes stronger. A French commentator on Alciati's em-blem writes of the figure as constituting *"une union tresforte."* [12]

Now, three brothers whose union in one body represents concord and thrice-multiplied strength figure largely in an earlier book of *The Faerie Queene*. They are the mighty and sympathetic three-brothers-in-one in Spenser's Legend of Friendship—which is really a Legend of Concord:

> Amongst those knights there were three brethren bold,
>> Three bolder brethren never were yborne,
>> Borne of one mother in one happie mold,
>> Borne at one burden in one happie morne,
>> Thrise happie mother, and thrise happie morne,
>> That bore three such, three such not to be fond;
>> Her name was Agape whose children werne

Tergeminos inter fuerat concordia fratres.
Tanta simul pietas mutua, & unus amor:
Inuicti humanis ut uiribus ampla tenerent
Regna, uno dicti nomine Geryonis.

FIGURE 24. Geryon. From Alciati's *Emblemata*, p. 42 (1548). Courtesy of the Rare Book Division, The New York Public Library, Astor, Lenox and Tilden Foundations.

> All three as one, the first hight Priamond,
> The second Dyamond, the youngest Triamond. . . .
> These three did love each other dearely well,
>   And with so firme affection were allyde,
>   As if but one soul in them all did dwell   (IV.ii.41,43)

These brothers, like Alciati's Geryon, are *tergemini*, *invicti*, and of *unus amor*. But though they are united in soul, they are separate in body; in accordance with the boon their mother begged of the fates, when one brother dies, his spirit and strength enters the body of the next, and accordingly the youngest gets to be of triple spirit—but he does not, like Geryon, get triple arms.

Yet in his emphatic three-i-tude Geryoneo is clearly a counterpart of the sons of Agape. It is all done with the same rhetorical gusto, too. Geryoneo

>   had three bodies in one wast empight,
> And th'armes and legs of three, to succour him in fight.   (x.8)

He brought Belge's land to subjection "Through his three bodies powre, in one combynd" (x.9). He has, too, "three double hands thrice multiplied" (xi.6). Finally Arthur puts an end to Geryoneo with a flurry of patterned threes:

> Through all three bodies he him strooke attonce;
>   That all the three attonce fell on the plaine:
>   Else should he thrise have needed, for the nonce
>   Them to have stricken, and thrise to have slaine.
>   So now all three one sencelesse lumpe remaine   (xi.14)

Spenser even sees the three-in-one-ness of the sons of Agape and of Geryoneo in terms of the same imagery. The sons of Agape are

> Like three faire branches budding farre and wide,
>   That from one roote deriv'd their vitall sap:
>   And like that roote that doth her life divide,
>   Their mother was, and had full blessed hap   (IV.ii.41)

In his battle with Geryoneo, Arthur succeeds in cutting off one of his adversary's arms; soon he again

> smote at him with so importune might,
> That two more of his armes did fall away,
> Like fruitless braunches, which the hatchets slight
> Hath pruned from the native tree, and cropped quight.
>
> (V.xi.11)

The sons of Agape represent the united power of concord; they are a prominent symbol in Spenser's Legend of Friendship. According to Renaissance interpretation, Geryon has the same significance. But Spenser's Geryoneo, though identical in his appearance and similar in some of his associations, is diametrically opposite from these. He is not noble or good, but evil. Far from being the embodiment of concord, he is, rather, the epitome of discord: the first thing he does when he has gained power in Belge's kingdom is "To stirre up strife" (x.13). The only thing that he has in common with the Geryon of myth and emblem is threefold power. Geryoneo represents a perversion or demonic parody of the power of just concord.

The whole of the Arthur-Geryoneo episode seems based on the theme of the threeness of Geryon. In the first place, there are three chief Geryoneo-associated enemies whom Arthur has to slay: the "Seneschall of dreaded might" (x.30–33), Geryoneo, and Geryoneo's monster. Similarly, altering tradition to his purpose, Spenser describes the three fearful creatures Arthur's predecessor, Hercules, had to slay: Orthrus, Geryon, and a guardian monster (which Spenser created as a composite of the *two* guardian monsters of legend).[13]

The general threeness of everything Arthur has to encounter in this episode is reiterated in the *three* knights who come out against him after he has defeated the Seneschall. The rhetorical device in this description is like that in the description of the threeness of the sons of Agape and of Geryoneo himself. "All"

and "attonce" unite the three knights into a prospective image
and variant form of the Geryoneo Arthur is yet to meet:

> But as he nigher drew, three knights he spyde,
>   All arm'd to point, issuing forth a pace,
>   Which towards him with all their powre did ryde,
>   And meeting him right in the middle race,
>   Did all their speares attonce on him enchace.
>   As three great Culverings for battrie bent,
>   And leveld all against one certaine place,
>   Doe all attonce their thunders rage forth rent,
> That makes the wals to stagger with astonishment.

> So all attonce they on the Prince did thonder;
>   Who from his saddle swarved nought asyde,
>   Ne to their force gave way, that was great wonder,
>   But like a bulwarke, firmely did abyde   (x.34,35)

Arthur fells the knight in the center. As soon as their solid front
is broken the knights lose their power; the remaining two flee and
are killed, one after the other, separately.

United, Geryon stands. Divided he falls. So observed the commentator to the 1583 edition of Alciati's *Emblemata*. He remarks that *Ceterum aiunt Geryones ab Hercule vinci nunquam
potuisse, nisi separatos & a se disiunctos*.[14] He is attempting to account for the contradiction between the nature of the Geryon who
symbolizes just concord and the nature of the Geryon whom Hercules slew. For Hercules, who was regarded in the Renaissance as
a supremely virtuous and just hero, would not have destroyed
Geryon if what Geryon represented was absolutely and only the
concord of just men. Ripa and Conti put forward two alternative
interpretations; both write that some say Geryon, being three
brothers in one body, or many limbs under one will, embodies
concord; but others say he was either the three brothers or the
one strong king who ruled the three kingdoms of Spain.[15] Thus

euhemerizing, Diodorus Siculus comments: "We know for an assurance Gerion had no iii bodies as is of him recounted." Diodorus begins his story of this adventure of Hercules: "Kinge Gerion, otherwise called Criseus, which is as much to say in our language as 'Golde,' so that for his great rychesse he was callyd Criseus. And he had iii sons. . . ." [16]

The Geryoneo whom Arthur rightly slays is like Diodorus's Geryon in that he is a wealthy tyrant. In that he is also, like the other aspect of traditional Geryon, an embodiment of threefold power—a figure which usually represents concord—Geryoneo is a supreme parody of the good. Just as a crocodile and a lion lie beneath justice's ladies, a penned man-dragon lies beneath the idol of Geryoneo's father. But Isis and Mercilla hold their power in check; Geryoneo uses his power for oppression and for gain. The threefold creature in whom mythographers saw invincible concord embodied is, in its obverse, a monument to perverted power.

Geryoneo and Geryon, with all their characteristics, attributes, and associations, constitute a marvelous image cluster. It stands in reciprocal, explicatory balance against two parallel icons elsewhere in the book. In all these icons is epitomized the book's thematic play with ideas of force and fraud. And Geryoneo and Geryon are, moreover, also superbly relevant to two of Spenser's other levels of allegory and thematic imagery.

There is in the first place the fact that Geryon was, in euhemerized mythology, a Spanish tyrant, rich as Criseus. This fits him impeccably into the historical allegory of the Legend of Justice. Throughout the final section of the book Spenser alludes to England's foreign affairs, which were, of course, dominated by Spain. In the episode of Belge the distressed heroine represents the Catholic-occupied Netherlands; Geryoneo is the perfect representative of the fabulously wealthy tyrannously extended power of Spain.

And then, finally, it was Hercules who slew him. He is yet another of the rebels and tyrants whom Jove- and Hercules-imitating Arthur rightly destroys. Indeed, this episode of Geryoneo is one of those which most firmly link the whole legend of the knights of justice with that of Hercules.

HERCULES

CHAPTER 10

THE CHAMPION OF
TRUE JUSTICE

It HAS long been recognized that in Book V of *The Faerie Queene* the figure of Hercules stands behind both Artegall and Arthur as a prototype of the just hero, and that in effect the myth of Hercules constitutes one of the Legend's levels of allegory.[1] Hercules's presence in the book is felt not only through the association of the roles of the knights of justice with that of Hercules, the archetypal hero of justice, but also through many clear images and references, and through a number of word-pictures which very closely match the iconography connected with Hercules.

Spenser makes Artegall's relationship to justice-maintaining Hercules specifically clear in the opening stanzas of the first canto:

> Though vertue then were held in highest price,
> In those old times, of which I doe intreat,
> Yet then likewise the wicked seede of vice
> Began to spring which shortly grew full great,
> And with their boughes the gentle plants did beat.
> But evermore some of the vertuous race

Rose up, inspired with heroicke heat,
That cropt the branches of the sient base,
And with strong hand their fruitfull rancknes did deface.

Such first was Bacchus, that with furious might
  All th'East before untam'd did overronne,
  And wrong repressed, and establisht right,
  Which lawlesse men had formerly fordonne.
  There Justice first her princely rule begonne.
  Next Hercules his like ensample shewed,
  Who all the West with equall conquest wonne,
  And monstrous tyrants with his club subdewed;
The club of Justice dread, with kingly powre endewed.[2]

And such was he, of whom I have to tell,
  The Champion of true Justice Artegall.   (i.1–3)

According to the old genealogies, Bacchus, or Libyan Jove, was
the father of Hercules; father and son set out to conquer and civ-
ilize all the known world, East and West, just as Spenser describes
them as doing. Furthermore, not only does the poet specifically
connect Artegall with Hercules in this introductory passage
and, by implication, throughout the Legend of Justice, but he
also identifies him, in that central analysis of the nature of justice, in the temple of Isis, with Osiris. Now Osiris and Bacchus
were commonly identified with one another.[3] Osiris was specifically renowned as a god of justice. Spenser appropriately associates, and to some extent identifies with one another, Osiris-
Bacchus and Hercules, father and son, the god and the hero of
justice.

   Like Hercules, Artegall and Arthur go through their world
subduing a succession of monstrous tyrants. There are incom-
parably more references to tyrants, tyranesses, and tyranny in the
Legend of Justice than in any other part of Spenser's work. According to the Concordance, these words recur thirty-seven times
in Book V of The Faerie Queene. Their next highest incidence is

in Book I, in which they recur only seven times. Almost all the enemies of justice—almost all of them, that is, which do not primarily represent guile—are tyrants. Pollente, the Souldan, Geryoneo, and Grantorto are tyrants. Radigund is a tyraness. (V.ii.6; viii.20, etc.; x.6, etc.; i.3, etc.; vi.11.)

The tyrant Geryoneo is specifically related to the Geryon whom Hercules slew: he resembles him in his monstrous shape and is actually said to be his son (x.9–11). It is of some interest, moreover, that the sacrifice-eating monster that Geryoneo keeps beneath the idol he has built for his father resembles another detail in the Hercules story. When Hercules was returning from his labor of destroying Geryon, he encountered and slew King Faunus: and Faunus was wont to sacrifice strangers at the altar of *his* father Hermes.[4]

Then there is the Souldan. The destruction of the Souldan is clearly associated with the myth of Hercules both through Spenser's specific reference and through the implication of some of the details. For the Souldan came forth in his terrible chariot

> Like to the Thracian Tyrant, who they say
> Unto his horses gave his guests for meat,
> Till he himself was made their greedy pray,
> And torne in peeces by Alcides great. (viii.31)

The Thracian tyrant was Diomedes, King of Thrace, the destruction of whom was another of the twelve labors of Hercules. Then, a herculean analogy having been initially set up, the reader may see traces of Hercules at two other points during Arthur's battle with the Souldan.

When Arthur receives a "griesly wound" from the Souldan, his reaction is explicable only in terms of a tradition associated with Hercules. For

> Much was he grieved with that haplesse throe,
> That opened had the welspring of his blood;
> But much the more that to his hatefull foe

He mote not come, to wreake his wrathfull mood.
That made him rave, like to a Lyon wood,
Which being wounded of the huntsmans hand
Can not come neare him in the covert wood,
Where he with boughes hath built his shady stand,
And fenst himselfe about with many a flaming brand.   (viii.35)

In allowing his pain and wrath to drive him to rave like a mad lion Arthur is behaving almost ridiculously. But the matter may be explained when one remembers the tradition of the noble madness and just wrath of Hercules. When Hercules put on the poisoned shirt it burst into flames (and Arthur, too, is faced with "many a flaming brand"); he went mad with pain and rage. Far from condemning such fury as immoderate and reprehensible, the Renaissance tended to regard it as nobly heroic. So it was that Tasso could celebrate, in his *Gerusalemme Liberata*, the Irefull Virtue as a positive good. Arthur's Hercules-like wrath is a fitting and indeed inevitable preliminary to his decision to unveil, two cantos later, his terrible shield. For his shield is like Jove's thunderbolt; and it is in his wrath that the god always strikes.

Now, we have already seen that the effect of Arthur's shield is like that of God's grace, Jove's lightning bolt, and the true sun.[5] The succession of metaphors suggests that it also resembles two frightful monsters: "the monstrous Scorpion" which put Phaeton's chariot horses to flight and the sea beast which terrified the chariot horses of Hippolytus (viii.40,43). Hercules, too, had a miraculous, monstrous, brilliantly shining shield. Hesiod describes it as

All glittering: no one ever broke it with a blow or crushed it. And a wonder it was to see; for its whole orb was a-shimmer with enamel and white ivory and electrum, and it glowed with shining gold. . . .

And there were heads of snakes unspeakably frightful, twelve of them; and they used to frighten the tribes of men on earth whosoever made war against the son of Zeus; for they would clash their teeth when

Amphitryon's son was fighting: and brightly shone these wonderful works.[6]

Arthur's shield is quite as bright, adamantine, and monster-terrible as was the shield of Hercules.

Geryoneo and the Souldan are the most clearly Hercules-related tyrants whom Spenser's heroes of justice destroy. But there are several other tyrannous characters. And there are the monsters. Spenser actually describes Artegall as having spent a monster-killing youth much as Hercules did. (He gives a more elaborate account of this hero's origins and antecedents than he does of any of the others'.) Indeed, as Hercules, though half a mortal, was suckled and tutored by goddesses and gods, the apparent foundling, Artegall, was "noursled" by Astraea.[7] Astraea taught Artegall "all the discipline of justice"; she showed him how to use the balance and how to mete out equity and rigor appropriately:

> Of all the which, for want there of mankind,
> She caused him to make experience
> Upon wyld beasts, which she in woods did find,
> With wrongfull powre oppressing others of their kind.   (i.7)

He becomes so powerful and skilful in fight

> That even wilde beasts did feare his awfull sight.   (i.8)

And Hercules's *enfances*, too, consisted largely of exploits against wild beasts and monsters; indeed, most of his twelve labors were also of this nature. According to the legends he was chiefly renowned and often moreover reproached for his dominion over animals.[8]

One notable Hercules-related monster whom Artegall and Arthur destroy in the course of their travels is Malengin. Though in this case there is no specific mention of any name associated with the Hercules legend, the heroes' destruction of shifty Malengin clearly reflects Hercules's conquest of the shape-changer Achelous.

Now Hercules's monster-killing career is significant not only in so far as it is part of his general maintenance of peaceable order. It is part, too, of his function as a cosmic figure. For many of the beasts which Hercules in one way or another slew went up to the skies to become, it was said, signs of the zodiac. It seems clear enough that Book V's setting, Artegall's predecessors and nurturing, the nature of several of his and Arthur's adventures, and the implications of some of the imagery connect the Legend of Justice very firmly with the myth of Hercules. Hercules, in his aspect of archetypal obtainer and maintainer of justice, is a supremely appropriate vehicle for the major theme of the book. But in its largest sense, this major theme is more than the destroying of monsters, tyrants, and villains. It is really a matter of maintaining universal order, in the heavens as well as on the earth. And Hercules is perfectly relevant to this larger theme, too.

In this connection it is interesting to notice a series of five illustrations of the deeds of Hercules by Anton Woensam von Worms

FIGURE 25. The deeds of Hercules. Anton Woensam von Worms. From a title page in an edition of the nine books of Herodotus (Cologne, 1526).

(Figure 25). The first little picture shows Hercules holding up the starry globe; the second, his wounding the Cerneian hind; the third, his choosing between two ladies; the fourth, his capturing Cerberus; and the fifth, his approaching the pyre on which he will die. The series covers all the aspects of Hercules which were allegorized and "moralized" in the Renaissance. The last two scenes in the series allude to the respects in which Hercules is Christ-like: he conquers hell and death. The central one depicts the hero at his most moral moment of choice: he chooses virtue rather than pleasure. The scene of his wounding the hind, a creature which was sacred to Artemis, was taken to represent the hero's pursuit and attainment of wisdom.[9] Finally, the first of the scenes is ostensibly of Hercules's holding up the globe for Atlas. But the reason this particular scene is chosen is that it shows Hercules in his cosmic aspect: the hero who so nobly at the end of the series approaches his own funeral pyre and his apotheosis is destined during his life to create some of the stars which he now

holds up and finally himself to enter among the constellations.

It is intersting that much as Anton Woensam von Worms starts his series on Hercules by an allusion to his stellar role, Spenser opens his Legend of Justice on the same note. The proem principally treats of the difference between the justice of the golden age and the conditions of the contemporary, fallen, iron age. That the time is out of joint indeed is confirmed by the fact that the stars have gone out of their proper courses and that the sun (which is, after all, the very symbol of Osiris and of justice) seems, according to Aegyptian wizards, to be forsaking men (Pr. 5–8). Astronomical miscarrying, decline, and decay was a common and understandable image of degeneration.[10] It is notable, though, that all the figures of the zodiac whose wanderings the poet deplores are associated with Hercules.

This is how Spenser describes the degenerating constellations:

> They all are wandred much; that plaine appeares.
> For that same golden fleecy Ram, which bore
> Phrixus and Helle from their stepdames feares,
> Hath now forgot, where he was plast of yore,
> And shouldred hath the Bull, which fayre Europa bore.

> And eke the Bull hath with his bow-bent horne
> So hardly butted those two twinnes of Jove,
> That they have crusht the Crab, and quite him borne
> Into the great Nemoean lions grove.   (Pr.5,6)

According to some Renaissance mythographers, the twelve-signed zodiac is named for and inhabited by beasts killed by Hercules in the course of his twelve labors, or by other signs, symbols, or objects associated with his labors. Astronomers and mythographers were divided in their ordering of these series and in their particular attribution of signs to labors, or vice versa; the coincidence of the figure twelve was no doubt enough to put them to their task.[11]

There was one point, however, on which all seemed agreed: the slaying of the Nemoean lion was generally regarded as the first and in a sense the definitive labor of Hercules, and this Nemoean lion was believed to have taken his place as Leo among the constellations.[12] This lion stands at the climax of Spenser's account of the displacing of the signs of the zodiac. The other mythological figures he mentions are less clearly associated with the labors of Hercules, but all of them do have some connection with Hercules in that he rescued them. He intervened when Phrixus was about to kill himself, putting Phrixus on the ram onto which the boy then took up his sister Helle. Then, too, the ram is, for Spenser as in tradition, specifically the "golden fleecy" one; and Hercules was one of the Argonauts. The bull which bore Europa was often identified with the Cretan bull, the capture of which constituted what was usually reckoned to be the seventh labor of Hercules. This bull is commemorated in the constellation Taurus.[13] The crab played an important part in Hercules's encounter with the hydra of Lerna, the object of his second labor. Juno sent the crab scuttling between Hercules's feet to impede him in the fight. Hercules crushed it. This crab became the constellation Cancer.[14] It has been well observed that Spenser's wording "crusht the Crab" seems to point specifically to this incident.[15] To all appearances least clearly associated with Hercules are "those two twins

FIGURE 26. Hercules as a sky map. Dürer, 1515.

of Jove," Castor and Pollux, who made up the constellation Gemini. Yet the association is firmly made by Coluccio Salutati, who wrote:

Hercules etiam, ut idem narravit Iginus, creditur a nonullis una cum Apolline Geminorum signum esse, quod tamen communiore sententia dicitur esse Castorum et Pollucem, qui simul maxima concordia vixerunt nullo modo de regno certantes.[16]

Hercules himself was, of course, a twin, the immortal brother of Iphicles; and indeed twins were very magic to the mythographers, one of the two usually being considered, like Hercules, a child of the gods.

It would be possible to argue that in the proem Spenser is merely using astronomical decline as an addition to his general vision of decay, and that Hercules's supposed association with the zodiac has no particular significance. Yet the final allusion to the Nemoean lion is unmistakeably deliberate. To confirm the effect, the first canto opens, a few stanzas later, with a direct invocation of Hercules's memory: it is the primary reminder that Hercules was the representative hero of justice, subduer of "monstrous tyrants."

It must be said, however, that the various zodiacal figures are presented in a less than magnificent way. One reader at least has found that "there are overtones of slapstick in the random motions of Jupiter's menagerie."[17] It was because of some particularly unpleasant marital complications in Jove's love life that Phrixus was doomed to die; and Europa's bull was, of course, the horny God himself. Because of these associations it is generally said that the signs of the zodiac whose wanderings the poet deplores are derived from Jove.[18] It is certainly true that one ancient theory explained the constellations as being Jove-related; but it does not seem to have been so widespread or so well attested as the Hercules theory. It is possible that in this passage Spenser is deliberately glancing at the idea of the sex-involved, Jovial origin of the zodiac as well as at the heroically herculean one. If this be so, the hints of Jove's ruthless love life may serve as a reminder of the concupiscent aspect of his son—whose other self was nevertheless the magnificent slayer of that "great Nemoean lion." It may be that Spenser is conveying, at this earliest moment of the Legend of Justice, the extraordinary contradictions that are present in his mythological prototype, Hercules, in his narrative hero, Artegall, and in the virtue of justice itself.[19]

In the literature and iconography of the Renaissance Hercules appears in three quite different aspects. For one thing, he was regarded as an admirable figure from both mythology and "history"—a just prince who maintained national and cosmic hierarchy and who traveled about the world destroying tyrants and monsters. For another, he was "moralized" into an allegorical figure, an emblem of temperate virtue and of Christ. Third, though, he was recognized, by those who read his story for what it was, to be what recent writers have variously termed a "social bandit" and a "herculean hero,"[20] an embodiment of magnificent violence, madness, and triumphant love.[21]

An awareness of the central dichotomy in the hero's character goes back a long way. Seneca's two plays about Hercules, which largely shaped the Renaissance concept of the hero, are very clear in this respect. For Seneca, Hercules was in the first place a champion of civilized order and a supreme giant-, tyrant-, and monster-killer. At the beginning of *Hercules furens*, for instance, the hero declares:

Myself will I frame prayers worthy of Jupiter and me: May heaven abide in its own place, and earth and sea: may the eternal stars hold on their way unhindered; may deep peace brood upon the nations; may the harmless country's toil employ all iron, and may swords lie hid; . . . may savage and cruel tyrants rule no more. If earth is still to produce any wickedness, let her make haste, and if she is preparing any monster, let it be mine.[22]

Again, at the end of *Hercules Oetaeus* the Chorus prays to the apotheosized Hercules to much the same effect:

But do thou, O mighty conqueror of beasts, peace-bringer to the world, be with us yet; still as of old regard this earth of ours; and if some strange-visaged monster cause us with dire fear to tremble, do thou o'ercome him with the forked thunder-bolts—yea, more mightily than thy father's self the thunders hurl.[23]

In Spenser as in Seneca, the heroes of justice have to maintain peace and cosmic order; indeed, the world desired in these prayers is much like the world regretted in the proem to Book V. And in Spenser as in Seneca, a herculean hero has for this purpose the use of the thunderbolt of Jove. Indeed, as maintainer of right hierarchy and punisher of wrongdoers Hercules would seem to be as effective as, if not interchangeable with, his classical father Jove. The idea that Hercules could wield a thunderbolt seems to have lingered on in emblem literature. There is an emblem of this kind, entitled "The Mask of Judgement," in Hermann Hugo's *Pia desideria* (Antwerp, 1628). In it a masked figure threatens with Jove's thunderbolt a woman who is as frightened as a rabbit; the mask is the lion-mask so often worn by Hercules.[24] The conjunction of Jovial and Herculean themes is of course very clear in Spenser: Artegall and Arthur imitate Hercules's deeds and wield Jove's weapons.

The main drift of Seneca's plays is to establish Hercules as the embodiment of heroic virtue. The hero who killed himself on Mount Oetaeus died, as Seneca presents it, an examplary Stoic death; and in general during his life, Seneca suggests, he exercised a virtue that rested upon a love of justice and capacity for heroic endurance. Yet Seneca is also well aware that most of the stories told about Hercules are very far from supporting such a noble view of the hero's character. His two plays are in fact based on an alternation between the conflicting aspects of the hero; in them, Hercules's heroic virtue seems at times to be shaded with dubiousness, depravity. In both *Hercules furens* and *Hercules Oeteaus* the first and last parts assert the hero's fortitude, endurance, and worthiness for deification. But in the center of both

Hercules appears in the extreme of his other aspect, as a cruel, lustful man. In *Hercules furens* the hero is not entirely responsible for or culpably guilty of the murder of his wife and children, since it is Juno who has made him mad; but the nature of his conversation with Megara before slaying her and the fact that he kills some of his children on stage emphasize the horror of his deed.[25]

In *Hercules Oetaeus* his excess of cruelty and passion is made even more plain. At the beginning of the play Iole herself appears with a chorus of captive maidens; Hercules has just avenged himself on her father for refusing her to him. The chorus declare: "No more is left to suffer—we have seen, oh, woe! the angry Hercules." Iole then says:

But I, unhappy one, bewail not temples fallen on their gods, or hearth-fires scattered, or fathers burned in mingled heaps with sons, and gods with men, temples with tombs,—nay, no common misfortune do I mourn.   (ll.171–77)

She goes on to describe how she saw her father and brother slain and to bewail her fate and her enslavement by Deianira.

But Deianira, though free, is no happier than Iole; she is madly jealous of Hercules's love for her rival. Deianira complains, " 'Tis the wont of Hercules to love captive maids." The nurse agrees, but points out that it is equally his wont not to love them for long:

'Tis true he loved the captive sister of Dardanian Priam, but he gave her to another; add all the dames, all the maids he loved before. A wanderer in love was he. Why, the Arcadian maid, Auge, while leading Pallas' sacred dance, suffered his lust's violence but fell from his regard, and Hercules retains no trace of his love for her. Why mention others? The Thespiades are forgotten; for them but with a passing flame Alcides burned.   (ll.362–70)

And so on. And soon Deianira, cynical in her distress, is reduced to interpreting the deeds of Hercules as most commonsense observers would be likely to do:

He is a trifler, nor does the charm of glory urge him on. He goes wandering o'er the earth, not in the hope that he may rival Jove, nor that he may fare illustrious through Grecian cities. Some one to love he seeks; his quest is maidens' chambers. If any is refused him, she is ravished; against nations doth he rage, midst ruins sees his brides, and unrestrained excess is called heroic.   (ll.417–22)

This is the ultimate condemnation, the complete debunking. It is an apt comment on the development of the whole Hercules legend: unrestrained excess *did* come to be called heroic. Deianira herself, at the end of the play, on hearing of her husband's heroic fortitude in his death, is wild with guilt and regret and lauds him as highly as does everyone else. Indeed, it is in effect the final poetry which justifies the hero's apotheosis. But the reader is not deceived. Though Seneca ultimately stands by the noble interpretation of the myth of Hercules, though his Hercules is, despite all aberrations, a virtuous, Stoic hero, and a god, the playwright has suggested a gaping alternative possibility at both plays' centers.

Coluccio Salutati, in the early years of the Renaissance, recognized the same duality in the figure of Hercules. He was much put to it to prove that Hercules was, despite all appearances to the contrary, a noble, Christian-like man. He wrote the first version of his *De laboribus Herculis,* in the form of a long letter to Giovanni da Siena, to deal with this very problem. As a contemporary scholar has phrased it,

How could Seneca let Hercules become a god in the *Hercules Oetaeus* after representing him as a murderer of his wife and children in the *Hercules furens?* That question perplexed Salutati, with his Christian ideology, and he wrote his treatise in the first instance to answer it. The explanation lies in allegory, he maintains.[26]

Salutati argued that Hercules represents the soul, Megara the flesh, and their three sons irascibility, sensuality, and concupiscence—so Hercules was clearly quite right to kill them. Salutati ends his account at the capture of Cerberus, so does not need to mention Iole; he deals with Omphale, Hercules's most voluptuous mistress, by explaining that it was in her realm that the virtuous hero killed the serpent of lust. Salutati's Hercules manuscripts did not have a wide circulation and were not very influential; [27] but they provide interesting evidence of a Renaissance awareness of, and an attempt to deal satisfactorily with, the anomalies in the Hercules story.

Salutati's interpretation of the Hercules myth is an inevitable derivative both from the tendency to "moralize" pagan mythology and from the penchant of theologians for dealing with unforgettable pagan figures by regarding them as *figurae* of Christian ones: [28] Hercules, who triumphed over hell in his capturing of Cerberus, who died a martyr's death, and who became a god, is conveniently analogous to Christ. Indeed, Salutati devotes the whole of his last chapter—a quarter of the entire work—to the subject of Hercules, Cerberus, and hell.

A promoter of the moralized Hercules who shows his awareness of the other Hercules by his omissions is Diodorus Siculus. Diodorus gives an account of Hercules in terms of his twelve labors, presenting him as "the noblest prynce of the world," and particularly admiring his feat of capturing the hind, on the grounds that it was accomplished "not by forcyble menys of daungerous ieobardy, but by his discrete & wyse circumspection." [29] But Diodorus neglects to mention either Omphale or Iole, and partly exonerates Hercules's killing of his wife and children by strongly emphasizing the madness in which the hero did the deed and his deep remorse on his recovery.

The matter which Diodorus omitted or apologized for is of course the most humanly interesting part of the Hercules legend. Not very surprisingly, it is this aspect of the legend which enters into the two Renaissance Italian epics which are (however indirectly) about Hercules. Ariosto, in his *Orlando Furioso* (1516), alludes by his title to Seneca's *Hercules furens;* and he picks up, bestows upon his Orlando, and mocks, that furious Hercules's proneness to fall both into love and into fits of violent madness.

As for Cinthio Giraldi's long epic, *Dell'Hercole* (1557): this gravely retells almost all the heroic, extravagant, ruthless Hercules adventures of legend. The whole thing is by way of compliment to the *illustrissimo et excellentissimo signore Hercole Secundo da Este, duco quarto di Ferrara*. The stated business in life of this Hercules is in accordance with tradition and is entirely praiseworthy: he acts *Contra i Tiranni, & contra i mostri crudi*.[30] But he is also violent and lustful to the degree that he seems hardly the ancestor to be so very proud of. His mad killing of his wife and children is described without comment (canto viii). So are his numerous exploits in love, many of which show impressive skill and stamina and a total lack of moral or social conscience; for instance, in one night he lies with all but one of the fifty daughters of Thespius, his host (canto xiii). Many stanzas of the epic are devoted to his relationship with the great love of his life, the enslaving and effeminating Omphale (canto xvi). (Unwilling perhaps to kill off his fictional Hercules during his real Hercules's lifetime, the poet never does get to Iole.)

Hercules's various appearances in literature, from Seneca's plays to Cinthio Giraldi's epic, show that there was a traditional awareness of the contradictions in the character of the "champion of true justice." Some writers, like Cinthio Giraldi, assimilate everything in a general amoral enthusiasm for Hercules's greatness. But others, like Seneca and Spenser, who are moralists, can observe and use the paradoxes. In the visual arts matters are usually rather different. Most painters and draftsmen use their art in such a way that they can only deal with one thing at a time, and present in their work just one aspect of Hercules or the other. These aspects are embodied and as it were embalmed in single, static memorable icons. And it is from the details and implications of certain recurrent icons of Hercules that we get the most interesting hints for interpreting some of the peculiarities in Artegall's character. (Yet on the other hand, that some artists could wonderfully capture fleeting, mysterious ambiguities will become apparent in the course of the following chapters.)

Hercules is usually depicted naked, bearing a massive club, and with a lion's skin thrown over his shoulders. Spenser actually writes of Hercules's "club of Justice dread" (i.2). Hercules was supposed to have derived from his lion's skin, probably that of the Nemoean lion, some of the lion's impregnability and some of his force and might. As Seneca wrote, Hercules *armatus venit/ leone et hydra.*[31] Valeriano Bolzani, too, in discussing the topic *Herculanus leo quid,* concludes that Hercules's lion represents the force by which the hero overcomes his foes.[32] Indeed, in Renaissance emblem books and iconographical dictionaries Hercules usually represented, quite simply, like the lion, force. (And so, in some respects, it may be remembered, does Artegall.) Hercules was conventionally regarded as the embodiment of *right* force; but at least one man in the Renaissance was less sanguine. To further his program for cosmic, social, and psychological improvement, Giordano Bruno exhorted his readers: "Let us banish the Hercules of Violence." [33] Spenser is as well aware as Bruno that the "force" of Hercules can be violent.

Hercules is very often depicted in the act of using his force in the right, justice-maintaining way: in the act of slaying one or another of all those monsters and tyrants—both those which were the objects of his twelve labors and those others which he met on his travels.[34] (The monstrous tyrant which Hercules is most often shown in the act of crushing is Cacus.[35] Perhaps this is because Cacus could be regarded as the most outrageous of all kinds of tyrants, a low-born one who perverts his natural calling; like Tamburlaine, Cacus was a shepherd.) But Dürer depicts Hercules in the act of destroying, not monsters or evil-doers, but a young girl's father and brother—and that brother his own friend. In his woodcut of "Hercules and Iole" Dürer portrays the hero at the height of his massacre of Iole's people; with looks of great

FIGURE 27. Hercules. Dürer, 1496.

ferocity, he stands with a foot on two slain foes (surely Eurytus and Iphitus); beside him, Iole throws her arms up in anguish and is assailed by an old woman—who is, I presume, Deianira [36]— just as her men are kept down, in parallel gesture, by Hercules. Artegall, like Hercules, is on the one hand a heroic destroyer of tyrants and on the other a cruel instigator of massacres, one who causes the death of a comrade [37] and who makes at least one neglected lady weep and tear her hair.

In all the Renaissance iconography of Hercules two scenes are depicted over and over again. And in spirit and implication these two scenes directly contradict one another. The scene which is represented most often of all is the scene in which Hercules makes a choice between two women, or sometimes between two paths: he chooses *virtus* rather than *voluptas*, wisdom rather than pleasure. This is the choice of the heroic, stoic Hercules. The other very common scene is the entirely contrary one in which Hercules abandons himself to the voluptuous pleasures of his amorous enslavement by Omphale. This is the Hercules of heroic, love-triumphant excess. It would seem impossible to reconcile these two scenes and these two views of Hercules. Yet this is precisely what, in a central scene in the Legend of Justice, Spenser magnificently does.

CHAPTER 11

THE CHOICE

THE WAY in which that strange central episode in the Legend of Justice, the Radigund affair, associates Artegall and Radigund with Hercules and Omphale has been pointed out by other readers; but the degree of sexuality that is implied in it has not been fully recognized. Similarly, scholars have suggested that Hercules's well-known choice of heroic virtue rather than pleasure affects the whole moral mode of *The Faerie Queene*; but none has seen how closely Artegall's confrontation with Radigund and acceptance of tutelage by Britomart resembles the iconography of Hercules's choice.[1] Iconographical parallels suggest that Artegall, in succumbing to Radigund, is chosen by—even if he does not choose—pleasure; Britomart, who is virtue and wisdom, rescues him from the consequences of his wrong choice.

In all Book V the episode in which Artegall is most clearly associated with Hercules is that of his enslavement by Radigund. For not only is Artegall's captivity in Radigund's Amazon realm twice specifically compared with Hercules's relationship with a mistress (v.24; viii.2), but, too, Radigund herself is clearly related to no fewer than three of the women in Hercules's life. Every one of these associations has a strong aura of sexuality.

We should in the first place understand that there is indeed an objection to reading any pleasure or sexuality into Artegall's relationship with Radigund. According to the narrative, he is a prisoner, sentenced to hard, or at any rate to uncongenial labor (doing woman's work), and punished by near-starvation for rejecting Radigund's amorous advances; even when he pretends to listen to Clarinda's offers and appeals on her mistress's behalf

> Yet never meant he in his noble mind,
> To his own absent love to be untrew. (v.6)

This is the poet's statement, and on one level we must accept it. Yet the weight of imagery and allusion, and of structure and diction makes the contrary implication. *The Faerie Queene* is, after all, an allegory, and an allegory of a very particular kind. In the episode of Radigund there are no imposing moral abstractions and no transparent political allusions; it appears to be a simple romantic narrative. But the episode so closely echoes analogous episodes in popularized and moralized mythology that we cannot in fact regard it as at all simple. Whatever the narrative may convey to the contrary, Spenser is deliberately creating if not an allegory, yet a potent evocation of sexuality. Popular readings of Freud have tempted us to regard sex as the basic reality, and to interpret most of our actions and images, in life and in art, as reflections of that reality. It was perfectly possible for Renaissance artists to work in the other direction and to use sex as a metaphor for something else. This, after all, is much what the neoplatonists did in relating human to divine love; and it is what Spenser himself may have been doing in conflating the political and sexual associations of the crocodile. Lust-enslavement is as good a metaphor as any other for Artegall's duty-neglecting sojourn with Radigund. At this time, though, it is less interesting to speculate whether or not Artegall was "really" lustful than to try to bear in mind simultaneously all the episode's ambiguities and apparently contradictory resonances. For it is these effects which are the essence of Spenser's allegory.

There has already been some suggestion of Artegall's sexuality in the hero's identification with the crocodile, emblem of lust. And it should be recalled that, even though Spenser's characters do not remain entirely the same from book to book, Artegall has shown a previous tendency to admire and desire false beauty: at the tournament in the Legend of Friendship he very much wanted the false Florimell and was very angry indeed when he could not get her (IV.v. 9, 21). The hero who succumbs to Radigund is promised and, in the very midst of the cantos describing his sojourn with the Amazon, is prophetically married to Britomart (vii.23); in falling into Radigund's hands he is in effect falling into adultery. Actually Artegall's relationship with Radigund begins, as readers have often pointed out, in just the same way as his relationship with Britomart began. It is another instance of evil being an exact inverse reflection, a demonic parody, of the good. Artegall engages, in Book IV, in single combat with Britomart, unseats her from her horse, holds her at his mercy— but sees her hair and her beautiful face beneath her shorn-off helmet: she is like an angel, divine; instead of killing her, he kneels to do her homage. Not long afterwards he woos her and wins her acceptance of his love (IV.vi.10–41). It is all much the same when Artegall combats Radigund. When she is at his mercy he unlaces her helmet in order to cut off her head; but he sees her beauty, "a miracle of natures goodly grace" (V.v.12), pities, and spares her. Not long afterwards, he is her slave.

Spenser's choice of wording for this incident supports the suggestions of its narrative structure. During their fight Radigund wounds Artegall in the thigh

> And like a greedie Beare unto her pray,
> With her sharpe Cemitare at him she flew,
> That glauncing downe his thigh, the purple blood forth drew.

(v.9)

A wound in the thigh which draws purple blood is the sexual wound of Adonis, as Spenser has clearly established it in Book III.[2] A bear with a curved sword: one could not come much nearer than this to the boar whose tusk wounded Adonis in the thigh, drawing that purple anemone blood. Then, too, Radigund's beauty causes a glance from her eye to pierce Artegall's heart just as, in the physiology and psychology of the literature of courtly love and Petrarchism, ladies' glances usually do. Artegall saw her beauty revealed:

> At sight thereof his cruell minded hart
> Empierced was with pittiful regard   (v.13)

(In the fifteenth and sixteenth centuries a usual meaning of a "regard" was a "look" or a "glance.") Commentators have recognized the pitying consideration which penetrated Artegall's heart at this moment, but not the love-glance. Then, in the light of a common sixteenth-century meaning of "will" some more of Spenser's lines become interestingly clear. "Will" meant sexual desire (and even both male and female sexual organs). It is upon these meanings that the puns in Shakespeare's Sonnet 135 depend.[3] Having unmanned Artegall by her beauty and her "pittiful regard," Radigund assails him "like as a Puttocke" (kite or buzzard) attacks a broken-winged falcon "with licentious will" (v. 15). The congruence of "licentious" and "will" seems suggestive. Two stanzas later the poet comments that

> after by abandoning his sword,
> He wilfull lost, that he before attayned.   (v.17)

This "will" primarily has its modern meanings: of his own volition, Artegall lost all; moreover, he rather wilfully, childishly lost all. But he lost partly on account of his falling into sexual temptation. Again, three stanzas later, as soon as he returns to the subject of Artegall, the poet repeats his analysis of his hero's fault; a rhetorical flourish underlines its centrality:

> Then tooke the Amazon this noble knight,
> Left to her will by his own wilfull blame   (v.20)

It seems that in the confrontation between Artegall and Radigund there is, in more than one sense, a meeting of wills.

The suggestions of sexuality which are made by the narrative parallels and the wording are strengthened by the fact that it is· "the Amazon," in fact the "Queene of Amazons" (iv.33), whose will wins Artegall. Radigund has several characteristics which make the identification fitting. It was the Amazon custom to make men do household tasks while the women fought and governed. This is Radigund's practice, too. Perhaps one office-holding male menial in Radigund's kingdom is mentioned: Eumenias, the jail-keeper. The rest, the knights she captures, dresses in women's clothes, and sets to work spinning, sewing, and washing, are her slaves (iv.31). Again, like the Amazons in the Greek story, Radigund carries a moon-like shield (v.3). (Though theirs, to be sure, were in the shape of half moons; Radigund's is like a full moon.) Even Artegall's single combat with Radigund resembles Hercules's with Hippolyte. When Hippolyte was thrown from her horse, the story goes, Hercules stood over her, club in hand, offering quarter; but Hippolyte chose to die rather than to yield. There is a moment when Artegall likewise stands above Radigund offering quarter; Radigund, less honorable than Hippolyte —an epitome, in fact, of guile—takes the opportunity to reverse their relative positions.

Obtaining the girdle of Hippolyte, queen of the Amazons, was one of Hercules's twelve labors. Now girdles, like Venus's *cestus* and indeed like Florimell's girdle, are sex-associated. To the moralizers of indecorous legend, Hercules's defeat of Hippolyte represented Heroic Virtue's conquest of lust. The commentary to Alciati's treatment of the twelve labors of Hercules makes this significance very clear. The Alciati item is in this case an allegorical stanza unaccompanied by any pictorial representation. The commentator explains to which labor of Hercules each line in the stanza refers, and what is the moral significance of each episode. Alciati's line

Vincit, Fœmineos spoliatque insignibus astus

refers, the commentator explains, to Hercules's obtaining the girdle of Hippolyte, emblem of woman's guile and lasciviousness.[4] It seems probable that a contemporary reader would expect to interpret a Hippolyte-associated figure as an embodiment of guile and lust. Spenser's imputation, during the course of the narrative, of these characteristics to Radigund seems by way of a confirmation of an emblem.

Hercules destroyed Hippolyte, making it possible for moralizing commentators to maintain that the virtuous hero destroys lust. Radigund, on the contrary, enslaves Artegall. Now, in the iconography and literature of Hercules the type of the temptress, the man-enslaver, the embodiment of lust is Omphale. Hercules gave the ax of conquered Hippolyte to Omphale, the next significant woman in his life.[5] And indeed the two women are parallel. Omphale made an effeminate slave of Hercules as Hippolyte had tried to make effeminate slaves of all men. In the Omphale legend the literal and allegorical levels merge: it is not merely, as in the case of Hippolyte, that the bondage of men to women should be taken as symbolizing the bondage of man to lust; but in the story of Omphale the queen symbolically debases her captive, Hercules, to a lascivious servitude, becoming (in both senses of the word) his mistress.[6]

A recent study has demonstrated the remarkable quantity and ubiquity of Renaissance portrayals of Hercules and Omphale.[7] Most of these paintings and drawings are entirely voluptuous, with the lovers represented in terms of, or echoing the tradition of those archetypal lovers, Mars and Venus.[8] Omphale is very often represented, like Venus, with the boy Cupid; sometimes a number of cupids flutter around her, and sometimes a bevy of voluptuous maidens attend her. Hercules occasionally wears armor, like Mars. But it is always clear from two or three unmistakable signs that the lovers are in fact Omphale and Hercules, not Venus and Mars. The lady sometimes wears a lion's skin. The man sometimes wears woman's clothing and almost always holds a distaff. And there is usually a club somewhere in the picture: often—with transparently sexual suggestion—a cupid rides or embraces the club; or he tries to draw it away from its bearer: this represents, like the putting off of the lion's skin, the emasculating of Hercules's strength and the stealing from him of his life's noble purpose. In Francisco Bassano's painting of Hercules's voluptuous sojourn with Omphale, a background hanging depicting heroic endeavor sets off all the delicate pleasures which surround the hero (Figure 28). Some of the details and most of the implications of these drawings and paintings are in one way or another present in the Artegall-Radigund incident. Radigund has Artegall divested "of all the ornaments of knightly name," and dressed instead "in womans weedes"; then his sword is broken. Finally she personally, as it would appear, "Into his hand a distaffe to him gave" (v.20–23). Radigund furnishes Artegall with the object which is veritably the emblem of Omphale-loving Hercules. Indeed the distaff was so thoroughly a symbol of women and womanhood that it has even survived in our language in the

FIGURE 28. Hercules and Omphale. Francesco Bassano (circa 1580). Vienna, Kunsthistorisches Museum.

idiom "the distaff side" (of the family). Artegall's distaff clearly shows him to be like the Hercules who abdicated his manhood for a masterful mistress. Spenser makes the analogy explicit; and he goes very particular lengths to emphasize its love elements. He writes of the enslaved Artegall:

> Who had him seene, imagine mote thereby,
>   That whylome hath of Hercules bene told,
>   How for Iolas sake he did apply
>   His mightie hands, the distaffe vile to hold,
>   For his huge club, which had subdew'd of old
>   So many monsters, which the world annoyed;
>   His Lyons skin chaungd to a pall of gold,
>   In which forgetting warres, he onely joyed
> In combats of sweet love, and with his mistresse toyd.   (v.24)

This might be a word sketch for one of the most voluptuous of the paintings of the love of Hercules and Omphale. But, as if this were not enough, Spenser even strengthens the amorousness of Hercules by running together two characters and writing "for Iolas sake" instead of something to the effect that it all happened when Hercules was Omphale's slave. Spenser runs together the figures of Omphale, Hercules's most famous paramour, and Iole, his last great love.

It was for Iole's sake that Hercules incurred his wife's jealous anger, and, as it were, it was for her sake that he donned the poisoned shirt which his wife sent, and then killed himself. Or so the romantic could argue. From this point of view, then, Iole was the mistress for whom Hercules died, as Antony died for Cleopatra. The legends run well together. The meaningful confusion between the two stories occurs, too, in Boccaccio, and also in the *Gerusalemme Liberata*, in Tasso's description of the palace of Armida. Upon its outside two scenes are sculptured: one of Hercules with that distaff and Iole with a club and lion's hide; the other of Antony and Cleopatra at Actium on Antony's great unmanning occasion.[9] Spenser, too, writes of Hercules and Antony as parallel figures when, at the end of the Radigund affair, he with retrospective irony commends Artegall's willingness to leave Britomart to return to his duty:

> Nought under heaven so strongly doth allure
>> The sence of man, and all his minde possesse,
>> As beauties lovely baite, that doth procure
>> Great warriours oft their rigour to represse. . . .

> So whilome learnd that mighty Jewish swaine,
>> Each of whose lockes did match a man in might,
>> To lay his spoiles before his lemans traine:
>> So also did that great Oetean Knight
>> For his loves sake his Lions skin undight:
>> And so did warlike Antony neglect
>> The worlds whole rule for Cleopatras sight.
>> Such wondrous powre hath wemens faire aspect,
>> To captive men, and make them all the world reject.

> Yet did it not sterne Artegall retaine   (viii.1–3)

The Jewish swain is, of course, Samson, whose case was very similar to Hercules's and who was very frequently paralleled with Hercules as a supernaturally strong, nation-sustaining, woman-effeminated, heroically martyred, Christ-like figure.[10] Spenser here calls Hercules "that great Oetean knight" so as to suggest, beyond the Omphale-loving Hercules who, shorn of his strength, neglected his duty, the Iole-loving Hercules who gave up, like Antony, his life for his love (on Mount Oetaeus).

The effect of the Iole undertone is merely to intensify the sense of passion and unlawfulness in the relationship between Artegall and Radigund. And even if we admit only a portion of the available evidence for Radigund's sexual attraction we must associate this incident in Artegall's story with Hercules's temptation by a similarly attractive lady: Pleasure.

The story of Hercules's choice of virtue rather than pleasure has no justification in legend. It was entirely the invention of Prodicus the Sophist.[11] Improbable though the story seems, absurdly though it contradicts all the usual accounts of Hercules's amorous conduct, it came to be regarded as the definitive, pivotal act in heroic Hercules's life.

Perhaps the view of Hercules as the embodiment of heroic restraint derives in some way from his role of maintainer of justice: according to the traditional platonic correspondence between man and state, as reason subdues the passions in man, the philosopher-king controls the various constituent elements of the state. Certainly, Salutati explains Hercules's destruction of the Nemoean and Theumasian lions (which, for the convenience of his allegorical interpretation, he treats as a pair) as reason's subduing of wrath and concupiscence.[12] Along the same lines, Valeriano explains Hercules's battle with the lion in terms of the force of reason contending with the force of the passions: *Rationes cum appetitu pugna.*[13]

This Hercules of platonic self-government is often pictured not as fighting and subduing but as choosing and rejecting. For instance, in van Veen's *Emblemata Horatiana* there is an emblem in which Hercules as *virtus* is shown making a typical decision. A stalwart robed man who carries Hercules's unmistakable club stands rejecting the crowns offered by Pride and Power; under his foot he crushes three cherubs representing varieties of desire—one reaches for a crown, another clutches a money bag, and the third holds cupid's bow. Virtue, meanwhile, from behind, crowns the hero who is rejecting crowns (Figure 29). Again, Ripa's emblem of the virtuous Hercules consists (as that iconographer describes it, for there is no illustration) of a picture of Hercules holding three Hesperidean apples; the emblem is said to exemplify "Heroic or Divine Virtue." The apples represent, respectively, moderation of anger, moderation of avarice, and scorn of pleasure.[14]

But the respect in which Hercules was most clearly stoically

FIGURE 29. *Quis dives? Qui nil cupit*. From *Emblemata Horatiana*, p. 84.

virtuous was in his famous choice between pleasure and virtue. And this is the act in which the Renaissance pictured him most often of all. Occasionally Hercules's choice was presented in terms of the Pythagorean Y-motif. As in Christian parable, the hero is envisioned as following a road which divides, in time, like a Y, into two paths, a broad one and a narrow one, between which he has to choose. A full-scale pictorial allegory of this kind is that by Jan Wierx after Crispin van den Broeck. On one side of the choosing Hercules is a wise old woman, men working and men laboring up a stony path, a laurel garland, justice with its scales, and a trio who represent, it would seem, the crowning of virtue. On the other side is beautiful young *voluptas,* with the sword and fasces laid aside, and with feasts and dancing and such men-turned-beasts as attended Circe and Acrasia. Beyond them is a city on fire, and the gates of hell.[15]

But most of the representations of the choice of Hercules present the hero with a choice, not between feasts and the stony straight path of duty, but between two women. Sometimes, indeed, the motifs of the two paths and the two women are combined. So it is in Christoff Murer's woodcut, in which Hercules stands between the Way of Life, symbolized by a woman with the appurtenances of religion and wisdom and with the properly used distaff of labor, and the Way of Death, presided over by a naked lady who offers wine, fruits, and music (Figure 30). The hero has to choose between *virtus* and *voluptas,* between wisdom and wordly joys, between Pallas and pleasure.

Now, whether Artegall "really" succumbs to or withstands Radigund and all that she represents, he certainly makes a final firm choice of Britomart and virtue. Lacking lion's skin and club, Artegall does not *look* much like the usual Hercules (though indeed the Hercules who loved Omphale is often painted in Martial and knightly armor and the Hercules who chooses is sometimes dressed like any gentleman), but it is clear that in many respects Artegall is to be identified with Hercules. In Britomart's case, as we shall soon see, the details of the rescuing lady's appearance and circumstances are very close indeed to those of the Virtue and Wisdom of iconography. Radigund, though, who overworks, starves, and kills her prisoners, would seem on the face of it to offer little pleasure. Yet in those respects in which she implies Omphale, she implies, too, the temptations of Pleasure. In their iconographical appearances these two ladies, Omphale and Pleasure, strongly resemble one another. This is to some extent inevitable since women must always depend upon the same few techniques. But there is at any rate one artist who has as it were put a signature to the similarity between Omphale and *voluptas*.

Omphale and Pleasure are both depicted, naturally enough, in various stages of voluptuous dress and undress.[16] Omphale and Pleasure are both often accompanied, like Venus, by the boy Cupid.[17] (Indeed, in one of the Choice of Hercules illustrations, as in several of the Hercules and Omphale paintings, *voluptas*-Venus's Cupid most suggestively embraces Hercules's weapon—in Pleasure's case, his spear.) [18] Omphale and Pleasure both often have at their sides a goblet, bowl of fruit, or musical instrument

FIGURE 30. The Choice of Hercules. Christoff Murer (died 1614). A. 48.

to indicate the breadth of the sensual charms they have to offer.[19] Most significantly, one painter, Annibale Carracci, painted both the scenes from the Hercules legend, and used the same symbol of his own in each of them. In Carracci's painting of Hercules and Omphale, Omphale holds Hercules's club and Hercules holds a tambourine, presumably Omphale's (Figure 31). And in his

FIGURE 31. Hercules and Omphale. Annibale Carracci (circa 1600). Rome, Palazzo Farnese.

painting of the Choice of Hercules, Carracci equips Pleasure with just such a similar tambourine.[20]

Radigund has no tambourine. But she is magnificently dressed; and the pleasures of food and drink are distinctly part of her temptation. She is dressed in the rich but practical garb that is conventional for hunting maidens, from Dido and the disguised Venus in the *Aeneid* to Belphoebe in Book II of *The Faerie Queene:* [21]

> So soone as day forth dawning from the East,
> > Nights humid curtaine from the heavens withdrew.   (v.1)

writes Spenser, Radigund prepared herself in her magnificent costume:

> All in a Camis light of purple silke
> > Woven uppon with silver, subtly wrought,
> > And quilted uppon satin white as milke,
> > Trayled with ribbands diversly distraught
> > Like as the workeman had their courses taught;
> > Which was short tucked for light motion
> > Up to her ham, but when she list, it raught
> > Downe to her lowest heele, and thereuppon
> She wore for her defence a mayled habergeon.
>
> And on her legs she painted buskins wore,
> > Basted with bends of gold on every side,
> > And mailes betweene, and laced close afore:
> > Uppon her thigh her Cemitare was tide,
> > With an embrodered belt of mickell pride. . . .
>
> So forth she came out of the citty gate,
> > With stately port and proud magnificence,
> > Guarded with many damzels, that did waite
> > Uppon her person for her sure defence,
> > Playing on shaumes and trumpets, that from hence
> > Their sound did reach unto the heavens hight.   (v.2–5)

In all this, Radigund resembles the disguised Venus, and, even more, the hunt- and love-ready Dido who, coming out, splendidly dressed, at dawn, attended by a great throng, was soon to try to deflect Aeneas from the course of his duty.[22] Radigund takes on some of the sensuous resonances of these other hunting maidens. She is a warrior maiden and huntress in the tradition, not of the chaste Diana, but of the voluptuously aggressive *Venus armata*.[23]

It is worth noticing that Artegall starts his fall into the hands of Radigund with the voluptuous experience which both Omphale and Pleasure often offer: that of eating and drinking. The matter might not be remarkable were it not that there is, in a later, more heroic episode, in which Artegall shows up rather less badly, a markedly contrasting rejection of the pleasures of the table. At Radigund's command Clarinda brings to the knight who is threateningly encamped outside her walls "wine and juncates fit" along with a challenge that demands too much of the knight's courtesy (iv.48–49). Talus meets the ambassadors:

> So he them streight conducted to his Lord,
>> Who, as he could, them goodly well did greete,
>> Till they had told their message word by word:
>> Which he accepting well, as he could weete,
>> Them fairely entertaynd with curt'sies meete,
> And gave them gifts and things of deare delight. (iv.51)

Artegall accepts the ambassadors well; he accepts, as Radigund had intended, her conditions along with her gifts. On the other hand, when Artegall has come before the town held by Grantorto, and has challenged him to single combat next day,

> That night Sir Artegall did cause his tent
>> There to be pitched on the open plaine;
>> For he had given streight commaundement,
>> That none should dare him once to entertaine:
>> Which none durst breake, though many would right faine
>> For fayre Irena, whom they loved deare.
>> But yet old Sergis did so well him paine,

That from close friends, that dar'd not to appeare,
He all things did purvay, which for them needfull weare.

(xii.10)

To be sure, this is a different, perhaps more historically conditioned occasion; but Artegall is distinctly wiser before this single combat in declining the entertainment even of friends than he was before that other single combat when he courteously accepted the wine and junkets of his enemy.

Whatever may be the truth about Radigund and pleasure, there can be no doubt that Britomart represents wisdom and virtue; she is as closely related to Pallas Athena as Artegall is to Hercules.[24] Indeed, just as Artegall is, as the French iconographers were accustomed to write, *un Hercule*, Britomart is the figure who very frequently accompanies this *Hercule* in the emblems: she is *une jeune Pallas*. It will be remembered that in connection with Britomart's visit to the temple of Isis we mentioned one of Alciati's emblems, that which represents *Custodiendas virgines* (Figure 20). The virgin who is standing outside the temple, guarded by the dragon, is Pallas Athena herself: the embodiment of wisdom. Alciati specifically says so:

Vera haec effigies innuptae est Palladis.

The virgin wears a helmet on her flowing fair hair, carries a shield embossed with the Medusa-head which characterizes wisdom, and has a lance in her hand. At her feet, in the emblem which illustrates the 1621 edition, has been added that traditional companion of Minerva, the owl.[25] Britomart, too, has each of these characteristics. To be sure, since she is in disguise, she hides her hair beneath her helmet; but it flows magnificently down, with a remarkable effect on male observers, every time she loosens or removes her helmet (III.i.63; ix.22; IV.i.13, vi. 19,20). On one occasion in Book III, in Malbecco's house, when Britomart removes her armor, the poet writes that it was

Like as Minerva, being late returnd
  From slaughter of the Giaunts conquered. . . .
  Hath loosd her helmet from her lofty hed,
  And her Gorgonian shield gins to untye
From her left arme, to rest in glorious victorye.[26]   (III.ix.22)

Spenser does mention that Britomart's shield is "of great power" (III.iii.60). But her most notable piece of equipment is her enchanted lance. Now Pallas Athena and Minerva were always represented as bearing lances; so is the Wisdom, and also the Virtue, of the emblem books. It is the ladies' standard, representative equipment. Spenser devotes a whole stanza to an account of Britomart's "mighty speare," "made by Magick art," which has "great virtues," and with which she can always unseat her foes (III.iii.60). Actually, though in Books III and IV it does her great service, Britomart does not have much occasion in Book V to use her lance. She does use it to destroy the "losels" on Pollente's bridge (vi.39).

Besides having flowing hair beneath a helmet, and a shield and lance, Pallas is usually provided in iconography with an owl. As we have seen, the engraver of an early edition of Alciati's emblems did not see fit to include an owl in his depiction of Pallas; a later engraver thought the owl essential, and added it. Van Veen sets an owl at the foot of Pallas in his representation of the truth that it is wisdom to grasp opportunity by the forelock (Figure 32). Valeriano Bolzani associates the owl with, in the first place, Minerva and, in the second place, *Sapientia:*

De Noctua:

  Minerva. Primarium Noctuae significitum est, ut Minerva per hieroglyphicum eius intelligatur, de qua ipsa Glaucopidis etiam cognomentum sumpsit. . . .[27]

Glaucopis is an epithet of Minerva. In Greek, Γλαυχη means owl. Now Britomart is accompanied, through a large part of her adventures previous to Book V, by a nurse named Glauce. It has

been pointed out that one contemporary at least was quick to associate Spenser's Glauce with the owl; however, he was struck only
by the (dubious) applicability of the horror and the harsh voice
of the owl.[28] By giving Britomart Glauce as mentor and companion, Spenser clearly associates his heroine with the owl-attended
goddess of wisdom.

FIGURE 32. Pallas. From *Emblemata Horatiana*, p. 67.

Britomart is actually introduced into *The Faerie Queene,* in Book III, as the hero-knight of what Spenser calls chastity— though it is in effect, rather, virtuous love. As the *Custodiendas virgines* emblem and many others show, Pallas and chastity are virtually synonymous. It is appropriate, too, that Isis, the goddess with whom Britomart is so clearly associated, was regarded as a goddess of wisdom. Plutarch says so, quite plainly, at the very beginning of his *De Iside et Osiride* (a book from the first few pages of which Spenser took many details for his description of the priests and the temple of Isis).[29] In the Legend of Justice Isis specifically, and quite without traditional authority, represents equity. So, clearly, does Britomart. But this meaning is superimposed upon the figure as an additional significance; it does not obliterate the accepted meaning. Isis traditionally represented wisdom. So, for some purposes, does Britomart.

This wise and chaste Britomart is a fine and morally fitting comrade for heroic Artegall. And actually, when Artegall is first mentioned, in the first part of *The Faerie Queene,* there is an indication that Spenser already had it in mind to associate this hero with Wisdom. Guyon assures Prince Arthur that if he does decide to serve "the mighty Queene of Faerie," as he is well worthy to do,

> Great guerdon, well I wote, should you remaine,
> And in her favour high be reckoned,
> As Arthegall, and Sophy now been honored.   (II.ix.6)

The knight of the art of making equal, of weighing justice, and the knight of wisdom fit well together. So, too, do justice-maintaining Hercules and wise Pallas.

In the myths Pallas was always intervening in some way on behalf of her son. This no doubt is the origin of the association the Renaissance saw between armed female wisdom and herculean strength. There would also appear to be a connection between these in Renaissance philosophy or psychology, or in its moral allegory and mystery. For Stephen Batman's verbal emblem of "Minerva, or Pallas" suggests that the tendency to pair Pallas and Hercules was something of an "unfolding" of the complex significance that could reside in the figure of Pallas alone (or, in the view of the Stoic moralizers, in the figure of Hercules alone.) [30] Batman wrote:

Pallas was portraicted all armed: her countenance menacing the beholder, having a Cloke of three coulers, in her righte hande a Speare, and on her lefte a Christalline Target, embossed with a Gorgons head. By her stoode a Greene Olive Tree, and a Dragon, with an Owle flyinge over them.

Signification. By Minerva is signified Wisdome, joyned to Force, to qualifie extremities. . . . She . . . steppeth forth all armed, that [sic] which Lawe cannot wynne by levity: it must compel by force.[31]

The development of these themes and combinations in some later emblem books is of interest. Ripa, in conventional and understandable manner, represented Virtue of Body and Mind, and Heroic Virtue, and, by clear implication, Force, in the person of Hercules with his lionskin and club.[32] Baudoin imitated him. But Baudoin also represented Strength or Force as a *woman* with a lion and club. (Figure 33). And Daniel de la Feuille's dictionary of 1700 has several similar figures.[33] *Force* is represented *comme la Déesse Pallas*, bearing a shield on which are depicted a monkey and a lion. We learn the significance of this shield from another of his emblems: one which depicts *un Hercule* with a club, a monkey, and a lion (the animals represent, respectively, *virtue du corps* and *courage*). The same emblematist's *Force d'esprit et de corps* consists of a woman with a helmet and a lance who bears a shield emblazoned with the club of Hercules. The emblem is accompanied by this rhyme:

> *Pallas, ainsi qu'on le decrit*
> *Dans cette Image symbolique,*
> *Est une peinture energique*
> *De la force du Corps, de celle de l'Esprit.*[34]

If body and spirit, heroic virtue and wisdom, Hercules and Pallas were by tradition so closely related that they could be expressed in one figure possessed of their peculiar attributes, it would seem that Spenser was doing a small enough thing in the direction of this sort of integration by proposing to marry Artegall to Britomart.

But Hercules and Pallas appear more often as comrades than as

FORCE.

FORCE D'ESPRIT ET DE CORPS.

FORCE ET PRVDENCE.

FORCE DE COVRAGE.

FIGURE 33. Force and prudence. From Baudoin's *Iconologie*, p. 65. Courtesy of the Art and Architecture Division, The New York Public Library, Astor, Lenox and Tilden Foundations.

a composite figure. Notably, the two of them stride together through many of the pages of the *Emblemata Horatiana,* in appearance, characteristics, and adventures much like Artegall and Britomart. In their separate appearances they have all the attributes we have noticed—Hercules or heroic virtue has lionskin and club; Pallas or wisdom has helmet, shield, lance, and owl. Together, they tend to drop all but their most salient and easily recognizable attributes, in this volume Hercules his club and Pallas her shield. The drunkard whose vice has brought him to the neglect of all honor and virtue is shown with the emblems of heroic virtue and wisdom thrown aside, together; the club of Hercules lies broken, and beside it lies the Medusa-headed shield of Pallas. Again, there is an emblem to illustrate the maxim:

> *Pecunia a bono et honesto abstrahit.*

It consists of a stalwart man and a woman with long fair hair who are literally pouring gold and coins into a trading enterprise; love of money has drawn them away from goodness and honesty and they have discarded, respectively, their lionskin and club, and Medusa-headed shield and lance.[35]

In a number of Choice of Hercules pictures the hero in effect chooses, between two eager candidates, the lady with whom he is afterwards to be so frequently associated—his life partner, as it were. For the virtue which Hercules chooses is very often embodied in a lady with helmet, spear, and Medusa-shield. In one early seventeenth-century representation of the Choice of Hercules, naked Pleasure embraces an equally naked hero, and emblematically appropriately clothed Pallas, complete with owl, urges him to go on his way (Figure 34).

Several of the pictures of the Choice suggest as this one does that Hercules has already been won by *Voluptas* before the armed maiden arrives to direct him to the path of duty. The artists must have had in mind the Hercules of excess who was much devoted to *voluptas,* and combined this Hercules with the moral Hercules of Stoic teaching by use of a chronological device: present virtue leads him out of his past devotion to pleasure. It may be that Spenser, as aware as anyone of the dichotomous nature of the Hercules legend, uses something of the same device: Britomart, or wisdom combined with virtue, draws Artegall from his (dubiously) pleasurable servitude to Radigund.

In Rubens's painting of The Choice of Hercules, Hercules

FIGURE 34. The Choice of Hercules. Ph. Trière after Gaspar de Crayer (d. 1669).

seems to be just in the act of moving out of the embrace of *Vo-luptas;* Cupid is holding his leg. On the other side a martial lady, wearing a helmet but with her Medusa-headed shield laid aside, draws the hero toward his horse.[36] In another similar painting Cupid and a maiden support *Voluptas* as she detains Hercules; armed and owled Virtue stands aside confidently waiting. Again, in an eighteenth-century painting by Pompeo Battoni, Pleasure sits with Hercules almost in her lap. But Virtue, with her helmet, shield, and spear, points upward to the steep and narrow path. All these works present Hercules as having almost chosen, or as having for a short time chosen, pleasure rather than virtue. Then —for all are chronological paintings, poised at the moment which divides before from after, and clearly implying the situations obtaining both before and after—then, Hercules leaves pleasure for Pallas.

The same sequence of choice which is implied in the Radigund episode and in all these rather later paintings is clearly laid out in Ben Jonson's masque, *Pleasure Reconciled to Vertue* (1617–18). Hercules is the hero or subject of the masque. It opens with a scene at the top of Atlas's bleak mountain—representing the austerity of virtue. It continues with a scene in the grove at the foot of the mountain—a pleasurable, even a libertine celebration around Comus. Then Daedalus conducts a dance to reconcile virtue and pleasure "in sacred harmony." This is the song of reconciliation:

> Come on, come on; and where you goe,
>   so enter-weave the curious knot,
> as ev'n th'observer scarce may know
>   which lines are Pleasures, and which not.
> First, figure out the doubtfull way
>   at which, a while all youth shold stay,
>   where she and Vertue did contend
>   which should have Hercules to frend.
> Then, as all actions of mankind

are but a Laborinth, or maze,
so let your Daunces be entwin'd [37]

The idea that youth should resolve the problem of "the doubtfull way" not by rejecting one but by entwining both suggests an interpretation of the Hercules story which iconography quite firmly bears out.

In some of the many Renaissance paintings, engravings, and drawings in which Hercules is presented in the act of choosing between two women the image is actually formalized into a sort of shorthand cliché representation. *Virtus*, Hercules, and *Voluptas* are several times presented as a trio oddly but conveniently grouped like the three Graces, arms and glances indissolubly interlinked.[38] Cristofano Robetta presents the three naked and looking entirely like the Graces in his painting of The Choice of Hercules (Figure 35). Prospero Fontana presents them in much the same manner; in his representation, though, pleasure and virtue are both dressed and Hercules is wearing ivy leaves.[39] But in both cases the figures are presented in a relationship of reciprocity, not in a relationship of the antagonism that necessitates choice. The artists who portrayed Hercules, pleasure, and virtue as interlinked were no doubt attempting to unify the strange contradictions in the Hercules story.

They were also presenting one of the concepts of Renaissance Neoplatonism: that men should choose unity and wholeness, neither overemphasizing nor neglecting any one of the important life-principles. As Ficino wrote to Lorenzo de' Medici: "No reasonable being doubts that there are three kinds of life: the contemplative, the active, and the pleasurable. And three roads to felicity have been chosen by men: wisdom, power, and pleasure." He indicates that to choose one at the expense of the others is wrong, even blasphemous. Among those who were punished for their singleness of life were: Paris, who chose only pleasure; Hercules, who chose only heroic virtue; and Socrates, who chose only wisdom.[40]

FIGURE 35. The Choice of Hercules.   Cristofano Robetta (circa 1500).
B. 20.   From Panofsky, *Hercules*, plate 48.

If Spenser does have any mystical sense that power, wisdom, and pleasure should be held in balance together he expresses it by "infolding" in Britomart, through the scene in the Temple of Isis with all its marital associations, pleasure as well as wisdom. He never suggests that commitment to Radigund is acceptable, though he does, perhaps, maintain that it is more or less inevitable. His final judgment on Artegall's association with her is the same as Jonson's final, considered opinion on the possibility of reconciling pleasure and virtue. The central implication in his masque is the understandable one that Hercules has a right, reasonably enough, to enjoy himself as well as to be a hero. But in the last song in the masque Mercury admonishes:

> An eye of looking back, were well,
>   or any murmur that wold tell
>   yor thoughts, how you were sent,
>   and went,
>   to walke with Pleasure, not to dwell.
> Theis, theis are howres, by Vertue spar'd
>   hirself, she being hir owne reward,
>   But she will have you know,
>   that though
>   hir sports be soft, hir life is hard.
>   You must returne unto the Hill,
>   and there advaunce
>   with labour, and inhabit still
>   that height, and crowne,
>   from which you ever may looke downe
>   upon triumphed Chaunce.   (ll.323–38)

Readers of the Legend of Justice have always seen that the hours of Artegall's captivity are hours spared by virtue which virtue cannot afford to spare. The narrative makes it plain. It is said that Irena almost loses her life on account of Artegall's tardiness (xi.39,40). Even though acceptance of pleasure and, for that matter, marriage to Britomart, are part of the whole herculean man,

Artegall leaves, within a few stanzas, both Radigund and Britomart to pursue "his avowed quest" (viii.3).

Thus, though Spenser makes no specific reference to pleasure or
virtue or wisdom, or to the choice of Hercules, that episode, with
all its ramifications and interpretations, was familiar enough to be
called upon to create a complex and mysterious restatement of the
poet's simple narrative theme—through allegory, or analogous
narrative, or implied emblem, or infolded mystery, or whatever it
is that we are to call Spenser's many-faceted effect.

CHAPTER 12

THE BLATANT BEAST

WHATEVER contrary implications may momentarily be made in the central cantos of Book V, the Hercules with which the Legend of Justice ends is a nobly heroic and stoic one. To be sure, it is not immediately apparent that the book does end, as it began, with a reference to Hercules. That this is the case is demonstrable, once again, through iconography—through the iconography of envy and of the mythological associations of that vice. Indeed, many of the details of the ending of the Legend of Justice, in which Artegall confronts but does not destroy Envy, Detraction, and the Blatant Beast, are remarkably iconographically orthodox; and an understanding of their emblematic meaning will help reveal the ending's full significance.

Spenser's Envy is, to begin with, in almost all respects like the envy of iconographical tradition. Artegall was returning to the Faerie Court in response to the Queen's summons,

> When as two old ill favour'd Hags he met,
> By the way side being together set,
> Two griesly creatures; and, to that their faces

Most foule and filthie were, their garments yet
Being all rag'd and tatter'd, their disgraces
Did much the more augment, and made most ugly cases.

The one of them, that elder did appeare,
  With her dull eyes did seeme to looke askew,
  That her mis-shape much helpt; and her foule heare
  Hung loose and loathsomely: Thereto her hew
  Was wan and leane, that all her teeth arew,
  And all her bones might through her cheekes be red;
  Her lips were like raw lether, pale and blew,
  And as she spake, therewith she slavered;
Yet spake she seldom, but thought more, the lesse she sed.

Her hands were foule and durtie, never washt
  In all her life, with long nayles over raught,
  Like puttocks clawes: with th'one of which she scracht
  Her cursed head, although it itched naught;
  The other held a snake with venime fraught,
  On which she fed, and gnawed hungrily,
  As if that long she had not eaten ought;
  That round about her jawes one might descry
The bloudie gore and poyson dropping lothsomely.

Her name was Envie, knowen well thereby. . . .   (xii.28–31)

By "knowen well thereby" Spenser means that his Envy should
be immediately recognized as such. Her appearance and attributes
are entirely in accordance with iconographical tradition.

The hair which Spenser calls loathsome was very often drawn as
literally snaky locks. Envy was usually, in fact, in one way or another represented with snakes. She was sometimes shown chewing
a snake, sometimes chewing a foul morsel of something or other,
but always with ugly, bony face, hanging breasts, and ragged
clothing. According to Alciati she is a wretched creature with serpents at her mouth.[1] Van Veen represents Envy as sitting by the

roadside, wearing only a ragged cloth, and chewing the snakes that form her hair; beside her stands an unpleasant-looking cur, his teeth bared (Figure 36). Ripa describes Envy in three different forms, although he does not illustrate any of them. *Invidia* may be represented, he writes, by an ugly old woman with bare breasts

FIGURE 36. *Grande malum invidia.* From *Emblemata Horatiana*, p. 97.

that a serpent nibbles, who is accompanied by a hydra; or it may
be represented simply by an ugly woman whose hair is formed of
serpents; or it may be represented by an ugly woman whose hand
touches her mouth and who is accompanied by a dog that is being
bitten by serpents.[2] Fully within this tradition is Spenser's Envy,
who waits in the road, with her rags, her foul hair, and her
snakes, chewing her own entrails as the Envy of the emblem
chews or is eaten by the snakes that are her hair—and attended by
a beast.

De la Feuille's use of one of Ripa's emblems of Envy is particularly interesting in connection with Spenser because the dic-
tionary-maker explains the significance of some of her attributes.
He represents Envy as a foul-looking woman with snaky locks and
hanging breasts; she is accompanied by a hydra. De La Feuille
supplies his hag with these verses:

> Le bonheur d'autrui fait mon mal,
> Peut-on rien voir de plus brutal? [3]

He explains that Envy hates to see her neighbor enjoying any
good: this is symbolized by the serpent which nibbles her breast;
and she rejoices to see her neighbor suffer evils: this is symbolized
by the hydra which she caresses. The psychology of Spenser's
Envy is just the same: she is one

> Whose nature is to grieve, and grudge at all,
> That ever she sees doen prays-worthily,
> Whose sight to her is greatest crosse, may falle,
> And vexeth so, that makes her eat her gall.
> For when she wanteth other thing to eat,
> She feedes on her owne maw unnaturall,
> And of her owne foule entrayles makes her meat;
> Meat fit for such a monsters monsterous dyeat.

> And if she hapt of any good to heare,
> That had to any happily betid,
> Then would she inly fret, and grieve, and teare
> Her flesh for felnesse, which she inward hid:

> But if she heard of ill, that any did,
> Or harme, that any had, then would she make
> Great cheare, like one unto a banquet bid;
> And in anothers losse great pleasure take,
> As she had got thereby, and gayned a great stake.   (xii.31,32)

Spenser proceeds directly to describe the other hag who met and assailed Artegall. This is Detraction.[4] Whereas Envy "did conceale" her evil thoughts "and murder her owne mynd," it is Detraction's joy to "spred abroad" all the evil slander she can (xii. 33). Envy and Detraction are, in Spenser, "together set"; in their dwellings they are next neighbors (xii.28,35). There are some iconographical instances of envy being accompanied by a female figure representing hate or calumny.[5] But these evils were most often symbolized by the dog or hydra that accompanies envy; and in *The Faerie Queene* it is somewhat the same. Envy and Detraction are accompanied by a creature which actually re-embodies both their vices: it is the Blatant Beast. Like Envy, the Blatant Beast thinks evil. Like Detraction, it speaks and spreads evil.[6] Its character and its very existence are surely the result of Spenser's running together the tradition of Virgil's *fama* and its descendants and the tradition of the companions of envy: dogs [7] and hydras.

The Blatant Beast is actually primarily dog-like. His first appearance is in order to support Envie and Detraction in their attack on Artegall:

> Thereto the Blatant beast by them set on
> At him began aloud to barke and bay
>
>   (xii.41. See also VI.i.9)

When Calidore has succeeded in muzzling the creature, he

> Like a fearefull dog him followed through the land.
>
>   (VI.xii.36)

The Blatant Beast was begot of Cerberus, the terrible guardian dog of the underworld (VI.i.8); he resembles Cerberus, too (VI.xii.35). But whereas Cerberus had three snake-maned heads,

the Blatant Beast has many tongues in one head. These tongues
are various, resembling the tongues of many different animals—
but the first animals which Spenser mentions in this connection
are, again, dogs. His mouth, the poet writes, was terrible:

> And therein were a thousand tongs empight,
>> Of sundry kindes, and sundry quality,
>> Some were of dogs, that barked day and night. . . .
>>>>>>>> (VI.xii.27)

The last creatures he mentions, which carry considerable weight
since they are not listed with the others, but are described in some
detail in a separate stanza—the grammatical logic making them
spokesmen for the whole—are serpents.

> And them amongst were mingled here and there,
>> The tongues of Sepents with three forked stings,
>> That spat out poyson and gore bloudy gere
>> At all, that came within his ravenings,
>> And spake licentious words, and hatefull things
>> Of good and bad alike, of low and hie.   (VI.xii.28)

The Blatant Beast is dog-like because the dog is the creature
who frequently accompanies Envy. He has many tongues because
the tongue is the instrument of slander and malice; the bad, slanderous poet Malfont is punished by having his tongue cut out (ix.
25–26). Some of his tongues are snaky because snakes are essential to envy and to evil-speaking. But, above all, the Blatant Beast
is associated with the hydra that Hercules slew, that terrible monster with seven, or some say fifty, some a hundred (cf.V.xii.41),
some a thousand (cf.VI.i.9) snaky heads.[8] Spenser, in Book VI,
specifically compares his thousand-tongued Blatant Beast with
Hercules's thousand-headed hydra. The monster fought off Sir
Calidore "like a feend,"

> Or like the hell-borne Hydra, which they faine
>> The great Alcides whilome overthrew,
>> After that he had labourd long in vaine,

To crop his thousand heads, the which still new
Forth budded, and in greater number grew.   (VI.xii.32)

The hydra often recurs in iconography and has a number of
significances. It appears in its primary significance in an emblem
that lies very close to Spenser. In Van der Noodt's *Theater for
. . . voluptuous worldlings,* to which Spenser himself contributed, there is an emblem of the Whore of Revelations riding
upon the seven-headed beast.[9] This beast, each of whose seven
heads grew again as soon as it was destroyed, fell naturally together with Hercules's similar hydra.[10] Spenser thus describes
the monster that Duessa, Whore of Babylon and Queen of Rome,
rides on in the Legend of Holiness. Orgoglio presented her with
it:

He gave her gold and purple pall to weare,
And triple crowne set on her head full hye,
And her endowd with royall majestye:
Then for to make her dreaded more of men,
And peoples harts with awfull terrour tye,
A monstrous beast ybred in filthy fen
He chose, which he had kept long time in darksome den.

Such one it was, as that renowned Snake
Which great Alcides in Stremona slew
Long fostred in the filth of Lerna lake,
Whose many heads out budding ever new,
Did breed him endless labour to subdew:
But this same Monster much more ugly was;
For seven great heads out of his body grew,
An yron brest, and back of scaly bras,
And all embrewd in bloud, his eyes did shine as glas.

His tayle was stretched out in wondrous length . . .
And underneath his filthy feet did tread
The sacred things, and holy heasts foretaught.
Upon this dreadfull Beast with sevenfold head
He set the false Duessa, for more aw and dread.   (I.vii.16–18)

Inevitably, this seven-headed beast often represents the seven deadly sins.[11] It occurs, too, as a symbol of vice in general. Daniel de la Feuille has an emblem of *Vice* which consists of a young man caressing a seven-headed monster, *un Hydre*. This stanza accompanies it:

> *Tout est souillé des ordures du vice,*
> *On ne void rein que fraud & qu'injustice,*
> *Le coeur de l'homme est double & plein de fiel,*
> *Et la vertu n'est plus que dans le ciel.*[12]

It is tempting to connect these ordures and the much emphasized filth of Duessa's mount with the "filth and ordure" which the hydra-like Blatant Beast uncovered in the monasteries, and the way in which he "Altars fouled, and blasphemy spoke" (VI.xii. 24,25).

Now, one of the principal, several times repeated features of the beast in Revelations is that "there was given unto him a mouth speaking great things and blasphemies." [13] And the hydra of the Hercules myth, too, tended to be associated with evil speaking. One reason for this is that the hydra, having many heads, has many tongues. Another is that these heads grow again as soon as they have been destroyed. It was on these grounds, too, that the moralizers of the Hercules story identified the hydra with sophistic argument. Salutati explained that the hydra with his many heads represents the sophists with their many arguments whom the virtuous man defeats.[14] Similarly, the commentator to the 1583 edition of Alciati's *Emblemata* interprets Hercules's defeat of the hydra as the defeat by virtue and eloquence of sophistic argument. This is why: *Hydra uno capite resecto septem alia repullulabant: quod notat artis sophisticae captionem.*[15] It would seem that this talkative hydra was crossed with Virgil's *fama* to influence an aspect of Spenser's Blatant Beast. Related to Spenser's beast, too, is Dr. John Dee's "Swift Sharpe Poysonable Tongued Monster of many heads that devoureth men—calumny.[16]

An interesting connection between virtue, Hercules, and calumny is suggested in Joseph Wibarne's *The New Age of Old Names* (1609). He writes:

Vertue according to the Stoickes, was divided into *Cathecon* and *Catorthoma,* that is into Vertue meane and possible, or Vertue transcendent and heroycall, such as the Scriptures ascribe to *Sampson,* the Poets their Apes to *Hercules,* and our writers to Prince *Arthur.* This vertue hath beene three wayes assaulted, First, by calumniation, for actions done by divine instinct have ever found some *Zoylus, Momus, Mastix,* or tongue of blattant beast, so called of βλαττω, to hurt.[17]

Envy, too, was thought to have assaulted the heroical and transcendent virtue of Hercules; this envy was symbolized by the hydra. Thus Valeriano Bolzani, in his chapter *De Hydra,* declares that the hydra Hercules slew represents *Invidia;* for envy, like the hydra, sprouts more venomous heads for every one that is destroyed.[18] Valeriano Bolzani assumes that Hercules did destroy the hydra of envy. But other iconologists were less sanguine. In fact moralizing tradition reiterates that the only foe whom Hercules was never able to destroy was envy. The whole matter is most strikingly illustrated and most interestingly explained in an emblem in the *Emblemata Horatiana* entitled *Post mortem cessat invidia* (Figure 37). In it, Hercules is depicted as triumphing over the Hydra, foot on the beast's neck or necks, club in hand, as Death with his billhook stands triumphing over Envy. (The hydra depicted here has the heads, be it noted, of, perhaps, a snake or dog, a boar, a crocodile or lizard, and a cat or tiger— just as the Blatant Beast has the tongues of various creatures of the kind). The emblematist quotes the passage from Horace which is, no doubt, the origin of the whole tradition (Valeriano Bolzani refers to it in the same connection):

> —*diram qui contudit Hydram,*
> *Notaque fatali portenta labore subegit,*
> *Comperit Invidiam supremo fine domari.*
> *Urit enim fulgore suo, qui praegravat artes*
> *Infra se positas: exstinctus amabitur idem.*[19]   (Lib.3, Epist.1)

Gomberville has an explication of the emblem in his edition of the *Emblemata Horatiana*. He writes that even the indomitable Hercules could not defeat the hydra of envy who in effect makes the hero turn his strength against himself. For as fast as the hero cuts off a head, another grows. Only death can destroy envy.

FIGURE 37. *Post mortem cessat invidia.* From *Emblemata Horatiana*, p. 173.

Cependant, ce Liberateur du monde, ce prodige de valeur, aussi bien que de justice, tenta mille fois en sa vie, cette grande avanture, & la manqua mille fois.[20]

If figures of heroic, herculean virtue have always had as their inevitable enemies foul-tongued envying beasts which they cannot destroy, Artegall's final experience in the Legend of Justice can be looked upon in a new light. On the level of political allegory Artegall's meeting with Envy, Detraction, and the Blatant Beast on his way home on his recall from Irena's land fairly clearly reflects the disgrace associated with Lord Grey's recall from Ireland. In the course of a slight change in Elizabeth's policy toward Ireland, Grey's previously quite satisfactory methods came under some criticism; the Lord Deputy was recalled. It was remarked by Grey's supporters that great men always have to pay for their greatness by being subject to calumny and envy. Hercules was the greatest of those who have suffered in this way. Though his name is not mentioned in the last canto of Book V, Hercules has so consistently been associated with Artegall throughout the Legend of Justice, and his experience with envy and calumny is so close to Artegall's, that we have to be conscious of his presence in the last episode as a kind of analogous echo.

On the level of moral or social allegory, the final confrontation of justice with rumor and malicious report emphasizes justice's dependence on truth. For rumor, guile, and wrong speech are essentially antithetical to justice and law, which depend upon rightly recorded history and accurate information: in other words, the truth.[21] Thus the larger associations of the Blatant Beast have the effect of raising the ending of the Legend of Justice from a particular apology for a small historical failure to a universal statement about the concomitants of greatness and the constituents of justice.

Artegall's final encounter is so unsatisfactory because he is no more able than was Hercules to make a triumphant conquest of his insidious foe. He can only endure. And yet in this too he resembles Hercules. For Hercules chiefly qualified as a stoic hero by virtue of his endurance of pain at the end of his life. Now the Legend of Justice ends, not, to be sure, in a flaming suicide, but at any rate in a most stoic endurance of adversity. The hags and their creatures are so slanderous

> That they the mildest man alive would make
> Forget his patience and yeeld vengeaunce dew.   (xii.42)

But Artegall restrains Talus (and himself) and endures the worst that they can do.[22] There may thus be a sense in which the greatness of the martyred Hercules closes the Legend of Justice as the greatness of the apotheosized Hercules—he whose works are commemorated among the stars—opens it.

Then, too, Artegall's final failure, like the final failures of the Red Cross Knight and Guyon, reflects man's condition in the actual fallen world. For in the iron age which is so clearly postulated in the proem to Book V, human justice *cannot* be finally successful.

It is worth remarking here on some of the Blatant Beast's other implications, especially as they appear in Book VI. In the Legend of Courtesy the Blatant Beast becomes the object of the quest of Calidore. After many vicissitudes, the hero captures, muzzles, and chains the beast; he "drew him forth, even in his own despight":

> Like as whylome that strong Tirynthian swaine,
>   Brought forth with him the dreadfull dog of hell,
>   Against his will fast bound in yron chaine,
>   And roring horribly, did him compell
>   To see the hatefull sunne, that he might tell
>   To griesly Pluto, what on earth was donne,
>   And to the other damned ghosts, which dwell
>   For aye in darkenesse, which day light doth shonne.
> So led this Knight his captyve with like conquest wonne.
>
> (VI.xii.35)

As we have seen, Hercules's labor of mastering Cerberus was allegorized as the hero's conquest of death, which proved him to be immortal and suited him to be a *figura* of Christ. Indeed, his descent to Hades was regarded as analogous to Christ's harrowing of hell. Christ harrowed hell and chained Satan for one (or more) thousand years, after which he escaped again into the world in which Spenser's contemporaries had the misfortune to live. For the author of the book of Revelations had declared:

And I saw an angel come down from heaven, having the key of the bottomless pit and a great chain in his hand.

And he laid hold on the dragon, that old serpent, which is the Devil, and Satan, and bound him a thousand years,

And cast him into the bottomless pit, and shut him up, and set a seal upon him, that he should deceive the nations no more, till the thousand years should be fulfilled: and after that he must be loosed a little season.[23]

The Blatant Beast was captured by Calidore as Cerberus was captured by Hercules and Satan by an angel or Christ:

> So did he eeke long after this remaine,
> Untill that, whether wicked fate so framed,
> Or fault of men, he broke his yron chaine,
> And got into the world at liberty againe.   (VI.xii.38)

It is understandable that the Blatant Beast and the hags should triumph at the end of Book V; the beast is left as it were triumphant for ever at the end of Book VI.

The ending of the Legend of Justice can seem an inexplicable anticlimax. It would appear to be petty-minded, to say nothing of inartistic, to round a study of the whole state-sustaining virtue of justice into a defense of a particular unmemorable and rather unsavory man. But history, iconography, and some relevant texts can suggest a series of analogous figures behind disappointed Artegall. The last episode can actually be regarded as a summation of the chief themes of the Legend of Justice. The divinely ordered, orthodoxly Christian basis of Justice is implied at the end as it is asserted at the beginning of the book. The fact that falsehood is the chief enemy of justice is reiterated: for in a sense the Blatant Beast is another monster of guile. And here is still the persistent shadow of Hercules, who, though he is in one aspect possessed of just about every vice that calumny could name, is in the other a warrior-Christ, a champion of true justice on earth.

Epilogue

THE POSSIBILITY that the most radically exploratory poetry is that which imitates the visual arts has become very present in the twentieth century: so was it with the surrealists and dadaists, so, most probably has it been with many American poets' new, as it were abstract expressionist emotionalism, so is it with concrete poetry and with isolated experiments with "pop" poetry. The visual arts have been equally seminal in other periods. It is indeed arguable that it was the Renaissance iconological tradition, with its detailed visual set-pieces, its automatic "significations," its propensity for allusion and cross-reference, and its often very complex philosophical content, that, as much as any other single influence, made *The Faerie Queene* the particular kind of extraordinary poem that it is.

Certainly, the only adequate illustrations for Spenser's poems would be those drawn from the iconography of his own time. The highlight of the first book would be a representation of the picture, from Van der Noodt's *A Theatre . . . of Voluptuous Worldlings,* of a gorgeous hag riding upon a hydra. For Duessa on Orgoglio's monster looks exactly like that figure. Now the emblem of the Whore of Babylon on the hydra-like monster of Revelations is a traditional one; it had certainly appeared in all the editions of Alciati and in several Dürer woodcuts. It must have been widely known. But Spenser's special connection with the Van der Noodt book—to which he is known to have contributed—emphasizes the immediacy of his use of iconographical material. It is further notable that not only does Spenser transpose the familiar emblem, detail by detail, into his poem as an intensely visual vignette but he also weaves the implications of the emblem into the whole fabric of his allegory. It is usual to say that in his Legend of Holiness Spenser makes use of the imagery of Revelations, and also of the contemporary application of that imagery to anti-Catholic polemic. But the nature of the Van der Noodt book suggests that Spenser came to the familiar material from a specifically iconographical starting point. In emblem literature vehicle and tenor, picture and signification, Whore and Catholicism are absolutely fused. And at some moments Spenser's allegory does exactly what these emblems do: it presents, less an interpretation of, than an elaborate pictorial correlative to a familiar abstraction.

There is nothing new in the observation that Spenser's poetry is close to the pictorial conventions of the Renaissance, that it is, in fact, intensely visual. Centuries of readers have remarked how fully Spenser's poetry is an application of the dictum, so often repeated in the Renaissance: *ut pictura poesis*. Many readers have chiefly come to Spenser to delight in his elaborate descriptions; some have impressionistically compared his style of depiction with that of a number of the Old Masters; some, in this century, have pointed to this or that particular iconographical analogue. But it has not been sufficiently recognized that in order to understand *The Faerie Queene* in its full richness the contemporary reader must rediscover the whole Renaissance iconological tradition. For Spenser's art and allegory, in its general concept and in its details, was created out of his consciousness of the visual arts and their iconological interpretations.

At times Spenser's stanzas might well be the descriptive and explanatory verse accompaniments to various emblem-drawings. This is the case, in Book I, with Duessa and the hydra. And in Book V this is most clearly the case with Envy, who is presented just as the vice always traditionally was as foul, snaky, beast-attended.

At many other times Spenser endows his characters with one or more iconographical details which firmly associate them with a traditional character or theme. In this way the poet creates motifs of recurring icons, chains of thematic imagery. The justice-heroes' so frequent use of literal or metaphorical swords, flails, thunder-bolts, and sun rays becomes a constant reiteration of the truth that God's terrible justice is executed by God's terrible weapons. Similarly, the series of adversaries who are described in terms of the familiar iconography of guile make it clear beyond the need for any explicit statement that fraud is justice's most insidious foe.

Thus Spenser uses recurrent and echoing icons as a unifying structural device and also as centers of allusive, emblematical imagery. Some of his icons become at once richer and more relevant when one understands that there is a significance not only in the details which Spenser does describe—which are, in effect, at the center of his picture—but also in the traditionally associated details which would surely lie at the margins of an actual pictorial representation of the subject. Because ladies with flowing hair beneath helmets and with lances and owls represent Pallas, it seems clear that similarly accoutred and accompanied Britomart also represents Pallas, and that Hercules may well be somewhere in her vicinity.

The fact that Envy is accompanied by a hydra in many of the emblems casts a suggestive light on the beast which accompanies Spenser's so orthodoxly iconographical Envy. In visualising Envy as the poet portrays her, the reader acquainted with iconography will, as likely as not, fill out his picture with the usual hydra or dog: he will then inevitably apply his vision and its various implications to the figure of the Blatant Beast. The Blatant Beast will then seem not only the natural attendant on Envy and Slander; but, as Hercules's final foe, the fitting climactic figure in Artegall's analogous progress; and, as resonant embodiment of vice and echo of the apocalyptic beast, that with which in the largest view justice is eternally confronted.

Some of Spenser's scenes are fully comprehensible only through reference to iconography. The most remarkable of these is the description of Arthur's defeat of the Souldan. In this passage, in the first place, the icons and allusions that make up the thematic imagery are consistent with the book's primary purpose. Arthur, the prince, with his magically effective shield, is like the sun and has the power of the sun; and he uses, moreover, as a representative of justice should, a lightning-like Jovial and godly bolt. The Souldan is the irreligious aspiring rebel whom right authority must strike down; he is, Spenser reveals in a stanza's clear analogy, a Phaeton, a false sun who aspires to displace the true sun, and whom Arthur with his true sun-like shield naturally destroys. But the Souldan's threat to order and his destruction are seen not only in terms of the thematic imagery of sun and thunderbolt, prince and god, but also in terms of the thematic imagery of Hercules: for Spenser compares the Souldan with the tyrant Diomedes whom justice-maintaining Hercules slew; and Arthur's magic shield, which is certainly both thunderbolt and sun, may also be the shield of Hercules. Now Arthur in *The Faerie Queene* on the political level represents England: with that honored name he can scarcely do otherwise. In Books I and II he has also represented the grace of God. The Souldan and his chariot would seem to represent Philip II of Spain, and the Armada which, Englishmen said, England with the grace of God destroyed. All these threads are magnificently combined in the light of the *impresa* through which Philip II claimed to be like Apollo in his sun-chariot. In declaring the Souldan to be a Phaeton, he who attempts to usurp the place which is truly that of sunny Mercilla alone, Spenser is also reversing Philip II's claim to a monarchial symbol which the poet regards as being properly that of only his queen. Here in marvelous conjunction are a narrative of bold fight, the thematic imagery of orthodoxly order-maintaining Hercules and of sun and thunderbolt, and a set of historical allusions that are in several respects apt. And the whole thing hinges upon an iconographical allusion.

But the most complex of Spenser's uses of icons are those by which he either associates a number of different icons, having different suggestions, with one figure or scene, or those by which he calls upon the various, perhaps quite self-contradictory significations of a single icon. Thus, in his description of Queen Mercilla, Spenser combines iconographical details appropriate to any monarch, iconographical details adopted by or commonly bestowed upon Spenser's own particular monarch, and iconographical details which illustrate the poet's personal philosophical position on justice and Elizabeth. Like almost any other monarch, Mercilla is seated beneath a sun and above a lion, and with scepter and sword to hand. But, particularly like Queen Elizabeth, Mercilla has laid her sword aside. Then, in keeping with Spenser's presentation of justice in this book, at Mercilla's threshold guileful speech is punished; around her hover the four daughters of God; above her, and in contrast to her, Jove and angry God threaten vengeance. Each of these icons is very briefly presented, or, indeed, in the case of the four daughters of God, very faintly suggested. Yet each clearly points to some theme or other that is intrinsically tied into Spenser's knot of meaning.

And then there is the crocodile, and the fact that crocodiles are iconographically associated on the one hand with Osiris, noble hero of justice and a god, and on the other with all kinds of bestiality—with fraud, and ravening violence, and lust. Spenser uses the crocodile's traditional ambiguity to body forth his dynamically ambiguous concept of Artegall and of justice. The crocodile is god of justice; Artegall is God-representing hero of justice. The crocodile is the symbol of the lustfulness, violence, and cunning which are the primary moving forces in natural man; forces which enable such heroes as Osiris and Artegall were supposed to have been to create societies, and such technicians as Machiavelli observes to maintain them; but forces which the temperate and just man must bridle, in himself as in the state, in order to achieve a just and godly commonwealth. The complex relationship between the force which it is right for justice to use and the force which it is right for justice to restrain is embodied in the icon of Isis and the crocodile and, with greater schematic clarity, in the icon of Mercilla and the lion—in which the lion is equally, shiftingly, interchangeably, the monarch's power, the monarch's passions, and monarchy's rebels and foes. Such interrelationships as these are weakened and made to seem merely contradictory in the course of discursive explication. In their knotty icons they are presented with the immediacy and simultaneity of the visual arts and are apprehended as a whole as true.

The most startling case in which a knowledge of Renaissance iconography can change the reader's understanding of the Legend of Justice is one which would appear to have no iconological reference whatever. In fact, many of Spenser's images whose significance is perfectly clear either from literary analogues or from the poet's own explication are actually verbal emblems or allegorical pictures. The reader, becoming attuned to an expectation of pictorial analogues, learns to look for icons even in passages which do not appear to have them. Thus in the case of Artegall's sojourn with Radigund he will become aware of the presence behind the scene of the two iconographical commonplaces of Hercules and Omphale and Hercules's choice. The reader will come to perceive that the scene's barely hinted iconological resonances run directly counter to the surface narrative statement, turning a simplistic love story into an ethical crux, and, beyond that, into complex psychological and philosophical speculation.

Spenser was as sage and serious as Milton knew him to be: not because his allegory teaches man *quid agas,* but because his icons —which demand explication though they remain inexplicable— infold the ironies of man's action and condition.

NOTES

INTRODUCTION

1. See William R. Mueller, *Spenser's Critics: Changing Currents in Literary Taste*, Introduction and *passim*.

2. William Empson, *Some Versions of Pastoral*, p. 139.

3. See Northrop Frye's seminal essay, "The Structure of Imagery in *The Faerie Queene*," in *The University of Toronto Quarterly*, XXX, 109–27, reprinted in *Fables of Identity*, pp. 69–87.

4. J. A. Mazzeo has demonstrated that Dante (and surely his Renaissance successors) knew that the fourfold interpretation technique was applicable only to the Bible, which is a given truth, and not to literary compositions, which are imitative artifacts. See *Structure and Thought in the Paradiso*, pp. 25–37.

5. Notably Lilian Winstanley, in the introduction to her editions of Books I and II; A. B. Gough, in the introduction to his edition of Book V; F. M. Padelford, in *The Political and Ecclesiastical Allegory of the First Book of The Faerie Queene*; and Edwin Greenlaw, in *Studies in Spenser's Historical Allegory*.

6. T. K. Dunseath, in *Spenser's Allegory of Justice in Book Five of The Faerie Queene* (Princeton, 1968), reads Book V as the "spiritual biography" (p. 235) of Artegall and Britomart. Professor Dunseath's study was published too late for me to make full use of it: a few of our findings duplicate and many of our findings complement one another's. But his thesis that Spenser delineates characters that develop and change for the better is not supported by the words and events of the poem; and it imposes an inappropriate modern viewpoint on a Renaissance text.

7. Herschel Baker and E. M. W. Tillyard, for instance, repeatedly,

with justification, quote from Spenser to illustrate the medieval-Renaissance view of order, and other concepts. See the indexes to Baker, *The Dignity of Man* and *The Wars of Truth,* and Tillyard, *The Elizabethan World Picture.*

8. William Nelson, in his authoritative study of *The Poetry of Edmund Spenser,* focuses much of his discussion on the poet's consistently, deliberately, philosophically presented dualisms. See his summary, p. 297. Some of his suggestive chapter-titles are "Prays-desire and Shamefastnesse" (Book II), "Maid and Woman" (Book III), and "The Idol and the Crocodile" (Book V).

Angus Fletcher, in *Allegory, The Theory of a Symbolic Mode,* maintains that all allegories are necessarily ambivalent. He has a special discussion of *The Faerie Queene,* pp. 269–73.

9. C. S. Lewis, *The Allegory of Love,* pp. 313–16, and *English Literature in the Sixteenth Century,* pp. 381–83.

10. Recent students of allegory have cast their nets very wide. Professor Fletcher discusses, among many other things, movies and eighteenth-century sublimity. Edwin Honig's *Dark Conceit: The Making of Allegory* embraces *The Faerie Queene* and *Moby Dick* and *Ulysses.* Indeed, he suggestively compares Spenser's and Joyce's use of allegory; this material was first published in "Hobgoblin or Apollo," *Kenyon Review,* (Autumn, 1948), 664–81.

11. The term "moralized narrative" may be used to distinguish the literary kind which critics have long condemned from the kind of "allegory" being redefined here.

12. W. K. Wimsatt, *The Verbal Icon,* p. [x].

13. See Rosemond Tuve, *Allegorical Imagery.* The "emblem" in the emblem books is properly the picture; a few Renaissance iconologists titled the verbal explanation of the picture the "signification." The basic studies of emblem literature are those by Mario Praz, *Studies in Seventeenth Century Imagery,* and by William S. Heckscher and Karl-August Wirth, "Emblem, Emblembuch," in the *Reallexicon zur deutschen Kunstgeschichte,* Nos. 49–50 (1959), cols. 85–228. There is some interesting information in the first chapter of Martha Hester Golden's dissertation, "The Iconography of the English History Play."

14. *English Emblem Books,* pp. 101–13. There have been two un-

published doctoral dissertations on Spenser's use of emblems. Both are largely devoted to the history of emblem literature and neither has any significant material on Book V of *The Faerie Queene*. They are: Sister Marie Louise Beutner, "Spenser and the Emblem Writers," and Jack Willard Jessee, "Spenser and the Emblem Books." There has also been an M.A. thesis on the topic: Ellen G. Ward, "Spenser and the Emblem Writers."

15. Especially Henry Peacham, several of whose emblems, and instructions for representing allegorical figures (in *Minerva Britanna* and *The Compleat Gentleman*) are, Miss Freeman suggests, drawn from Spenser. *English Emblem Books*, pp. 71, 80–82.

16. In *Allegorical Imagery*. Samuel C. Chew's *The Pilgrimage of Life* illustrates the interrelationship between iconography and literature from medieval times to the seventeenth century.

17. *Mythology and the Renaissance Tradition in English Poetry*, p. 93.

18. Notably A. C. Hamilton in *The Structure of Allegory in The Faerie Queene*.

19. Harry Berger, Jr., in *The Allegorical Temper*, discusses a case of "conspicuous irrelevance" in Spenser's Book II; he finds that an apparently irrelevant incident and image in fact admirably serves Spenser's larger purpose and even has an immediate aptness in many of its details.

One of Angus Fletcher's insights into the typical characteristics of allegory is that it is a form in which the images tend to be in isolation from one another—separate, clear, detailed, surrealistic, ornamental. (*Allegory*, p. 87, etc.) Traditional readings of *The Faerie Queene* have always assumed Spenser to be an allegorist of the kind which Professor Fletcher so interestingly analyzes. But, as Fletcher also maintains, especially in his forthcoming study of Book V, Spenser is as much a mythopeic or "prophetic" writer as he is an allegorist; many of his apparently discrete images in fact fulfill a mythic pattern or purpose.

20. *Elizabethan and Metaphysical Imagery*, p. 97*n*.

21. Since 1957 there has been a remarkable number of books by critics who have rediscovered or discovered interesting aspects of Spenser's poetry. Many of them may be criticized on the grounds I have

mentioned. A. C. Hamilton's study traces particularly strange narrative patterns and structures of Christian allegory in *The Faerie Queene*. The numerological study is by Alastair Fowler: *Spenser and The Numbers of Time*. Though certainly rather far-fetched, and sometimes irresponsible in its manipulation of evidence, it does open fascinating possibilities. I have found a number of Fowler's particular details very suggestive.

22. Graham Hough, "First commentary on *The Faerie Queene:* Annotations in Lord Bessborough's copy of the first edition of *The Faerie Queene*," *Times Literary Supplement*, April 9, 1964, p. 294. See also "MS Notes to Spenser's 'Faerie Queene,'" *Notes and Queries N. S.*, IV (1957), 509–15, and A. S. Fowler, "Oxford and London Marginalia to *The Faerie Queene*," *Notes and Queries N. S.*, VIII (1961), 416–19.

I. JOVE'S JUDGMENT SEAT

1. Enid Welsford, *The Court Masque*, p. 50.

2. *The Myth of the State*, pp. 97–105.

3. See G. R. Elton's commentaries on the various sixteenth-century statements on justice which he has gathered into an anthology in *The Tudor Constitution*, pp. 20, 147, 158–61.

4. *Six Books of the Commonwealth*, translated by M. J. Tooley, p. 134 (Book IV, Chap. v).

5. *The Works of Edmund Spenser: a Variorum Edition*, edited by Edwin Greenlaw, C. G. Osgood, F. M. Padelford, et al., 11 vols. Volume V, p. 237. Hereafter referred to as *Works*, V, 237.

6. William Nelson, "Queen Elizabeth, Spenser's Mercilla, and a Rusty Sword," *Renaissance News*, XVIII, 113–17.

7. *The Virtues Reconciled: An Iconographical Study*, pp. 35–68. Donald Cheyney comments on this aspect of Book V in his *Spenser's Image of Nature: Wild Man and Shepherd in "The Faerie Queene,"* p. 167, and so does Angus Fletcher, in his study of Book V.

8. *Iliad*, IX, 498 ff., *Theogony*, 901–2. See *Works*, V, 241–42.

9. Nelson, *Edmund Spenser*, p. 267, and Hamilton, *The Structure of Allegory*, p. 186. Hamilton associates Britomart rather than Mercilla

with the New Law; but the two ladies are closely parallel in function and significance.

10. Hymne XXIII. I quote from the facsimile edition of Sir John Davies's *Poems*, edited by Clare Howard. See also the discussion by Frances A. Yates, "Queen Elizabeth as Astraea," *Journal of the Warburg and Courtauld Institutes*, X, (1947), 27–82.

11. See two articles by James E. Phillips, Jr., "The Background of Spenser's Attitude toward Women Rulers," *Huntington Library Quarterly*, V (1941–42), 5–32, and "The Woman Ruler in Spenser's Faerie Queene," *ibid.*, pp. 211–34; and Kerby Neill, "Spenser on the Regiment of Women," *Studies in Philology*, XXXIV (1937), 134–37.

12. Batman, *The Golden Booke*, pp. 1–2.

13. *Q. Horatl Flaccl Emblemata* (Studio Othonis VaenI, Antwerp), p. 79. I shall use the running head as the most convenient short title of this work, to which I shall often be referring. Mario Praz discusses the works attributed to Van Veen in his *Studies in Seventeenth Century Imagery*, II, pp. 168–69.

14. In another similar emblem a king is shown ruling by the sword; above him, his model and governor, a divine sword threatens him as he threatens the people. See Chew, *The Virtues Reconciled*, p. 95. Chew refers the reader to Emile Mâle, *L'Art Religieux du XIIIe siècle en France*, p. 314 and fig. 169. But I can find in Mâle's book no emblem resembling Chew's description.

15. Marin Le Roy Gomberville, *Le Theatre moral de la vie humaine*, p. 34.

16. *Works*, V, 281–82, 287–88, 292–97.

17. *Maxims of State*, in *Works*, I, p. 19.

18. London, 1618, Embleme 16. I have used the photolith facsimile edited by Henry Green and James Croston.

19. *Works*, V, 226–28.

20. Alastair Fowler, in *Spenser and the Numbers of Time*, pp. 192–221, associates Arthur and Britomart with Jove's thunderbolt and believes that Artegall's sword and Talus's flail are associated with Jove.

2. The Giants' Rebellion

1. See Chapter 10, "The Champion of True Justice."

2. Alastair Fowler suggested aspects of this theme. *Numbers of Time*, pp. 204–6.

3. Robert Graves, *The Greek Myths*, I, 39–41, 131–32. There is a coincidental relevance in the fact that Hercules, archetypal defender of justice and the status quo, was Jove's chief instrument in the suppression of the giants' rebellion.

4. Talus, flail, and sword are associated, too, with the club of Hercules—"The club of Justice dread, with kingly powre endewed" (i.2).

5. London, 1639, Vol. II, Bk. iii, Emblem 12.

6. Vol. II, Bk. iv, Emblem 4.

7. In *The Mirrour of Majestie* there is an emblem in which a mailed hand is depicted holding Jove's thunderbolt (Figure 3). A few pages further on there is a similar emblem of a mailed hand emerging from heaven's cloud; this hand is holding a sword. The writer of the accompanying verse declares that he who draws his "revenging rod" in a cause other than God's and his country's, "gives a *sword* withall/To Heavn's high Justice, by invoking downe/*Revenge,* in lieu of *Guerdon,* or a Crowne" (Embleme 12). Edgar Wind, in *Pagan Mysteries in the Renaissance*, p. 87, discusses the icon of a sword or dagger hovering overhead as a symbol of the wrathful God of Vengeance.

8. See the appropriate entry in the unpublished dissertation by Joel Jay Belsen, "The Names in *The Faerie Queene*."

9. Fowler, *Numbers of Time*, p. 201.

10. Richard Hurd first made the suggestion in his *Letters on Chivalry and Romance*. See *Works*, V, 169–70. G. R. Elton discusses the problem of the "overmighty subject" (his quotation marks) in *The Tudor Constitution*, pp. 30–31.

11. These epithets occur in *Works*, V, 345; M. Pauline Parker, *The Allegory of The Faerie Queene*, p. 205; Leo Kirschbaum, *Edmund Spenser: Selected Poetry*, p. xxxi; Graham Hough, *A Preface to The Faerie Queene*, p. 195; etc.

12. Frederick M. Padelford, "Spenser's Arraignment of the Anabaptists," *Journal of English and Germanic Philology*, XII (1913), 434–48. Quoted in *Works*, V, 336–41.

13. See *Works*, V, 175–81; 336–45.

14. Sir Philip Sidney's original version of *The Countess of Pembroke's Arcadia*, pp. 122–25.

15. *The true subject to the rebel, or the hurt of sedition, how grevious it is to a Common-wealth*, pp. 11–12. The work was first published as *The hurt of sedition* in 1549. The change in name underlines the work's oratorical bent.

16. *Ibid.*, p. 64.

17. The work was attributed to Raleigh and published with his *Maxims of State*. The quotation is from pp. 95–96.

18. I have conflated more than one account, as the men of the Renaissance tended to do. See Graves, pp. 131–33, 136–37.

It is interesting in this connection that one of the number of things that Hercules represented for the Renaissance was Eloquence. Valeriano lists Hercules's significance as *Eloquentia* first. See Giòvanni Pierio Valeriano Bolzani, *Hieroglyphica*, p. 733. Hercules's significance as eloquence was derived rationally from his primary significance as force. Jean Bodin wrote in *Six Books of the Commonwealth*: "There is nothing which has greater influence over men's souls than the art of eloquent speech. Our forefathers portrayed the Celtic Hercules as an old man, trailing after him a crowd of people fastened by the ears with chains issuing from his mouth. They thus intimated that the powers and armed forces of kings and princes are not so potent as the vehemence of an ardent and eloquent man. He can excite the most cowardly to overcome the bravest, he makes the proudest cast aside their arms, turns cruelty into gentleness, barbarity into humanity, revolutionizes a commonwealth, and plays upon the people at will. I don't say all this in praise of eloquence, but to show what force it has, for it is a force more often used for evil than good ends" (IV, vii. Tr. Tooley, p. 143). Precisely the emblem Bodin describes occurs in Alciati's popular and frequently reissued *Emblemata*, p. 144 in the 1548 edition. And it reappears in a mid-seventeenth-century emblem dictionary. See I. Baudoin, *Recueil d'Emblemes Divers*, I, 532. The commentator on an unillustrated allegorical verse by Alciati, on the subject of the labors of Hercules, explains Hercules's slaying of the Nemoean lion in terms of eloquence's victory over force. *Emblemata cum commentariis* . . . *per Claudium Minoem*, p. 460.

3. POWER AND LAW

1. In this Spenser is being untraditional. During the Golden Age, when Astraea was still on earth, perfect justice presiding over a perfect society of men, there should have been no need of a judge, let alone of an executor. As Ovid wrote, "Golden was that first age, which, with no one to compel, without a law, kept faith and did the right. There was no fear of punishment, no threatening words were to be read on brazen tablets; no suppliant throng gazed fearfully upon its judge's face; but without judges lived secure" (*Metamorphoses*, I, 89–93). But Spenser, perhaps too much of a hierarchy-ridden Elizabethan to be able to conceive of a functionless justice, even in the Golden Age, writes that in that virtuous, perfectly peaceful time, "Justice sate high ador'd with solemne feasts,/And to all people did divide her dred beheasts." (Pr. 9.) That the Justice of the Golden Age should be *dread*, and that she should have to occupy herself with an Aristotelian *dividing* of things (see *Nichomachean Ethics*, V, v) is inconsistent with the implications of tradition.

2. *Allegory of Love*, p. 349.

3. John Upton, *The Faerie Queene of Edmund Spenser* . . . , II, 632–33. Quoted in *Works*, V, 269.

4. *Fables of Identity*, pp. 84–85. Among other critics who think that Talus represents power or force are R. E. Neil Dodge, editor of *Complete Poetical Works*, p. 281, and B. E. C. Davis, *Edmund Spenser*, p. 125.

5. In his "manie" Spenser no doubt intends to include the meanings of two different words as recorded in the O. E. D.: *meanie*, which meant "many," and *meinie*, which meant "mob" or "retinue."

6. Thomas Warton was the first to point out the similarities between the two Taluses. *Observations on the Fairy Queen of Spenser*, I, 97–100. Quoted in *Works*, V, 165–66. The most detailed discussion

of the sources of the Talus legend is by John W. Draper, "Spenser's Talus Again," *Philological Quarterly*, XV (1936), 215–17.

7. *Myths*, I, 36.

8. *Works and Days*, 143–51. Translated by Hugh Evelyn-White. Loeb Classical Library, 1914.

9. Talus assails Munera, who is helpless, and a woman, "Withouten pitty of her goodly hew," and "without remorse." The knightly Artegall does rue her plight, although in the interests of justice he controls his feelings (ii. 25, 26).

10. *Hesiodi Asraei*, edited by Cornelius Schrevellius, p. 21.

11. "The Georgicks of Hesiod," *Homer's Batrachomyomachia*, lines 242–43.

12. "Works and Days," *The Works of the English Poets From Chaucer to Cowper*, XX, 746.

13. Jean Seznec, *The Survival of the Pagan Gods*, translated by Barbara F. Sessions, pp. 191–93. See figures 42, 74, 75, 76, 77, 78, 79.

14. See *F.Q.* V. ii.51–54; iv.24,44; vi.30; vii.35; xi.59; xii.7. It may not be irrelevant to note that Hesiod's brazen men wore bronze armor, but that Talus of Crete was *made* of bronze; and that Mars wore iron armor, but that Spenser's Talus was *made* of iron.

15. John P. Daly, S. J. " 'Talus' in Spenser's *Faerie Queene*," *Notes and Queries*, N.S., VII (1960), 49. See also *Works*, V, 167.

16. See B. E. C. Davis, *Spenser*, p. 124.

17. *Partenay*, XXII, 2999; *Melusine*, xxxviii. See O.E.D. "Flail:3."

18. See Stephen Batman's account of Mars: "A Wolfe went before him with a Sheepe in hys mouth. . . . The Wolfe with the Sheepe in his mouth representeth Mars, whose Souldiers are as great raveners of other mens goodes, as the wolf is of seely sheep." *The Golden Booke*, p. 6.

19. Cesare Ripa, in his many-times translated and reprinted *Iconologia* [First Edition, 1593. My references are to the edition entitled *Nova Iconologia*—Padua, 1618] has a number of emblems with wolves in them. Wolves are central in his emblems of *Armi, Avarizia, Carro di Marto, Nocumento di ogni cosa*, and *Rapina* (pp. 35, 41, 67, 369, 439).

20. Angus Fletcher discovered this interesting parallel; he discusses

it in his chapter on "Talus and Time" in his study of Book V. *Stair Ercueil Ocus a Bas* (*The Life and Death of Hercules*), [c.1475– 1500], edited and translated by Gordon Quin, pp. 83, 111, 246. Fletcher also notes that in Egyptian art Osiris is shown holding a shepherd's crook and a flail. S. H. Hooke, *Middle Eastern Mythology* (Penguin, 1963), Figure 3.

21. John M. Steadman, "Spenser and the *Virgilius* Legend: Another Talus Parallel," *Modern Language Notes*, LXXIII, 412–13.

22. Seznec, *Survival of the Pagan Gods*, p. 191.

23. *The Poems of John Dryden*, edited by James Kinsley, I, 267. Line 89.

24. Guy de Tervarent, *Attributs et Symboles dans l'Art Profane: 1450–1600*, col. 195. ("Fouet: 1. Jupiter.")

25. *Saturnalia*, I, 23.

26. See Seznec, p. 253 and Figure 98.

27. Angus Fletcher, in his chapter on "Talus and Time" recalls the popular conflation of Chronos with Saturn as scythe-bearing figures; he associates both of them with Talus and his flail.

28. The author of *The Pilgrimage of Perfection* (1526), wrote that "The flayle tryeth ye corne from the chaffe." P. 134 b. See O. E. D. "Flaile: 3."

29. "Talus: The Law," *Studies in Philology*, XV (1918), 97–104. Quoted in *Works*, V, 276–80.

30. Henry Gibbons Lotspeich, *Classical Mythology in the Poetry of Edmund Spenser*, p. 40.

31. Draper, "Spenser's Talus Again," pp. 215–17.

32. *Works*, IX, 78.

33. *Six Books of the Commonwealth*, Book I, Chapter viii. (Tooley, p. 28).

34. *Ibid.*, I.viii (p. 32).

35. *Ibid.*, I.x (p. 43).

36. Notably H. S. V. Jones, in *A Spenser Handbook*, pp. 379–80, and in "Spenser's Defence of Lord Grey," *University of Illinois Studies in Language and Literature*, V, 151–219, *passim*. See also Index to *Works*, IX; W. L. Renwick and other scholars repeatedly refer to passages from Bodin in their explications of Spenser's prose works.

William Nelson quotes from him to illuminate Spenser's concept of equity (*Spenser*, pp. 268–69).

37. Thomas Jenner, *The Soules Solace* (1626). The emblem is reproduced in Freeman, *English Emblem Books*, plate 14.

38. See Aristotle, *Nicomachean Ethics*, translated by H. Rackham, V.ix.10.

39. In Ripa's *Nova Iconologia* only simple Justice herself is illustrated (p. 223). However, Jean Baudoin, Ripa's French translator and follower, has a plate on which all four are represented as Ripa describes them. *Iconologie*, II (1644), 56.

40. Ripa, p. 223.

4. LION

1. Strong, *Portraits, passim*.

2. Ripa, pp. 316–17; Strong, pp. 100–2, etc. There is no entry on Monarchy in the copy of the 1618 edition of the *Nova Iconologia* which I have seen. *Monarchie* appears, however, in the Baudoin translation (II, 92–95), and *Monarchia Mondana* in Cesare Orlandi's 1764 edition: *Iconologia del Cavaliere Cesare Ripa, Perugino, Notabilmente accresciuta d'Immagini, di Annotazioni, e di Fatti*, IV, 153–54. (The plates in this edition are new, and stylistically in accordance with eighteenth-century taste; but they faithfully reproduce each emblematical detail of the original.)

3. Embleme 2, p. 3.

4. Nelson, "Elizabeth, Mercilla, and a Rusty Sword," pp. 113–17.

5. Kathleen Williams, in *Spenser's World of Glass*, p. 176n., notes the relevance of a cameo of the Virgin with a lion under her feet which symbolizes "the superseding of the Old Covenant by the New, Justice by Mercy." *Journal of the Warburg Institute*, II, 219.

6. Described in Ripa, pp. 82–83. Illustrated in Baudoin, II, 114–15, and in Orlandi, II, 1. Baudoin legitimately interprets *saetta* as "arrow," and represents his personification of clemency as wielding an arrow and a spear. Orlandi equally legitimately represents Clemency's *saetta* as a thunderbolt. (Spenser's Mercilla is represented as imitating thunderbolt-wielding Jove—ix.31,32.)

7. Baudoin, *Recueil d'Emblemes Divers*, I (1638), 596.

8. "Lion d'Atlas," 1829. Prints Collection, New York Public Library.

9. Ripa, p. 207.

10. The emblem is missing in the 1618 edition of the *Iconologie* which I have seen. It appears in Orlandi's 1764 edition. I have reproduced Baudoin's version (*Iconologie*, II, 92).

11. Strong, Woodcut 2.

12. Baudoin, II, 92–95; Orlandi, IV, 154. Though the Italian *serpente* may be translated either as "serpent" or "dragon," both emblematists draw dragons. It is notable that Mercilla's evil counterpart in Book I, Lucifera, or Pride, has a dragon beneath her throne as Mercilla has a lion (I.iv.10). (Northrop Frye has written of "demonic parody" and "the principle of symbolic parody" in *The Faerie Queene*, in which one event or image is so often echoed in reverse in another. *Fables of Identity*, p. 79.) It is not traditional for pride to be associated with a dragon. Samuel Chew finds no analogue for Spenser's seating his Lucifera on such a beast: see his essay, "Spenser's Pageant of the Seven Deadly Sins," *Studies in Art and Literature for Belle Da Costa Greene*, p. 43. However, it must be said that in Ripa's *Iconologia* Beauty is presented much like Spenser's Pride; like Lucifera, Beauty holds a mirror (symbol of vanity) and is seated on a dragon (p. 28).

13. Angus Fletcher suggests that there is a royal pun in Spenser's coinage, "to royne."

14. *Essay d'un dictionnaire contenant la connoissance du monde, des sciences universelles, et particulièrement celle des medailles, des passions, des moeurs, des vertus et des vices.* . . . (1700), plate 115, Figure 1. De la Feuille's is a vast and delightful collection of emblems, drawn from the work of Alciati, Baudoin, Ripa, Van Veen, and others. Each plate contains fifteen little contiguous circles, each containing a different tiny emblem. In view of the collection's late date it is, of course, possible that De la Feuille was indebted to Spenser as well as to all the many other preceding emblematists and artists; or Spenser and De la Feuille may both have drawn upon the same pictorial traditions.

15. *Emblemata* (1548), p. 32. *Recueil d'Emblemes*, I, 476–83.

16. *Hieroglyphica*, pp. 15–16.

17. *Iconologie*, II, 114–15. I have reproduced the whole page on

which the two emblems occur because the reciprocal relevance of the other pair on the page—Charity and Chastity—is so clear that it confirms the reader's sense of a connection between clemency and self-command. (The emblem of *Charité* will, too, interest those who remember Spenser's Charissa—I.x.29–31.)

18. For Hercules, lions, restraint, and the passions, see Chapter 10.

5. SUN

1. Jacobi a Bruck, in his *Emblemata Politica* (1618), has an emblem which shows the sun representing both monarchy and justice: *"Jure Laeditur."* Emblem xxx, p. 117.

2. Beneath her feet there are two white lions which Strong explains as allusions to the Northampton family, pp. 100–2.

3. Hymne XI, p. 207.

4. In Book I there is a closely analogous description of a sun-bright queen who is as excessive as Mercilla is moderate. This is Lucifera:

> High above all a cloth of State was spred,
>   And a rich throne, as bright as sunny day,
>   On which there sate most brave embellished
>   With royall robes and gorgeous array,
>   A mayden Queene, that shone as Titans ray,
>   In glistring gold, and peerelesse pretious stone:
>   Yet her bright blazing beautie did assay
>   To dim the brightnesse of her glorious throne,
> As envying her selfe, that too exceeding shone.
>
> Exceeding shone, like Phoebus fairest childe,
>   That did presume his fathers firie wayne,
>   And flaming mouthes of steedes unwanted wilde
>   Through highest heaven with weaker hand to rayne;
>   Proud of such glory and advancement vaine,
>   While flashing beames do daze his feeble eyen,
>   He leaves the welkin way most beaten plaine,
>   And rapt with whirling wheeles, inflames the skyen,
> With fire not made to burne, but fairely for to shyne.   (I.iv.8,9)

5. See especially I.ii. Emblem 15 (facing p. 98), and II.v.14 (facing p. 109).

6. Fowler, *Spenser*, p. 209.

7. Hamilton, *Structure of Allegory*, pp. 188–89.

8. Plutarch, *De Iside et Osiride*, 12, 41, 51. Diodorus Siculus, *Bibliotheca Historica*, I, II.

9. See Henry Reynolds' "Mythomystes" (1632). The work is reprinted in *Critical Essays of the Seventeenth Century*, edited by J. E. Spingarn, II, 141–79.

10. *Hieroglyphica*, pp. 484, 732.

11. *F.Q.* V.vii.1,2. Osiris was also identified with Bacchus, fabled exemplar of justice. See Isabel E. Rathborne, *The Meaning of Spenser's Fairyland*, pp. 88–89. Spenser associates Artegall with Bacchus in V.i.2.

12. Artegall actually bears "Achilles arms" (III.ii.25). Spenser seems to have had it in mind to associate Artegall with Achilles as well as with Hercules; but the Achilles relationship is not worked through.

13. Julius Guilielmus Zincgreff, *Emblematum Ethico-Politicorum Centuria* (1664), Emblem 36.

14. *Metamorphoses*, II, 198–201.

15. Graves, *Myths*, I, 156.

16. Angus Fletcher, in his unpublished book on The Legend of Justice.

17. *Impresa* of Philip II from Girolamo Ruscelli, *Imprese illustri*, 1566, p. 232. See René Graziani, "Philip II's *Impresa* and Spenser's Souldan," *Journal of the Warburg and Courtauld Institutes*, XXVII (1964), pp. 322–24.

18. *Works*, V, 225–26.

19. *Works*, V, 227.

6. CROCODILE

1. See Frances A. Yates, *Giordano Bruno and the Hermetic Tradition*, pp. 1–168, *passim*.

2. *The Golden Booke*, p. 16.

3. Irwin Panofsky, "Triciput," in *Hercules am Scheidewege*.

4. It is of some interest, in view of Artegall's association with Jove, that in one thirteenth-century lapidary of engraved stones, in a series of emblems of the planets, Jupiter is represented by a horse and a crocodile. "The illustrative portion of this work gives emblems of the seven planets, beginning under Mercury with a man sitting upon a plough, holding a fox and a vulture, with four men around his neck; Mars is represented by an armed figure of a man, Jupiter by a horse and crocodile, Venus by a man and a woman, Saturn by a horse with a kingly rider." Quoted by Jessee pp. 38–39, from Joan Evans, *Magical Jewels of the Middle Ages and the Renaissance*, p. 102.

5. E. A. Wallis Budge, *Osiris and the Egyptian Resurrection*, I, 21.

6. I. I. Boissard, *Theatrum Vitae Humanae* (1596), pp. 71–74.

7. *Hieroglyphica*, p. 731.

8. *De Iside et Osiride*, 75.

9. *Hieroglyphica*, p. 345.

10. *Spaccio della bestia trionfante*, Dialogue 3. Quoted and translated by Yates, in *Bruno*, p. 212.

11. *De Iside*, 18.

12. A. B. Gough made this point. See *Works*, V, 252, and Plutarch. *De Iside*, 71.

13. London, 1567, pp. 77–78.

14. *Hieroglyphica*, p. 349.

15. *Iconologia*, pp. 507–8; *Hieroglyphica*, p. 118.

16. The role of Echidna is discussed in Chapter 9, "Geryoneo."

17. William Nelson, in his book on *Spenser*, subtitles his chapter on The Legend of Justice "The Idol and the Crocodile."

18. Spenser writes "Himself before her feete he lowly threw" (vii.6); here and throughout the passage the feminine pronoun may refer either to Britomart or Isis. No doubt Spenser intentionally runs the two ladies into one through his use of an ambiguous pronoun. At the beginning of the passage it is clearly Isis who beats back the crocodile; at the end, it is as clearly Britomart who awakes. "She" begot a lion in the dream: since the lion, the royal progenitor, is more essentially Britomart's than Isis's, I have regarded Britomart as the dominant figure in the composite lady, and have phrased my text accordingly.

19. The only attempt at an explanation of this puzzling matter which

I have seen is one which oddly interprets it as historical allegory. René Graziani believes that the crocodile's devouring of the flames and tempest represents Elizabeth's punishment of Mary's supporters, that his threat to devour Britomart represents Elizabeth's self-endangering clemency, and that the subjugation of the crocodile represents the restoration of proper order. "Elizabeth at Isis Church," *Publications of the Modern Language Association,* LXXIX (1964), 376–89.

20. J. H. Walker, "*The Faerie Queene:* Alterations and Structure," *Modern Language Review,* XXXVI (1941), 51.

21. *Ethics,* V, i.

22. "Nature and Grace in *The Faerie Queene,*" *English Literary History,* XIV (1949), 216.

23. See also Hamilton, *The Structure of Allegory,* pp. 179–80; he notes that both the temple flames and the crocodile probably symbolize lust. Donald Cheyney thinks that Britomart's dream indicates her proclivity toward lust; he interprets her defeat of Radigund as in part her defeat of the Radigund-like elements in her own character. *Images of Nature,* pp. 170–71.

24. *Works,* V, 215. A. B. Gough, too, notes the oddly discrepant conjunction between the "faithful lover" and the crocodile. He writes: "This is proof, if any is needed, that Spenser's allegory is not rigidly systematic, but adapts itself spontaneously to the mood of the moment." See the notes to his edition of Book V, p. 248.

25. *Iconologia,* p. 320. See also Baudoin, *Iconologie,* I, 107–8, and De La Feuille, *Dictionary,* plate facing [p. 35], Figure 2.

26. Reprinted in Chew, *Pilgrimage,* fig. 114. Chew writes that the engraving was designed and published by Nicolas Guérard, but gives no other bibliographical details.

27. Lyons, 1548, p. 44; Paris, 1583, p. 99; Padua, 1621, p. 122. Graziani, too, in "Elizabeth at Isis Church," mentions this emblem as throwing light on Britomart's dream. C. S. Lewis uses the same emblem to explicate Spenser's account of Cupid with a wounded dragon beneath him—*F.Q.* III.xi.48. *Studies in Medieval and Renaissance Literature,* pp. 164–66.

28. Ripa, pp. 315–16. See also Chew, *Pilgrimage,* pp. 48, 50*n.*

29. *Hieroglyphica,* p. 348.

30. *Hieroglyphica,* under *De vipera,* p. 173.

31. *Emblemata* (1548), p. 154.

32. According to Angus Fletcher, in his study of Book V, "While virtue grows and can be cultivated, its champions will have to learn to control their own daemonic energy, which Spenser calls 'heroic heat.' Throughout Book V there is an interplay of this fearsome daemonic energy, one of whose aspects is sexual desire, and the attenuating, softening, gentling restraints of Christian charity."

7. FORCE AND FRAUD

1. See the article by J. A. Mazzeo, "Hell vs. Hell: From Dante to Machiavelli," *Symposium,* XVII (1963), 249–50.

2. *Politics,* V.iii.8 (translated by H. Rackman).

3. Cicero, *De Officiis,* I.x (translated by W. Miller).

4. Frances A. Yates, "Queen Elizabeth as Astraea," *Journal of the Warburg and Courtauld Institutes,* X (1947), 27–82.

5. See Cheyney, *Image of Nature,* pp. 150–51.

6. *Works and Days,* 174–201; *Metamorphoses,* I, 132–49.

7. Note Bodin's comment in his *Six Books,* I.iii (Tooley, p. 14): "There are innumerable cases of parents setting at defiance both divine and positive law in order to advance the interests of their children by fair means or foul."

8. See also *F.Q.,* V.Pr.4.

9. *Works and Days,* 190–201.

10. *Metamorphoses,* I, 128–31.

11. *Iconologia,* pp. 168–69.

12. *English Emblem Books,* p. 117.

13. I: 17; V: 19. The next highest frequency is in Book II, with 13 (three of which have reference to Archimago). III: 8; IV: 7; VI: 5.

14. Angus Fletcher points this out in his study of Book V.

15. *Works,* V, 234.

16. C. K. Allen, *Law in the Making,* p. 379. Angus Fletcher, in his study of Book V, quotes this passage and points out its relevance to Britomart and Dolon.

17. Leicester Bradner, *Edmund Spenser and the Faerie Queene,* pp.

92, 102; Gough, pp. 272, 284; Davis, pp. 124–25; Hamilton, pp. 170–77.

18. *The Allegory of Love*, p. 348.

19. A. C. Judson, *The Life of Edmund Spenser*, *Works*, VIII, 91–105; Gough, p. 273.

20. J. A. Froude, *A History of England*, Chapter 62. Quoted by Gough, p. 272.

21. Judson, p. 186.

22. Geoffrey Wagner, "Talus," *English Literary History*, XVII (1950), 79–86.

23. Britomart: vii.36,37; Artegall: xi.65, xii.8. Compare Gough's comment on the book's cruelties (p. xlviii): "[Spenser's] head approved while his heart wavered, and he subordinated his instincts to arguments. His uneasiness is seen in those passages where contrary to the facts Talus is called off like a hound that has tasted blood."

24. See Chapter 12, "The Blatant Beast."

25. See the sections on "Principle" and "Practice" in "The Tudors and Political Thought," the first chapter in Felix Raab's *The English Face of Machiavelli*, pp. 8–29.

26. *Six Books*, II.iv.

27. Niccolò Machiavelli, *The Prince*, Chapter XVIII, translated by Luigi Ricci, p. 64. I am indebted to Professor Mazzeo for pointing out to me the analogy between Machiavelli's thought and Spenser's. See his article, "Hell vs. Hell."

28. Compare the fox in Spenser's *Mother Hubberd's Tale*. For Valeriano Bolzani, the fox is the symbol of *calliditas dolosa* (p. 157), and Ripa describes *Insidia* as an armed woman with a fox on her helmet and *Astuzia ingannevole* as a woman with a fox at her feet (pp. 40, 263).

29. Bodin, *Six Books*, V.i: "Northerners succeed by means of force, southerners by means of finesse, people of the middle regions by a mixture of both. . . . Northern races . . . resort to force for all purposes, as do lions; those of the temperate regions to reason and law. Southern races rely on diplomacy and finesse, as do foxes, or they appeal to religion" (Tooley, pp. 148–52).

Cabinet Council: "A Prince being forced to use the Condition of Beasts, must among them make choice of the Fox and the Lion; for the

Lion cannot take heed of the Snares, and the Fox is easily overcome by the Wolves: it behoveth him therefore to be a Fox to discover the Snares, and a Lion to terrify the Wolves." (Raleigh, *Works*, I, 119.)

30. *Iconologia*, p. 475. The standard young man who goes about carrying the pelt of a lion is Hercules. Having taken the new, Machiavellian line about force and fraud, Ripa grafts it on to a traditional image where it sits rather oddly. Hercules, one feels, wouldn't have been seen dead in foxskin.

31. *Iconologia*, p. 505. See Mazzeo, "Hell vs. Hell," p. 267*n*. on the phrase's origin in Cicero and Plutarch.

32. Several of Spenser's close friends—Sidney, Raleigh, and Harvey —are known to have read, admired and, with circumspection, made use of Machiavelli's work. Spenser's own *View of . . . Ireland* is probably influenced by Machiavelli's thought; see Edwin Greenlaw, "The Influence of Machiavelli on Spenser," *Modern Philology*, VII (1909–1910), 187–202.

Book V of *The Faerie Queene* seems to be related to the *View;* several critics have found it similarly Machiavellian. In particular, B. E. C. Davis has declared that in Book V Spenser's representation of justice "is more Machiavellian than classical" (p. 109); and Angus Fletcher has found in the book an ambivalence in which orthodox and Machiavellian ideas of justice "are self-destructively intermingled" (*Allegory*, p. 271).

33. As it happens, Machiavelli's discussion of the prince's man-beast nature, and of his need to use both force and fraud, is all by way of demonstration that "Therefore, a prudent ruler ought not to keep faith when by so doing it would be against his interest, and when the reasons which made him bind himself no longer exist." (*The Prince*, p. 64.) It is precisely in his failure to keep faith with Radigund that Artegall seems most dishonorably guileful.

34. In Book VI, however, in an incident that is significantly parallel to this, Arthur gets into a "forbidden hall" by a similarly guileful method. His justification is in both books the same; for guile is as much the inevitable enemy of true courtesy as it is of ideal justice. He legitimately attacks the base and guileful Turpine and Blandina with their own weapons (VI.vi.17–20).

8. SNAKES AND SNARES

1. *Iconologia,* pp. 504–9.

2. *Guizor,* too, is a guileful name. It implies one who is wont to take on a guise that is not his own.

3. Graziani explains Dolon's trap as a political reference to a Catholic attempt to blow up Queen Elizabeth's bedroom; he associates it with the name of one of the principals in the plot, Leonard des Trappes (pp. 388–89).

William B. Bache points to Deloney's account of a similar incident and suggests that both may reflect a traditionally or a contemporarily notorious murder case. "Spenser and Deloney," *Notes and Queries,* N.S. 1 (1954), 232–33.

4. It has been pointed out that Malengin's appearance resembles that of one of the lowest members of Elizabethan society—the thieving "hooker," who carried a pole with a hook on the end with which to filch from a distance. Burton Milligan, "Spenser's Malengin and the Rogue-book Hooker," *Philological Quarterly,* XIX (1940), 147–48.

5. Greenlaw, for instance, states that guile is "described like one of the wretched outcasts that continually warred on the English in Ireland." *Historical Allegory,* p. 144.

6. From *View,* in *Works,* IX, 99.

7. *Iconologia,* p. 257.

8. *Works,* V, 235.

9. *Works,* V, 206.

10. Andreas Capellanus explains (c. 1185) that *amor* is derived from *amus,* a hook, "for he who is in love is captured in the chains of desire and wishes to capture someone else with his hook. Just as a skillful fisherman tries to attract fishes by his bait and to capture them on his crooked hook, so the man who is a captive of love tries to attract another person by his allurements. . . ." *The Art of Courtly Love* (*De arte honeste amandi*), translated by John Jay Parry, p. 31. It is the figure upon which Donne's poem "The Bait" depends, as does Dylan Thomas's "Ballad of the Long-Legged Bait."

11. *Iconologia,* p. 210.

12. Under the general heading of *Luxuria* Alciati has an interesting emblem entitled *In amatores meretricum* (*Emblemata,* 1548, p. 63). It consists of a picture of a fisherman, in idyllic surroundings, in a boat just off a pleasant shore, drawing in a net full of fish; but the fisherman has the horns of a goat—most lustful of animals. This emblem casts light on another Spenserian scene. Florimell, we may remember, in Book III, fell into the hands and the boat of just such a fisherman of extreme lustfulness—one who had "deceiptfull eyes" (III.viii.24).

13. See *Works,* V, 204, 297.

14. *De Officiis,* I.x.

15. *Six Books,* I.3.

16. *Iconologia,* p. 209.

17. See the discussion of "the knight hermit" in H. C. Chang's *Allegory and Courtesy in Spenser,* pp. 109–13.

18. *Works,* V, 236. Graves, II, 191. Achelous is a protean character in the Hercules story. Where Spenser most clearly follows the myth of Proteus, in the episode of Proteus's capture of Florimell, he describes the sea god's turning himself into the forms most likely either to attract or to terrify the lady whose love he desires to win: Proteus becomes in turn a Faerie knight, a king, a giant, a fiend, a centaur; he suitably culminates his effects by turning into a sea storm (IV.viii.39–41).

9. Geryoneo

1. *Mythologiae,* IX, 18.

2. "Father Time," *Studies in Iconology,* pp. 86–91.

3. *Iconologia,* pp. 209, 256, 257.

4. *Ibid.,* p. 209.

5. See also the discussion of the subject in Chew, *Pilgrimage,* pp. 99–100.

6. See Upton's note in *Works,* I, 182.

7. See John M. Steadman, "Spenser's *Errour* and the Renaissance Allegorical Tradition," *Neuphilogische Mitteilungun,* XVII (1961), 22–38.

8. Merritt Y. Hughes, editor, *Milton: Complete Poems and Major Prose*, p. 247*n*.

9. *Iconologia*, p. 209.

10. *Mythologiae*, VII. 1. Translated by C. W. Lemmi, *Works*, V, 255.

11. *Emblemata* (1548), p. 42; *Iconologia*, p. 95.

12. *Emblemes d'Alciat, de nouveau translatez en François vers pour vers iouxte les Latins*, p. 64.

13. V.x.10. Warton particularly comments on Spenser's omission of the dragon. *Works* V, 250.

14. *Emblemata* (1583), p. 167.

15. *Iconologia*, p. 95; *Mythologiae*, VII, 1.

16. *Bibliotheca Historica*, VII, 17. This translation is by John Skelton, before 1490, pp. 361, 390.

10. THE CHAMPION OF TRUE JUSTICE

1. William Nelson suggests in effect that the myth of Hercules is as much the base motif of Book V as the legend of St. George is of Book I and the *Aeneid* and the *Odyssey* of Book II. *Spenser*, p. 257. See also *Works*, V, 162, etc.

2. Compare Bodin's observation that "it is highly honourable, and befitting a prince, to take up arms in defence of a whole people unjustly oppressed by a cruel tyrant. Such a one was Hercules when he went about the world destroying monsters of tyranny everywhere" (II.iv. Tooley, p. 66). Such, too, of course, are Spenser's Artegall and Arthur, especially in that they go to the defense of the people of Irena and Belge, destroying the monsters of tyranny Grantorto and Geryoneo.

3. Rathborne, *Meaning of Spenser's Fairyland*, pp. 88–89.

4. Graves, II, 137.

5. See Chapters 1 and 5, "Jove's Judgment Seat" and "Sun."

6. "The Shield of Heracles," *Hesiod: The Homeric Hymns and Homerica* (translated by Hugh Evelyn-White), ll. 139–43; 161–65.

7. Artegall received martial gifts from his goddess-sponsor Astraea, including a golden sword obtained from Jove; similarly, Hercules received from Jove that magnificent shield of his, from Mercury a sword,

and from Phoebus, Vulcan, and Minerva other gifts of the same kind. (Graves, II, 101–2. In fact in almost all his encounters Hercules used only his club and his naked hands; but that, it is clear, was not for lack of the best martial equipment.)

8. Eugene M. Waith, *The Herculean Hero*, pp. 26–27.

9. Coluccio Salutati, *De Laboribus Herculis*, edited by B. L. Ullman, p. 182. It is in connection with this labor, and by way of explication of it, that Salutati mentions Prodicus's Choice of Hercules story.

10. In *Spaccio della bestia trionfante*, Giordano Bruno exhorts men to rid themselves of the evils connected with the degenerating constellations in preparation for a new period of justice, for an era governed by the truths of the ancient religion of Egypt, for the renewed day of Isis. See Frances A. Yates, *Giordano Bruno and the Hermetic Tradition*, p. 217. Bruno's book was dedicated to Sidney; Spenser may well have read it.

A well known lament for the degeneration of the constellations after the departure of Astraea is Donne's first Anniversary poem (1611).

11. Graves, II, 106, 108, 114, 116, 149. Coluccio Salutati confined his analysis neither to labors nor to signs of the zodiac; he associated with Hercules and the various incidents in his life the planet Mars, the sun, Ursus, Sagittarius, Serpens, Leo, and Gemini. See the chapter *Quibus sideribus Hercules fuerit ascriptus ab astrologis et poetis*, in *De Laboribus Herculis*, pp. 168–72. In Cartari's *Imagine dei Dei*, lxviii, the twelve labors of Hercules are identified with the twelve signs of the zodiac. See G. Kunoth, "Francisco Pacheco's Apotheosis of Hercules," *Journal of the Warburg and Courtauld Institutes*, XXVII (1964), 335–37. In iconography a notable representation of Hercules among the stars is in Dürer's Sky-map (Figure 26).

12. Graves, II, 106, 157. Salutati thought it the third labor (p. 184).

13. Graves, II, 121.

14. *Ibid.*, p. 108.

15. Fowler, *Numbers of Time*, p. 204n.

16. *De laboribus Herculis*, p. 171.

17. Cheyney, *Spenser's Image of Nature*, p. 153.

18. Fowler, in *Numbers of Time*, uses these Jove-associations to

help support his theory that the Legend of Justice is, thematically and numerologically, what he calls The Book of Jupiter (p. 204).

19. And in God. The second stanza of the proem alludes to an incident in which Jove was at his Godliest. Describing the degeneration of the world, Spenser says that men are now, worse than iron, stony like the stones which Pyrrha and Deucalion threw behind them (Pr.2). Angry at the impiety of men, Jove, like God in the biblical story, sent a flood which destroyed all but two human creatures—Deucalion and his wife, Pyrrha, who were saved in an ark. The story shows both Jove's God-like righteous vengeance and his God-like mercy: he recreated the race of man out of stones. In the fifth stanza of the proem Jove's presence is again invoked: but this time it is that very different Jove who was all too irresponsibly wont to make step-dames jealous and to ravish maidens.

20. "Social bandit" is Angus Fletcher's term. Eugene Waith's study of *The Herculean Hero* studies Hercules's appearances in and effect on the protagonists of heroic drama, from Euripides to Dryden.

21. Fashions in heroes have not changed much. The demi-god Hercules, slayer of magically strong monsters and villains, is the perennial Superman. The adventurer Hercules who may be regarded (depending on your point of view) either as a magnificent hero and lover or as a cruel and lustful "operator" is first in the line of adventurers that led to James Bond.

22. In *Seneca's Tragedies*, I (translated by Frank Justus Miller), ll. 926–39.

23. *Ibid.*, II, ll. 1989–96.

24. Reproduced in Fowler, *Numbers of Time*, plate 3(a).

25. See Waith, *Herculean Hero*, p. 33.

26. Berthold L. Ullman, *The Humanism of Coluccio Salutati*, pp. 21–26.

27. *Ibid.*, p. 26.

28. See Erich Auerbach, "Typological Symbolism in Medieval Literature," *Yale French Studies*, 9 (1952), 3–10, and "Figura," *Scenes From the Drama of European Literature*, pp. 11–76.

29. *Bibliotheca Historica*, IV, 13. Translated by John Skelton.

30. Canto ix, p. 110.

31. *Hercules furens,* ll. 45–46. Hercules was said to have carried arrows dipped in the hydra's poisonous gall.

32. *Hieroglyphica,* p. 13.

33. *Spaccio della bestia,* Dialogue 1. Quoted in Yates, *Bruno,* p. 217.

34. See the Hercules pictures collected by E. W. Bredt in *Die Welt der Künstler,* Band 3.

35. See bibliography in Will Tissot, *Simson und Hercules in den Gestaltungen des Barock,* pp. 132–40.

36. *The Complete Woodcuts of Albrecht Dürer,* edited by Willi Kurth, p. 99. Kurth mentions the theory that the figure behind Iole is "an old man . . . intended to personify Iole's feelings of distress" (p. 20). But the figure is quite clearly a woman and is quite clearly attacking Iole. In Seneca, the fact that Iole has to become Deianira's slave is the last and perhaps worst of the evils she bewails.

37. Terpine's death is a direct result of Artegall's yielding to Radigund (v.18). It is notable that Terpine makes the absolutely noble choice of death rather than dishonor (iv.32); Machiavellian Artegall looks out for himself better than that.

11. The Choice

1. Hallet Smith argues that choice-making Hercules is the typical hero of Renaissance epic and heroic poetry. He claims that "There is no hero in Spenser's *Faerie Queene* who is not conditioned by this picture of the dilemma of the heroic choice." *Elizabethan Poetry,* pp. 292–302.

Cheyney also sees heroic Hercules as central to *The Faerie Queene,* being particularly basic to Book V and the character of Arthur. *Image of Nature,* pp. 173–74.

2. III.i.34–38,65; iv.16; v.20,42; vi.48.

3. See Alan Brien, "Down with all Bowdlers," *New Statesman,* 198–99.

4. *Emblemata* (1583), p. 463.

5. Graves, II, 127.

6. Compare Seneca's account of the matter. Deianira's nurse thus describes the relationship between Hercules and Omphale: "When a

guest on Timolus, he caressed the Lydian woman and, daft with love, sat beside her swift distaff, twisting the moistened thread with doughty fingers. His shoulders, indeed, had laid aside the famous lion's skin, a turban confined his hair, and there he stood like any slave, his shaggy locks dripping with Sabaean myrrh." (ll. 370–76) In this view, Hercules's affair with Omphale is less an attempt to mitigate the discomforts of a literal slavery than a love-mania, an unmanly self-chosen condition which makes him *"like* any slave."

7. Georg Poensgen, "Herkules und Omphale," *Bibliotheca Docet: Festschrift Carl Wehmer*, pp. 303–[334].

8. See also Edgar Wind, *Pagan Mysteries in the Renaissance*, pp. 78–88. Mars is sometimes represented as more clearly the captive of Venus than, in any of the pictures I have seen, Hercules is of Omphale. In a painting by Francesco Cossa, Mars is chained to Venus's throne (Wind, Figure 57). In a Paolo Veronese painting, Cupid ties Mars' and Venus's legs together (Wind, Figure 56). The only ropes in any Omphale paintings are those occasionally suggested by the winding threads from the distaff.

9. *Works*, V, 204. Antony was reputed to have changed clothes with his mistress. Shakespeare's Cleopatra ecstatically remembers the episode (*A & C*, II.v.18–23).

10. Chaucer's Jankin, in the course of his wife-mastering campaign, reads about the similar destruction by their women of Adam, Samson, and Hercules (Wife of Bath's Tale, ll. 720–26).

11. Irwin Panofsky discusses the matter in his *Hercules am Scheidewege*, pp. 42–52.

12. *De laboribus Herculis*, pp. 184–91.

13. *Hieroglyphica*, p. 733.

14. *Iconologia*, p. 568. There is a picture of it in Baudoin, *Iconologie*, II, 83. Guyon, the knight of temperance in Book II, is the figure who most closely follows Hercules's heroically virtuous choosing and rejecting. In the book as a whole he rejects anger and concupiscence; in the Cave of Mammon he rejects riches and worldly glory. His final trial in the Cave is centered on the golden apples of the Hesperides— the bait which in his hunger and exhaustion he almost has to take (II.vii.53–66). Ripa claims that the apples represent moderation;

Spenser demonstrates that in his context they represent temptation toward excess.

15. Panofsky, *Hercules*, plate 61.

16. In the Choice of Hercules paintings, both ladies may be naked, or both may be clothed, or one lady may be naked and the other clothed. There is traditional justification for all these presentations. Naked Pleasure represents, obviously enough, lascivious abandon; naked Virtue represents unadorned truth. Magnificently clothed Pleasure represents voluptuous luxury; clothed Virtue, inevitably, modesty (Wind, pp. 123–24).

17. Poensgen, plates 1, 8, 9, etc. Panofsky, *Hercules*, pl. 5, 45.

18. Poensgen, pl. 24, 34, 39; Panofsky, *Hercules*, pl. 62.

19. Poensgen, pl. 29, etc. Panofsky, *Hercules*, pl. 44, 46, 60, etc.

20. Panofsky, *Hercules*, pl. 65.

21. Belphoebe closely resembles Radigund (see II.iii.26–31). For the iconography of Amazons and hunting maidens, see Rosamond Tuve, "Spenser and Some Pictorial Conventions, With Particular Reference to Illuminated Manuscripts," *Studies in Philology*, XXXVII (1940), 149–76.

22. *Aenead*, IV, 136–42. Dido wears *Sidoniam picto chlamydem circumdata limbo*, and *purpuream vestem*. Radigund's purple camis is a direct descendant of these.

23. See the discussion of this tradition in Wind, pp. 84–88.

24. Fowler has argued that Britomart is Minervan. But he does not connect Artegall and Hercules. *Numbers of Time*, pp. 124–28; 197–205.

25. *Emblemata* (1583), p. 99; (1621), p. 122.

26. In the 1590 edition the stanza began "Like as Bellona. . . ." Spenser's change suggests that by the time he had come to write Book V he was beginning to see his heroine as a specifically Minerva-like figure.

27. *Hieroglyphica*, p. 188.

28. Fowler, "Marginalia," pp. 416–19.

29. Plutarch writes of: "that goddess whom you worship, a goddess exceptionally wise and a lover of wisdom, to whom, as her name at least seems to indicate, knowledge and understanding are in the highest

degree appropriate. For Isis is a Greek word. . . ." F. C. Babbitt explains that Plutarch is trying to connect Isis with οἶδα, know. *De Iside*, p. 9.

30. For "infolding" and "unfolding," see Wind, p. 168.

31. *Golden Booke*, pp. 5–6.

32. *Iconologia*, pp. 567–68.

33. Daniel de la Feuille, *Essay d'un dictionnaire*. The emblems referred to in my text are: pl. 16, fig. 8; pl. 91, fig. 6; pl. 107, fig. 9. The emblem of Hercules leading a monkey and a lion is from Ripa, p. 568.

34. De la Feuille, p. 109.

35. *Emblemata Horatiana*, pp. 41, 105.

36. The works mentioned in this paragraph are reproduced in Panofsky, *Hercules*, pl. 54, 56, 82.

37. In *Ben Jonson*, edited by Ch. Herford and P. and E. Simpson, VII. Lines 253–68.

38. For the graces, see Wind, pp. 31–56. Wind interprets a painting of Hercules meeting the three graces in the way in which I am interpreting some of the illustrations of the Choice of Hercules. He also, most significantly, sees the Venus-and-Mars combination as expressing the mystery of virtue reconciled with pleasure (Wind, pp. 78–88).

39. Panofsky, *Hercules*, plates 48, 49.

40. *Epistolae. Opera*, pp. 919f. Quoted by Wind, p. 79.

12. THE BLATANT BEAST

1. *Emblemata* (1548), p. 65 (text only); fig. in 1583 edition, p. 250. The iconographical background to Spenser's Envy has been noted by Samuel Chew, "Spenser's Pageant of the Seven Deadly Sins," *Studies in Art and Literature for Belle Da Costa Greene*, pp. 37–54. Also by Jessee, "Spenser and the Emblem Books," pp. 132–33.

2. *Iconologia*, pp. 268–69.

3. *Dictionnaire*, pl. 91, fig. 15.

4. Spenser's Detraction has the same snake's tongue as Ripa's; I

have found, though, no iconographical analogue for Spenser's Detraction's distaff. (*F.Q.* V.xii.36; Ripa, *Iconologia*, p. 134.)

5. I have not seen them. They are mentioned in an anonymous work, *Collection of Mythological and Allegorical figures reproduced from the works of various artists.*

6. It is true that the Blatant Beast attacks the guilty as well as the innocent; and indeed, I have argued that Artegall is, on one level, in fact as cruel and guileful as the Blatant Beast's mistresses say he is. This ambiguity lends some credence to the old theory that the Blatant Beast represents the Puritans. But I think the Blatant Beast is basically evil, and his choice of victims more governed by chance than by moral purpose, more analogous to yellow journalism and muckraking than to Marprelate tracts.

7. Curs. Well-groomed hounds typically represent faithfulness; but messy-looking curs are mean. Envy and Detraction themselves resemble envy's creature: they are like "shepheards curres" (xii.38).

8. Graves, I, 110.

9. *Works*, II, 23. Compare Alciati, *Emblemata* (1548), p. 9. The Beast is described in Revelations xiii, xvii.

10. On Greek coins the hydra was depicted with seven heads; in most of the myths, though, it had many more (Graves, II, 110).

11. Chew, *Pilgrimage*, pp. 72–74.

12. *Dictionnaire*, pl. 91, fig. 15.

13. Rev. xiii. 1–6.

14. *De laboribus Herculis*, pp. 449–582.

15. *Emblemata*, p. 463.

16. On the title page of Dee's appeal against his calumniators (1599). Reproduced in Chew, *Virtues Reconciled*, fig. 11.

17. Leslie Hotson quotes this in the course of his argument that the Blatant Beast is a Blăttant, not a Blătant one. "The Blatant Beast," *Studies in Honor of T. W. Baldwin*, pp. 34–37.

18. *Hieroglyphica*, p. 200.

19. *Emblemata Horatiana*, p. 173. See also *Hieroglyphica*, p. 172.

20. Marin Le Roy Gomberville, *Le Theatre moral de la vie humaine*, p. 168.

21. I am indebted for this argument to Professor Angus Fletcher.

22. Gough has observed that in this he is like the David who endures the stones that are cast at him and passes on without taking any vengeance, (note to V.xii.42). David and Hercules were both *figurae* for Christ.

23. Rev xx. 1–3. In Revelations "that old serpent" is not identical with the beast which we have associated with the hydra; it is, rather, "the dragon which gave power unto the beast" (xiii.4).

LIST OF WORKS CITED

Alciati, Andrea. *Emblemata*. Lyons, 1548.

—— *Emblems d'Alciat, de nouveau Translatez en François vers pour vers iouxte les Latins*. Lyons, 1549.

—— *Emblemata: Cum commentariis . . . per Claudium Minoem*. Paris, 1583.

—— *Emblemata cum Commentariis Claudii Minois*. Padua, 1621.

Allen, C. K. *Law in the Making*. Oxford, 1930.

Aristotle. *Nichomachean Ethics*. Translated by H. Rackham. Loeb Classical Library, 1926.

—— *Politics*. Translated by H. Rackham. Loeb Classical Library, 1932.

Auerbach, Erich. *Scenes from the Drama of European Literature*. New York, 1959.

Bache, William B. "Spenser and Deloney," *Notes and Queries*, N.S., I (1954), 232–33.

Baker, Herschel. *The Dignity of Man*. Cambridge, Mass., 1947.

—— *The Wars of Truth*. Cambridge, Mass., 1952.

Batman, Stephen. *The Golden Booke of the Leaden Goddes*. London, 1577.

Baudoin, Jean. *Iconologie, ou explication nouvelle de plusieurs images, emblemes, at autres figures . . . tirée des Recherches et des Figures de Cesar Ripa*. Paris, 1644.

—— *Recueil d'Emblemes Divers*. Paris, 1638.

Belsen, Joel Jay. "The Names in *The Faerie Queene*," unpublished Ph.D. dissertation, Columbia University, 1964.

Berger, Harry J. *The Allegorical Temper*. New Haven, 1957.

Beutner, Sister Marie Louise. "Spenser and the Emblem Writers," unpublished Ph.D. dissertation, St. Louis University, 1943.

Bodin, Jean. *Six Books of the Commonwealth*. Abridged and translated by M. J. Tooley. Oxford, 1955.

Boissard, I. I. *Theatrum Vitae Humanae*. Metz, 1596.

Bolzani, Giovanni Pierio Valeriano. *Hieroglyphica*. Frankfurt, 1678.

Bradner, Leicester. *Edmund Spenser and the Faerie Queene*. Chicago, 1948.

Bredt, E. W., editor. "Herkules," Band 3, *Die Welt der Kunstler*. Ravensburg, 1913.

Brien, Alan. "Down with all Bowdlers," *New Statesman* (August 5, 1966), 198–99.

Bruck, Jacobi a. *Emblemata Politica*. Strassburg, 1618.

Bruno, Giordano. *Spaccio della bestia trionfante*. London, 1584.

Budge, E. A. Wallis. *Osiris and the Egyptian Resurrection*, 2 vols. London and New York, 1911.

Bush, Douglas. *Mythology and the Renaissance Tradition in English Poetry*. New York, 1957.

Capellanus, Andreas. *De arte honeste amandi*. Translated by John Jay Parry. New York, 1941.

Cartari. *Imagine dei Dei*. Venice, 1556.

Cassirer, Ernst. *The Myth of the State*. New Haven and London, 1946.

Chang, H. C. *Allegory and Courtesy in Spenser*. Edinburgh, 1955.

Chapman, George, translator. "The Georgicks of Hesiod," *Homer's Batrachomyomachia*. London, 1858.

Cheke, Sir John. *The true subject to the rebel, or the hurt of sedition, how greivous it is to a Common-wealth*. London, 1641.

Chew, Samuel. *The Pilgrimage of Life*. New Haven and London, 1962.

—— "Spenser's Pageant of the Seven Deadly Sins," *Studies in Art and Literature for Belle Da Costa Greene*. Princeton, 1954.

—— *The Virtues Reconciled: An Iconographic Study*. Toronto, 1947.

Cheyney, Donald. *Spenser's Image of Nature*. New Haven and London, 1966.

Cicero. *De Officiis*. Translated by W. Miller. Loeb Classical Library, 1913.

Cinthio. See Giraldi.

Collection of Mythological and Allegorical figures reproduced from the works of various artists. Liége [? 187–].

Cooke, Thomas. "Works and Days," The Works of the English Poets from Chaucer to Cowper, XX. London, 1810.

Daly, S. J., John P. " 'Talus' in Spenser's Faerie Queene," Notes and Queries, N.S., VII (1960), 49.

Davies, Sir John. Poems. Edited by Clare Howard. New York, 1941.

Davis, B. E. C. Edmund Spenser. New York, 1933.

Diodorus Siculus. Bibliotheca Historica. Translated by John Skelton. Early English Text Society, 1956.

Dodge, R. E. Neil, editor. Spenser: Complete Poetical Works. Boston and New York, 1908.

Draper, John W. "Spenser's Talus Again," Philological Quarterly, XV (1936), 215–17.

Dunseath, T. K. Spenser's Allegory of Justice in Book Five of The Faerie Queene. Princeton, 1968.

Dürer, Albrecht. The Complete Woodcuts of Albrecht Dürer. Edited by Willi Kurth. New York, 1946.

Elton, G. R. The Tudor Constitution. Cambridge, 1960.

Empson, William. Some Versions of Pastoral. Norfolk, Connecticut, 1960.

Evans, Joan. Magical Jewels of the Middle Ages and the Renaissance. Oxford, 1922.

Feuille, Daniel de la. Essay d'un dictionnaire contenant la connoissance du monde, des sciences universelles, et particulièrement celle des medailles, des passions, des moeurs, des virtus et des vices, etc. Amsterdam, 1700.

Fletcher, Angus. Allegory, The Theory of a Symbolic Mode. Ithaca, 1964.

—— MS of study of The Faerie Queene, Book V, and of Elizabethan concepts of justice and prophecy.

Fowler, Alastair. "Oxford and London Marginalia to The Faerie Queene," Notes and Queries, N.S., VIII (1961), 416–19.

—— Spenser and the Numbers of Time. London, 1964.

Freeman, Rosemary. English Emblem Books. London, 1948.

[Friedrich, Andreas]. *Emblemes Nouveaux: desquels le cours de ce monde est depeint et representé par certaines Figures, desquelles le sens est expliqué par rimes.* Frankfurt, 1617.

Frye, Northrop. *Fables of Identity.* New York, 1963.

Giraldi, Giovanbattista Cinthio. *Dell'Hercole.* Modena, 1557.

Golden, Martha Hester. "The Iconography of the English History Play." Unpublished Ph.D. Dissertation, Columbia University, 1964.

Gomberville, Marin le Roy. *Le theatre moral de la vie humaine, representée en plus de cent tableaux divers, tirez du poëte Horace, par le Sieur Otho Venius, et expliquez en autant de discours moraux par le Sieur de Gomberville.* Brussels, 1672.

Gough, A. B., editor. *The Faerie Queene, Book V.* Oxford, 1918.

Graves, Robert. *The Greek Myths,* 2 vols. Baltimore, 1955.

Graziani, René. "Elizabeth at Isis Church," *PMLA,* LXXIX (1964), 376–89.

—— "Philip II's *Impresa* and Spenser's Souldan," *Journal of the Warburg and Courtauld Institutes,* XXVII (1964), 322–24.

Greenlaw, Edwin A. "The Influence of Machiavelli on Spenser," *Modern Philology,* VII (1909–1910), 187–202.

—— *Studies in Spenser's Historical Allegory.* Baltimore, 1932.

Hamilton, A. C. *The Structure of Allegory in The Faerie Queene.* Oxford, 1961.

Heckscher, William S., and Wirth, Karl-August. "Emblem, Emblembuch," *Reallexicon zur deutschen Kunstgeschichte,* Nos. 49–50 (1959), cols. 85–228.

Hesiod. *The Homeric Hymns and Homerica.* Translated by Hugh Evelyn-White. Loeb Classical Library, 1914.

Hesiodi Asraei. Edited by Cornelius Schrevellius. Leipzig, 1684.

Honig, Edwin. *Dark Conceit: The Making of Allegory.* Evanstown, 1959.

Hotson, Leslie. "The Blatant Beast," *Studies in Honor of T. W. Baldwin.* Urbana, 1958.

Hough, Graham. "First Commentary on the *Faerie Queene,*" *Times Literary Supplement* (April 9, 1964), 294.

—— *A Preface to The Faerie Queene.* New York, 1962.

Jessee, Jack Willard. "Spenser and the Emblem Books." Unpublished Ph.D. dissertation, University of Kentucky, 1955.

Jones, H. S. V. *A Spenser Handbook.* New York, 1930.

—— "Spenser's Defence of Lord Grey," *University of Illinois Studies in Language and Literature,* V (1919), 151–219.

Jonson, Ben. "Pleasure Reconciled to Vertue," *Ben Jonson,* VII. Edited by C. H. Herford and P. and E. Simpson. Oxford, 1941.

Judson, A. C. *The Life of Edmund Spenser.* Baltimore, 1945.

Kirschbaum, Leo, editor. *Edmund Spenser: Selected Poetry.* New York, 1961.

Kunoth, G. "Francisco Pacheco's Apotheosis of Hercules," *Journal of the Warburg and Courtauld Institutes,* XXVII (1964), 335–37.

Lewis, C. S. *The Allegory of Love.* London, 1936.

—— *English Literature in the Sixteenth Century.* Oxford, 1954.

—— *Studies in Medieval and Renaissance Literature.* Cambridge, 1966.

Lotspeich, Henry Gibbons. *Classical Mythology in the Poetry of Edmund Spenser.* Princeton, 1932.

Machiavelli, Niccolò. *The Prince.* Translated by Luigi Ricci. New York, 1950.

Mâle, Emile. *L'Art Religieux du XIIIe siècle en France.* Paris, 1919.

Mazzeo, J. A. "Hell vs. Hell: From Dante to Machiavelli," *Symposium,* XVII (1963), 245–67.

—— *Structure and Thought in the Paradiso.* Ithaca, 1958.

Milligan, Burton. "Spenser's Malengin and the Rogue-book Hooker," *Philological Quarterly,* XIX (1940), 147–48.

Milton, John. *Complete Poems and Major Prose.* Edited by Merritt Y. Hughes. New York, 1957.

The Mirrour of Majestie: or, the Badges of Honour conceitedly emblazoned; with emblemes annexed, poetically unfolded. London, 1618. Photolith facsimile edited by Henry Green and James Croston. Manchester, 1870.

"MS Notes to Spenser's 'Faerie Queene,'" *Notes and Queries,* CCII (1957), 509–15.

Mueller, William R. *Spenser's Critics: Changing Currents in Literary Taste.* Syracuse, 1959.

Neill, Kerby. "Spenser on the Regiment of Women," *Studies in Philology*, XXXIV (1937), 134–37.

Nelson, William. *The Poetry of Edmund Spenser.* New York, 1963.

—— "Queen Elizabeth, Spenser's Mercilla, and a Rusty Sword," *Renaissance News*, XVIII (1965), 113–17.

Orlandi, Cesare. *Iconologia del Cavaliere Cesare Ripa, Perugino, Notabilmente accresciuta d'Immagini, di Annotazioni, e di Fatti,* 5 vols. Perugia, 1764.

Padelford, F. M. *The Political and Ecclesiastical Allegory of the First Book of the Faerie Queene.* Boston, 1911.

Panofsky, Irwin. *Hercules am Scheidewege.* Leipzig and Berlin, 1930.

—— *Studies in Iconology.* London and New York, 1939.

Parker, M. Pauline. *The Allegory of The Faerie Queene.* Oxford, 1960.

Phillips, James E. "The Background of Spenser's Attitude toward Women Rulers," *Huntington Library Quarterly*, V (1941–42), 5–32.

—— "The Woman Ruler in Spenser's *Faerie Queene.*" *Ibid.*, pp. 211–34.

Plutarch. "Isis and Osiris," *Moralia*, V. Translated by Frank Cole Babbitt. Loeb Classical Library, 1936.

Poensgen, Georg. "Herkules und Omphale," *Bibliotheca Docet: Festschrift Carl Wehmer*, pp. 303–[334]. Amsterdam, 1963.

Praz, Mario. *Studies in Seventeenth Century Imagery,* 2 vols. London, 1939.

Quarles, Francis. *Emblems Divine and Moral.* London, 1639.

Raab, Felix. *The English Face of Machiavelli.* London and Toronto, 1964.

Raleigh, Sir Walter. *Works,* 2 vols. London, 1751.

Rathborne, Isabel E. *The Meaning of Spenser's Fairyland.* New York, 1937.

Reynolds, Henry. "Mythomystes," *Critical Essays of the Seventeenth Century*, 2 vols. Edited by J. E. Spingarn. Bloomington, 1957.

Ripa, Cesare. *Nova Iconologia.* Padua, 1618.

Salutati, Coluccio. *De Laboribus Herculis.* Edited by B. L. Ullman. Zürich [1947].

Seneca. *Tragedies,* 2 vols. Translated by Frank Justus Miller. Loeb Classical Library, 1927.

Seznec, Jean. *The Survival of the Pagan Gods.* Translated by Barbara F. Sessions. New York, 1953.

Sidney, Sir Philip. *The Countess of Pembroke's Arcadia.* Cambridge, 1962.

Smith, Hallett. *Elizabethan Poetry.* Cambridge, Mass., 1952.

Spenser, Edmund. *The Works of Edmund Spenser: A Variorum Edition,* 11 vols. Baltimore, 1932–1957.

—— *Stair Ercueil Ocus a Bas (The Life and Death of Hercules,* [c. 1475–1500], edited and translated by Gordon Quin. Irish Text Society, XXXVIII. Dublin, 1939.

Steadman, John M. "Spenser and the *Virgilius* Legend: Another Talus Parallel," *Modern Language Notes,* LXXIII (1958), 412–13.

—— "Spenser's *Errour* and the Renaissance Allegorical Tradition," *Neuphilologische Mitteilungen,* XVII (1961), 22–38.

Strong, Roy C. *Portraits of Queen Elizabeth I.* Oxford, 1963.

Tervarent, Guy de. *Attributs et Symboles dans l'Art Profane: 1450–1600.* Geneva, 1958.

Tillyard, E. M. W. *The Elizabethan World Picture.* London, 1956.

Tissot, Will. *Simson und Hercules in den Gestaltungen des Barock.* Griefswald, 1932.

Tuve, Rosemond. *Allegorical Imagery.* Princeton, 1966.

—— *Elizabethan and Metaphysical Imagery.* Chicago, 1947.

—— "Spenser and Some Pictorial Conventions," *Studies in Philology,* XXXVII (1940), 149–76.

Ullman, Berthold L. *The Humanism of Coluccio Salutati.* Padua, 1963.

Valeriano. See Bolzani.

[Van Veen, Otto]. *Q. HoratI FlaccI Emblemata.* Antwerp, 1607.

Wagner, Geoffrey. "Talus," *English Literary History,* XVII (1950), 79–86.

Waith, Eugene M. *The Herculean Hero.* New York and London, 1962.

Walker, J. H. "*The Faerie Queene:* Alterations and Structure," *Modern Language Review,* XXXVI (1941), 51–84.

Ward, Ellen G. "Spenser and the Emblem Writers." Unpublished Master's thesis, Duke University, 1936.

Welsford, Enid. *The Court Masque*. Cambridge, 1927.

Williams, Kathleen. *Spenser's World of Glass*. Berkeley and Los Angeles, 1966.

Wimsatt, W. K. *The Verbal Icon*. Lexington, Kentucky, 1954.

Wind, Edgar. *Pagan Mysteries in the Renaissance*. New Haven, 1958.

Winstanley, Lilian. *The Faerie Queene, Books I and II*. Cambridge, 1915.

Woodhouse, A. S. P. "Nature and Grace in *The Faerie Queene*," *English Literary History*, XVI (1949), 194–228.

Yates, Frances A. *Giordano Bruno and the Hermetic Tradition*. Chicago, London, and Toronto, 1964.

—— "Queen Elizabeth as Astraea." *Journal of the Warburg and Courtauld Institutes*, X (1947), 27–82.

Zincgreff, Julius Guilielmus. *Emblematum Ethico-Politicorum Centuria*. Heidelberg, 1664.

INDEX